Managing MBS Portfolios

Frank J. Fabozzi, CFA
School of Management
Yale University

and

David Yuen, CFA
Susquehanna Advisors Group

Published by Frank J. Fabozzi Associates

FJF

To my wife, Donna,
and my two children, Francesco and Patricia

DY

To my wife, Mandy,
and my two children, Kevin and Ryan

© 1998 By Frank J. Fabozzi Associates
New Hope, Pennsylvania

This publication is designed to provide accurate and authoritative information in regard to the subject matter covered. It is sold with the understanding that the publisher is not engaged in rendering legal, accounting, or other professional services.

ISBN: 1-883249-38-4

Printed in the United States of America

Table of Contents

List of Advertisers

BARRA

Capital Access International

Derivative Solutions

Interactive Data Corporation

Intex Solutions

Wall Street Analytics

Chapter 1

Introduction

The broad-based bond market indexes published by Lehman Brothers, Salomon Brothers, and Merrill Lynch include three sectors: governments/agencies, corporates/asset-backed securities, and mortgage-backed securities. While the mortgage-backed securities sector represents about one-third of these indexes, residential mortgage and mortgage-related debt is actually the largest sector of the U.S. debt market.

The purpose of this book is to explain the various mortgage-related products (their features and investment characteristics) and how to manage a portfolio of securities of mortgage-related products. In this chapter we provide a description of the development of the mortgage-backed securities market and an overview of managing a portfolio of mortgage-backed securities. We conclude the chapter with a summary of the chapters ahead.

DEVELOPMENT OF THE MBS MARKET

Until late 1969, the only means for investing in mortgages was by originating loans and retaining them in a portfolio or purchasing loans originated by mortgage originators. While these instruments offered yields greater than that of Treasury securities, they exposed investors to several risks. First, they were not liquid instruments. Second, there was credit risk. Third, unlike Treasury securities and other publicly traded bonds, these instruments required servicing. Most investors were not equipped to service loans. Finally, there was prepayment risk. This is the risk that the cash flow was uncertain because the borrower (the mortgagor) had the option to pay off the loan in whole or in part at any time. Actually, at the time, there was very little concern by investors with prepayments because of the absence of significant interest rate volatility, the presence of prepayment penalties that were imposed on borrowers, and the significant cost faced by borrowers to refinance their loans when rates declined.

As a result of these drawbacks of investing in mortgages, there were only a few major players in this sector of the debt market — savings and loan associations, commercial banks, and life insurance companies. Given the huge size of the mortgage debt market, there was a need to encourage more investors into the market — or as investment bankers are fond of saying, "broadening the investor base." In 1969, the U.S. government intervened in the market by issuing securities backed by a pool of mortgage loans. This overcomed several of the drawbacks of investing in whole loans. First, it mitigated the liquidity problem in two ways. In the creation of mortgage-backed securities, the demand for mortgage loans

1

improved the liquidity for whole loans. Also, mortgage-backed securities were more liquid than the underlying pool of mortgage loans. Second, there was no credit risk since the securities were issued by an entity of the U.S. government that guaranteed the payment of principal and interest. Third, investors did not have to service the mortgage loans. Finally, and what was not fully appreciated at the time because prepayment risk was not a major concern, was that the pooling of a large number of mortgage loans increased the ability of investors to statistically predict the prepayment behavior of the borrowers compared to when only a limited number of mortgage loans were held in a portfolio.

As a result of these advantages and additional help by the U.S. government, the market for mortgage-backed securities grew. The particular type of mortgage-backed security that was issued was a mortgage passthrough security. Investors in this security received a pro rata share of the cash flow of the underlying mortgage loans, reduced by servicing and guarantor fees. There were different government agencies involved in the creation of passthrough securities and these securities were consequently referred to as *agency securities*. Throughout the 1970s, when market players talked about mortgage-backed securities they meant agency passthrough securities. In the late 1970s, there was limited issuance of securities not issued or guaranteed by an agency of the U.S. government. These securities were called *private label passthrough* securities.

The market for passthrough securities continued to grow. However, in the early 1980s in an environment of high and volatile interest rates, institutional investors became more conscious of managing assets relative to the nature of their liabilities. Sophisticated institutional investors began to recognize that while agency passthrough securities were unquestionably preferred to whole loan investing, these securities still did not provide a good match against liabilities because of prepayment risk. There was considerable uncertainty about the cash flow of an agency passthrough security, including how long the security would be outstanding. This uncertainty was due to prepayment risk. In a declining interest rate environment, refinancing by mortgagors could significantly shorten the life of a passthrough security relative to the expected life at the time of purchase — a property of a mortgage-backed securities referred to as *contraction risk*. In contrast, in a rising interest rate environment, the life of a passthrough could be significantly longer than the expected life at the time of purchase — a property referred to as *extension risk*.

To mitigate these adverse consequences due to prepayment risk, in 1983 investment bankers created a *collateralized mortgage obligation* (CMO). Basically, with a CMO the cash flows of a pool of passthrough securities were redistributed among different classes of bonds (called *tranches*) based on a set of rules for allocating principal and interest. The net effect was to mitigate the uncertainty about cash flows and the life of a security. The first generation of CMO deals basically reallocated the cash flows (or equivalently, reallocated the extension and contraction risks) so that institutional investors with different needs would find tranches that were more acceptable from an asset/liability perspective than mortgage passthrough securities. Now the mortgage-backed securities market included passthroughs and CMOs.

While the first generation of CMOs mitigated prepayment risk, there were still institutional investors uncomfortable with mortgage-backed securities and sought greater protection from prepayment risk. In 1987, the second generation of CMOs was created with that purpose in mind. Specifically, included within a CMO deal were tranches with a schedule of principal payments in which the certificate holders had priority over all other tranches in the structure with respect to the payment of the scheduled principal amount. These tranches were originally called Stabilized Mortgage Reduction Term (SMRT) bonds, Planned Redemption Obligation (PRO) bonds, and Planned Amortization Class (PAC) bonds. Today, they are popularly referred to as PACs. These tranches became extremely popular for institutional investors seeking reduced prepayment risk and a better matching of assets to liabilities.

However, a fundamental property of a pool of mortgage loans is that if prepayment protection is provided to one or more tranches, prepayment risk must be increased for the other tranches in a structure. In the first generation of CMOs, this was done by just redistributing the different forms of prepayment risk (extension risk and contraction risk) among the tranches so that some tranches had a reduction in contraction risk but greater exposure to extension risk, while others had a reduction in extension risk but greater exposure to contraction risk. With the introduction of PACs, the PAC tranches received protection against both contraction risk and extension risk. This protection came from the non-PAC tranches, popularly referred to as the *support* or *companion tranches*. By design, these tranches had the greatest prepayment risk. In fact, the prepayment risk for support tranches was greater than the prepayment risk from the underlying pool of passthroughs that was the collateral for the CMO deal.

Since the introduction of PAC bonds in 1987, the demand for these bonds has been tremendous. Wall Street firms accommodated this demand by issuing CMO deals with a variety of PAC tranches. The ability to issue such CMO deals depended on the ability of Wall Street firms to sell the support tranches. Because of the significant prepayment risk, these tranches were offered to institutional investors at a significant spread over Treasury securities. However, the offered spread over Treasuries may or may not quantify their substantial prepayment risk. Basically, there were too many institutional investors in the market who did not understand the characteristics of the support tranches that they owned. There was nothing wrong with the support tranches, they just had to be purchased by institutional investors who could bear their prepayment risk and were smart enough to extract from the Wall Street firms the proper compensation. The problem in the CMO market was a human capital problem — lack of skill to assess the prepayment risk — not a problem with the securities created. It also did not help that reporters documented the difficulties in the CMO market in a biased manner. Too often these reporters lacked an understanding of the CMO product. If few institutional money managers were properly trained to handle these products because CMOs were not a subject covered by most graduate business schools, certainly this was not a hot topic in schools of journalism!

Throughout the 1980s and early 1990s, institutional investors were concerned with credit risk (as well as prepayment risk). The vehicle of choice for investing in the mortgage market was the agency mortgage-backed security. As the economy improved in the 1990s, institutional investors started moving to mortgage-backed securities that were not backed by an agency of the U.S. government or a government sponsored enterprise. These securities, called *nonagency mortgage-backed securities*, expose investors to prepayment risk and credit risk. They are sometimes referred to as "credit spread products" because the spread that they offer over Treasury securities reflects not only prepayment risk, but credit risk.

Today, there is a wide range of nonagency products. In fact, it is difficult to distinguish a nonagency mortgage-backed from an asset-backed security. The Securities Data Corporation keeps the "league tables" telling us which investment banking firms are the leaders in the underwriting of particular investment products. The SDC provides a definition for purposes of creating league tables of what the difference is between nonagency mortgage-backed securities and asset-backed securities. In general, throughout this book we refer to a security in which the underlying collateral is a mortgage-related product as a mortgage-backed security.

OVERVIEW OF MBS PORTFOLIO MANAGEMENT

The process of managing an MBS portfolio involves three steps: (1) determining investment objectives and establishing investment policy, (2) selecting a portfolio strategy; and (3) selecting the assets. A manager may be employed as an internal manager of a financial institution or retained by a financial institution as an external manager. The client in either case is the financial institution for which the money is being managed.

Determining Investment Objectives and Establishing Policy Guidelines

The client specifies the investment objectives. The investment objectives should set forth what is expected of the manager. The key element in setting investment objectives is defining what the benchmark is and what the manager is expected to do versus that benchmark. For institutional investors, there are three possible benchmarks: (1) a liability, (2) a broad-based bond market index, and (3) a specialized mortgage market index. The broad-based bond market indexes include the Lehman Brothers Aggregate Index, the Salomon Brothers Broad-Investment Grade Index, and the Merrill Lynch Domestic Index. The specialized mortgage market indexes are the mortgage components of each broad-based bond market index.

In establishing the investment policy to meet the investment objectives, the risk tolerance of the client must be considered, as well as other constraints that might be imposed based on regulatory considerations and tax considerations. Here are a few examples. In managing an MBS portfolio for a pension fund, the client would specify that the securities must be Employee Retirement Investment Securities Act (ERISA) eligible. For depository institutions, mortgage-backed securities acquired must satisfy the Federal Financial Institutions Examination Council (FFIEC) tests. Thus, the client will restrict the manager to invest in only FFIEC qualified mortgage-backed securities. For credit unions, there are further restrictions beyond the FFIEC tests that limit the acceptable universe of mortgage-backed securities that a credit union client will impose on its manager.

The investment policy may restrict the manager to invest in only agency mortgage-backed securities. If nonagency mortgage-backed securities are permitted, there is typically a minimum credit rating specified by the client (reflecting the risk tolerance of the client) and the procedure that must be followed if there is a down grading of a nonagency security held below the minimum credit rating. The client might specify that the security must be sold immediately or permit the manager to hold the security subject to the approval of the client.

There are some mortgage-backed securities that have characteristics that call for the specific identification as to their permissibility for the manager to invest in. For example, a client may restrict permissible investments to agency mortgage-backed securities. But there are agency securities called interest-only securities. While an agency may guarantee that the interest for an interest-only security is paid if there are mortgages outstanding, there is no guarantee as to how much interest will be paid over the security's life. For example, a manager could buy an agency interest-only security for $5 million and by the time all the underlying mortgages in the pool are paid off, only $2 million is received by the investor. We'll discuss interest-only securities in Chapter 3 and why it could have the pay off just described. What is critical is that the client have a general understanding of the products in the mortgage-backed securities market and impose restrictions on products that it might find unacceptable.

Other restrictions imposed deal with the degree of leveraging, the use of derivative instruments (futures/forwards, swaps, options, caps, and floors), and exposure to interest rate volatility. This last restriction is specified in terms of a portfolio's duration. As explained in Chapter 10, duration is the approximate change in the value of a portfolio for a 100 basis point change in rates.

When the benchmark is a broad-based bond market index or a specialized mortgage index, the client may specify that the manager maintain the portfolio's duration within a specified range relative to the index. For example, suppose that the benchmark's duration is 4 and the client specifies that the portfolio's duration can deviate from the benchmark's duration by ± 0.5. Then the manager must maintain a duration of no less than 3.5 (4 minus 0.5) and no greater than 4.5 (4 plus 0.5). If the benchmark's duration increases to say 5, then the permissible range for the portfolio's duration is 4.5 to 5.5.

For depository institutions, there are interest rate risk-based capital requirements. If the interest rate risk exposure of a portfolio is greater than a specified level, additional capital requirements are imposed. Consequently, a manager of a depository institution will be restricted by this requirement.

Selecting the Portfolio Strategy

The manager must select the portfolio strategy that is consistent with the objectives and policy guidelines of the client. To understand how the portfolio strategy is tied to the investment objectives, consider the three general categories of benchmarks: (1) a liability, (2) a broad-based bond market index, and (3) a specialized mortgage market index.

In the first case, a client may have a liability that it must satisfy. Its minimum benchmark then would be to satisfy that liability. For example, suppose a client borrows funds for six months at say, LIBOR plus 20 basis points. The minimum investment objective would be to earn LIBOR plus 20 basis points. However, the client will seek to earn a spread over its funding cost. Suppose that spread is 80 basis point. Then the investment objective is to earn LIBOR plus 100 basis points. Insurance companies issue policies where they must pay a fixed rate. The investment objective is to earn that fixed rate plus a minimum spread. In the case of pension funds, a plan sponsor will seek to meet the actuarially determined liabilities at minimum cost.

The portfolio strategy must be structured so as to reduce the risk that the liability will not be satisfied. For example, suppose that the benchmark established by a client is a 6% 1-year return reflecting a liability of 5% and a desired spread of 100 basis points. The manager is considering two portfolio strategies and the outcomes of these two strategies, measured in terms of a 1-year total return, are as follows for different interest rate scenarios:

	Outcome of	
Change in rates	Strategy 1	Strategy 2
+250 basis points	+4.0%	−3.5%
+200 basis points	+4.5%	−2.0%
+100 basis points	+5.0%	−1.0%
+ 50 basis points	+6.0%	+2.0%
rates unchanged	+6.4%	+5.0%
−50 basis points	+6.8%	+7.5%
−100 basis points	+7.2%	+8.5%
−200 basis points	+7.4%	+10.1%
−250 basis points	+7.7%	+13.4%

Certainly, portfolio strategy 2 has more attractive upside potential if rates decline. For example, if rates decline by 200 basis points, the spread income that will be generated is 510 basis points for portfolio strategy 2 but only 240 basis points for portfolio strategy 1. Nevertheless, there is greater risk of not meeting the benchmark. If rates are unchanged, portfolio strategy 2 will just meet the liabilities. If rates rise, the portfolio's return would not be sufficient to satisfy the liabilities.

When the benchmark is a broad-based bond market index, the investment objective may be to either outperform the index or match the index. A portfolio strategy seeking to match an index is called *indexing*. Portfolio strategies seeking to outperform an index are called *active strategies*.

When a broad-based bond market index is the benchmark, there are several active strategies. The first is to underweight or overweight the fixed income sectors comprising the index based on expected relative performance. For example, suppose that one third of the index is the mortgage sector. If the manager expects the mortgage sector to outperform the government/agency and corporate/asset-backed securities sectors, then more than one third of the portfolio's assets will be allocated to mortgage-backed securities. This strategy is referred to as a "sector rotation" strategy, where funds are reallocated based on the manager's expectations of which sector will be the best performing sector.

A second active strategy is selecting securities within the mortgage sector component of the broad-based bond market index that is expected to outperform the securities comprising the index. In the mortgage index the securities included are generic agency passthrough securities. A manager can outperform the mortgage sector of the index by selecting securities that will outperform the securities in the index. This can be done by overweighting or underweighting the passthroughs in the index or by purchasing securities not included in the index that are expected to outperform the index. For example, CMOs, principal only, interest only, and nonagency mortgage-backed securities are not included in the index. The second portfolio strategy described above is also used when the mortgage index itself is the benchmark.

A third active strategy is to alter the duration of the portfolio based on expectations subject to the duration restrictions imposed by a client. So, if a manager believes that interest rates will decline, the manager may decide to increase the portfolio's duration to the maximum permissible. This is simply a bet on interest rates. There are other strategies that are basically bets on interest rate movements because, as we will see later in this book, there are certain mortgage-backed securities that will perform better in certain interest rate environments than other securities.

Selecting Assets

Once a portfolio strategy is specified, the next step is to select the specific mortgage-backed securities to be included in the portfolio. This step requires an evaluation of individual securities in terms of their price and investment characteristics (i.e., how they will perform when rates change and their credit risk).

It is most interesting to hear managers discuss the virtues of different sectors of the mortgage-backed securities market at professional conferences. For example, it is not uncommon to hear one manager say that CMOs are securities that he would not invest in because there is no benefit to doing so and, as a result, this manager restricts the mortgage portfolio to passthroughs. Yet, another manager at the same conference might say that CMOs are the vehicle of choice when investing in the mortgage sector. The reason for the differences in the views of the two managers can be traced to their investment objectives.

For example, the first manager who espouses limiting exposure to CMOs may be managing funds for clients where the benchmark established is a broad based bond market index or a specialized mortgage index. Basically, that manager feels that he will be able to outperform the index without the use of CMOs. As noted earlier in discussing active portfolio strategies, this can be done by identifying which passthroughs will outperform the index. In contrast, the manager who invests primarily in CMOs may be managing client funds in which the benchmark is a liability. As we will see when we discuss CMOs, fixed-rate passthrough securities are unattractive because they do not have characteristics that usually match the nature of the liabilities faced by financial institutions. CMOs overcome this problem.

OVERVIEW OF BOOK

With this background, let's look at the chapters ahead. The various types of mortgage loans are described in Chapter 2. Chapters 3, 4, and 5 provide a description of the products that we call mortgage-backed securities. Chapter 3 discusses passthroughs, mortgage strips (i.e., interest only and principal only securities), and callable passthroughs. Chapter 4 covers agency CMOs. In presenting this product, we don't simply describe the different types of CMO tranches available in the market. Rather, we take a passthrough security and show how a CMO is created from it, why they are created, and the interaction among the tranches in a CMO structure. A reader unfamiliar with the structuring process will find this chapter useful. Credit sensitive mortgage-backed securities are the subject of Chapter 5. Some of the products created have been typically classified as asset-backed securities. These include home equity loan-backed securities and manufactured housing loan-backed securities. The credit enhancement mechanisms for these products as well as nonagency CMOs are explained.

Prepayment analysis is covered in Chapter 6. We discuss the factors considered in prepayment models for agency and nonagency mortgage-backed securities. While there is sometimes an artificial distinction made between mortgage-backed securities and home equity loan-backed securities, the key is the prepayment characteristics of the underlying loans. We explain the difference in prepayment characteristics of first mortgage loans and home equity loans in this chapter.

Chapters 7 and 8 investigate further the factors that affect derivative mortgage products (CMOs and mortgage strips). In Chapter 7 we explain why collateral analysis is critical. Specifically, using illustrations we demonstrate why a systematic methodology analyzing all aspects of the collateral in a particular deal should precede evaluation of the structure itself. We then turn to the analysis of the structure in Chapter 8.

The various ways to leverage an MBS portfolio are explained in Chapter 9. Traditional reverse repos can be used. This agreement is simply a collateralized loan. A specialized repo transaction created for the mortgage-backed securities market is the dollar roll. We explain this form of collateralized borrowing and explain the uncertainties involving the funding cost when borrowing using a dollar roll. Finally, we discuss mortgage swaps and how they can be used to create leverage.

In Chapter 10, we look at how to measure the interest rate risk of a mortgage-backed security. There are two dimensions to interest rate risk: level risk and yield curve risk. We explain how duration is a measure of level risk and the relationship between convexity and duration. There are two measures of duration that market participants refer to — modified duration and effective duration. We explain each and why effective duration is the measure that should be used. The duration for a floating-rate mortgage-backed security is also explained. Yield curve risk is measured by a portfolio's key rate durations.

In Chapter 11, we look at the valuation of mortgage-backed securities. The traditional approach of determining the yield of a mortgage-backed security (called the cash flow yield) is severely limited as a measure of relative value. In fact, portfolio managers who used cash flow yield and the spread of that yield relative to a comparable Treasury were typically those who purchased CMO support tranches and failed to recognize the substantial prepayment risk. In the chapter we explain the option-adjusted spread (OAS) methodology. We explain what OAS means and how it is computed. What is critical is that the computed OAS is based on critical assumptions. Thus, the OAS value is subject to modeling risk. We demonstrate how to assess that risk. As emphasized in Chapter 10, the ability to measure a security's duration depends on access to a valuation model that can be relied upon to provide a reasonable estimate of how the security's price will change when interest rates change.

In Chapter 12 we decompose complex derivative mortgage products to understand their investment characteristics. We then look at how to hedge complex derivative mortgage products based on these investment characteristics.

In Chapter 13, we look at total return analysis of an MBS portfolio. In that chapter we explain how Monte Carlo simulation can be used to assess the potential performance of a portfolio. We also show how to construct an optimal MBS portfolio given typical constraints that are imposed. A byproduct of the optimization model is that a constraint can be recast into opportunity cost (i.e., a lower potential total return). This type of analysis is critical in working with clients to demonstrate the impact of actual and contemplated constraints.

Chapter 2

Mortgage Loans

A *mortgage loan*, or simply mortgage, is a loan secured by the collateral of some specified real estate property which obliges the borrower to make a predetermined series of payments. The mortgage gives the lender the right if the borrower defaults (i.e., fails to make the contracted payments) to "foreclose" on the loan and seize the property in order to ensure that the debt is paid off. The interest rate on the mortgage loan is called the *mortgage rate* or *contract rate*. Our focus in this book is on residential mortgage loans.

There are many types of mortgages available to borrowers. In this chapter we will describe the types of mortgages that have been used as collateral for a mortgage-backed security.

ALTERNATIVE MORTGAGE DESIGNS

There are many types of mortgage designs. By a mortgage design we mean the specification of the interest rate (fixed or floating), the term of the mortgage, and the manner in which the principal is repaid. We summarize the major mortgage designs below.

Fixed-Rate, Level-Payment, Fully Amortized Mortgage

The basic idea behind the design of the fixed-rate, level payment, fully amortized mortgage is that the borrower pays interest and repays principal in equal installments over an agreed-upon period of time, called the maturity or term of the mortgage. The frequency of payment is typically monthly. Each monthly mortgage payment for this mortgage design is due on the first of each month and consists of:

1. interest of 1/12th of the annual interest rate times the amount of the outstanding mortgage balance at the beginning of the previous month, and
2. a repayment of a portion of the outstanding mortgage balance (principal).

The difference between the monthly mortgage payment and the portion of the payment that represents interest equals the amount that is applied to reduce the outstanding mortgage balance. The monthly mortgage payment is designed so that after the last scheduled monthly payment of the loan is made, the amount of the outstanding mortgage balance is zero (i.e. the mortgage is fully repaid or amortized).

11

Exhibit 1: Amortization Schedule for a Fixed-Rate, Level-Payment, Fully Amortized Mortgage

Mortgage loan: $100,000   Monthly payment: $742.50
Mortgage rate: 8.125%   Term of loan: 30 years (360 months)

Month	Beginning mortgage balance ($)	Monthly payment ($)	Monthly interest ($)	Scheduled principal repayment ($)	Ending mortgage balance ($)
1	100,000.00	742.50	677.08	65.42	99,934.58
2	99,934.58	742.50	676.64	65.86	99,868.72
3	99,868.72	742.50	676.19	66.31	99,802.41
25	98,301.53	742.50	665.58	76.91	98,224.62
26	98,224.62	742.50	665.06	77.43	98,147.19
27	98,147.19	742.50	664.54	77.96	98,069.23
74	93,849.98	742.50	635.44	107.05	93,742.93
75	93,742.93	742.50	634.72	107.78	93,635.15
76	93,635.15	742.50	633.99	108.51	93,526.64
141	84,811.77	742.50	574.25	168.25	84,643.52
142	84,643.52	742.50	573.11	169.39	84,474.13
143	84,474.13	742.50	571.96	170.54	84,303.59
184	76,446.29	742.50	517.61	224.89	76,221.40
185	76,221.40	742.50	516.08	226.41	75,994.99
186	75,994.99	742.50	514.55	227.95	75,767.04
233	63,430.19	742.50	429.48	313.02	63,117.17
234	63,117.17	742.50	427.36	315.14	62,802.03
235	62,802.03	742.50	425.22	317.28	62,484.75
289	42,200.92	742.50	285.74	456.76	41,744.15
290	41,744.15	742.50	282.64	459.85	41,284.30
291	41,284.30	742.50	279.53	462.97	40,821.33
321	25,941.42	742.50	175.65	566.85	25,374.57
322	25,374.57	742.50	171.81	570.69	24,803.88
323	24,803.88	742.50	167.94	574.55	24,229.32
358	2,197.66	742.50	14.88	727.62	1,470.05
359	1,470.05	742.50	9.95	732.54	737.50
360	737.50	742.50	4.99	737.50	0.00

To illustrate this mortgage design, consider a 30-year (360-month) $100,000 mortgage with a mortgage rate of 8.125%. The monthly mortgage payment would be $742.50. Exhibit 1 shows for selected months how each monthly mortgage payment is divided between interest and repayment of principal. At the beginning of month 1, the mortgage balance is $100,000, the amount of the original loan. The mortgage payment for month 1 includes interest on the $100,000 borrowed for the month. Since the interest rate is 8.125%, the monthly interest rate is 0.0067708 (0.08125 divided by 12). Interest for month 1 is therefore $677.08 ($100,000 times 0.0067708). The $65.42 difference between the monthly mortgage payment of $742.50 and the interest of $677.08 is the portion of the monthly mortgage payment that represents repayment of principal. The $65.42 in month 1 reduces the mortgage balance.

The mortgage balance at the end of month 1 (beginning of month 2) is then $99,934.58 ($100,000 minus $65.42). The interest for the second monthly mortgage payment is $676.64, the monthly interest rate (0.0067708) times the mortgage balance at the beginning of month 2 ($99,934.58). The difference between the $742.50 monthly mortgage payment and the $676.64 interest is $65.86, representing the amount of the mortgage balance paid off with that monthly mortgage payment. Notice that the last mortgage payment in month 360 is sufficient to pay off the remaining mortgage balance.

As Exhibit 1 clearly shows, *the portion of the monthly mortgage payment applied to interest declines each month and the portion applied to reducing the mortgage balance increases.* The reason for this is that as the mortgage balance is reduced with each monthly mortgage payment, the interest on the mortgage balance declines. Since the monthly mortgage payment is fixed, an increasingly larger portion of the monthly payment is applied to reduce the principal in each subsequent month.

Servicing Fee and the Cash Flows

Every mortgage loan must be serviced. Servicing of a mortgage loan involves collecting monthly payments and forwarding proceeds to owners of the loan; sending payment notices to mortgagors; reminding mortgagors when payments are overdue; maintaining records of principal balances; administering an escrow balance for real estate taxes and insurance purposes; initiating foreclosure proceedings if necessary; and, furnishing tax information to mortgagors when applicable.

The servicing fee is a portion of the mortgage rate. If the mortgage rate is 8.125% and the servicing fee is 50 basis points, then the investor receives interest of 7.625%. The interest rate that the investor receives is said to be the *net interest* or *net coupon*. The servicing fee is commonly called the *servicing spread*.

The dollar amount of the servicing fee declines over time as the mortgage amortizes. This is true for not only the mortgage design that we have just described, but for all mortgage designs.

Prepayments and Cash Flow Uncertainty

Our illustration of the cash flows from a fixed-rate, level-payment, fully amortized mortgage assumes that the homeowner does not pay off any portion of the mortgage balance prior to the scheduled due date. But homeowners do pay off all or part of their mortgage balance prior to the maturity date. Payments made in excess of the scheduled principal repayments are called *prepayments*. We'll look more closely at the factors that affect prepayment behavior later in Chapter 6.

The effect of prepayments is that the amount and timing of the cash flows from a mortgage are not known with certainty. This risk is referred to as *prepayment risk.* For example, all that the investor in a $100,000, 8.125% 30-year FHA-insured mortgage knows is that as long as the loan is outstanding, interest will be received and the principal will be repaid at the scheduled date each month; then at the end of the 30 years, the investor would have received $100,000 in principal payments. What the investor does not know — the uncertainty — is for how long the loan will be outstanding, and therefore what the timing of the principal payments will be. This is true for all mortgage loans, not just fixed-rate, level-payment, fully amortized mortgages.

Adjustable-Rate Mortgages

While most mortgage-backed securities are backed by fixed-rate mortgages, adjustable- rate mortgages (ARMs) have become more and more popular among home buyers. The popularity of ARMs in the 1990s can be attributed to the historically steep yield curve in the early part of the decade. Many first time home buyers find an ARM to be more affordable in the mortgage's early years and are willing to take on the risk of higher rates in the future. ARMs have also gained popularity in the investment community since the early 1990s. Depository institutions found ARMs provided a better match against their liabilities. In 1988, there was only one mutual fund which would invest the majority of its assets in securities backed by ARMs and it had about $20 million in assets. By the early 1990s, there were at least 25 ARM mutual funds with total assets in excess of $20 billion.

The Basic Structure

As the name implies, an ARM has an adjustable or floating coupon instead of a fixed one. The coupon adjusts periodically — monthly, semiannually or annually. Some ARMs even have coupons that adjust every three years or five years. The coupon formula for an ARM is specified in terms of an index level plus a margin. We'll discuss the common indices that are used below. The margin is typically 2% to 3%.

At origination, the mortgage usually has an initial rate for an initial period (*teaser period*) which is slightly below the rate specified by the coupon formula. This is called a *teaser rate* and makes it easier for first time home buyers to qualify for the loan. At the end of the teaser period, the loan rate is reset based on the coupon formula. Once the loan comes out of its teaser period and resets based on the coupon formula, it is said to be *fully indexed.*

To protect the homeowner from interest rate shock, there are caps or ceilings imposed on the coupon adjustment level. There are periodic caps and lifetime caps. The *periodic cap* limits the amount of coupon reset upward or downward from one period to another. The *lifetime cap* is the maximum absolute level for the coupon rate that the loan can reset to for the life of the mortgage.

Since the borrower prefers to be warned in advance of any interest rate adjustment, the coupon determination actually has to take place prior to the coupon reset. This is called the *lookback period.* A typical lookback period for CMT ARMs is 45 days, meaning that the CMT rate 45 days before the anniversary date is being used to reset the coupon for the next period.

There are ARMs that can be converted into fixed-rate mortgages at the option of the borrower. These ARMS, called *convertible ARMs,* reduce the cost of refinancing. When converted, the new loan rate may be either (1) a rate determined by the lender or (2) a market-determined rate. A borrower can typically convert at any time between the first and fifth anniversary dates from the origination date.

Due to the caps and conversion feature, the value of an ARM and securities backed by ARMs must be valued using the methodology described in Chapter 11. This is because the methodology described, option-adjusted spread, considers the potential path of interest rates over the life of the ARM and how that path affects the coupon rate after adjusting for periodic and lifetime caps and whether the borrower will exercise the conversion option.

Indices Used

Two categories of indices have been used in ARMs: (1) market determined rates and (2) calculated cost of funds for thrifts. The index will have an important impact on the performance of an ARM and its value. The most common market determined rates used are the 1-year, 3-year or 5-year Constant Maturity Treasury (CMT) and 3-month or 6-month London Interbank Offered Rate (LIBOR).

The cost of funds index for thrifts is calculated based on the monthly weighted average interest cost for liabilities of thrifts. The most popular is the Eleventh Federal Home Loan Bank Board District Cost of Funds Index (COFI). About 25% of ARMs are indexed to this reference rate. The Eleventh District includes the states of California, Arizona, and Nevada. The cost of funds is calculated by first computing the monthly interest expenses for all thrifts included in the Eleventh District. The interest expenses are summed and then divided by the average of the beginning and ending monthly balance. The index value is reported with a one month lag. For example, June's Eleventh District COFI is reported in July. The mortgage rate for a mortgage based on the Eleventh District COFI is usually reset based on the previous month's reported index rate. For example, if the reset date is August, the index rate reported in July will be used to set the mortgage rate. Consequently, there is a two month lag by the time the average cost of funds is reflected in the mortgage rate. This obviously is an advantage to the borrower when interest rates are rising and a disadvantage to the investor. The opposite is true when interest rates are falling.

Describing ARMs

The attributes needed to describe an ARM are the teaser rate, teaser period, index, margin, reset frequency, periodic cap, and lifetime cap. Of course, maturity is important too but almost all ARMs are 30-year loans, unlike 5-year, 7-year, 15-year, and 20-year fixed-rate loans.

For example, a "6% 1-year CMT + 3% ARM with 2/12 caps" means the loan has a 6% coupon for the first year. It will reset the second year coupon to the then 1-year CMT index rate plus 3% on the anniversary date subject to the 2%

periodic cap and 12% lifetime cap constraints. If the prevailing CMT rate is 4.8%, the coupon will simply reset to 7.8% (4.8% + 3%). If the prevailing CMT rate is 5.5%, the coupon can only reset to 8% (not 5.5% + 3%) because the 2% periodic cap only allows a maximum of 2% movement (plus or minus) in the coupon rate from one period to another. The 12% lifetime cap limits the coupon to 12% during the life of the loan.

Agency ARM Programs

In the next chapter we will discuss mortgage passthrough securities issued by three agencies — Ginnie Mae, Fannie Mae, and Freddie Mac, These agencies have several standardized ARM programs to promote uniformity and liquidity in TBA trading of passthrough securities backed by a pool of ARMs (although ARMs also trade on a specified pool basis). The three most common programs are summarized in Exhibit 2.

While the programs in Exhibit 2 are the most common standardized ARM programs sponsored by the agencies, there are many variations. For instance, there are 3-year CMT ARMs that reset every three years off the 3-year CMT index and 5-year CMT ARMs that reset every five years off the 5-year CMT index. There are also 6-month Treasury bill ARMs that reset off the 6-month Treasury bill rate semiannually with a 1% periodic cap. There are semiannual and annual COFI ARMs that work exactly like CMT ARMs. There are also quarterly reset LIBOR ARMs that reset off the 3-month moving average LIBOR.

There exists another group of hybrid fixed/ARM loans that look like both fixed- and adjustable-rate mortgages. For instance, a "10/1 loan" has a fixed coupon for ten years, then it will convert to a 1-year CMT ARM starting the 11th year. A "7/23 loan" is a fixed rate loan that will reset only once for the life of the loan at the end of the 7th year to the prevailing market rate which will then be fixed for the remaining 23 years.

Exhibit 2: Agency ARM Programs

	PROGRAMS			
	Ginnie ARM	CMT ARM	COFI ARM	LIBOR ARM
Agency	GNMA	FNMA FHLMC	FNMA FHLMC	FNMA FHLMC
Teaser Period	1 year	1 year	6 months	6 months
Reset Frequency	annually	annually	monthly	semi-annually
Index	1-year CMT	1-year CMT	11th COFI	6-month LIBOR
Margin	2%	2% to 4%	2% to 4%	2% to 4%
Periodic Cap	1%	2%	none	1%
Lifetime Cap	teaser rate +5%	teaser rate +6%	teaser rate +6%	teaser rate +6%
Lookback	45 days	45 days	3 months	45 days
Convertability	No	Yes/No	No	Yes/No

Balloon Mortgages

In a *balloon mortgage*, the borrower is given long-term financing by the lender but at specified future dates the contract rate is renegotiated. Thus, the lender is providing long-term funds for what is effectively a short-term borrowing, how short depending on the frequency of the renegotiation period. Effectively it is a short-term balloon loan in which the lender agrees to provide financing for the remainder of the term of the mortgage. The balloon payment is the original amount borrowed less the amount amortized. Thus, in a balloon mortgage, the actual maturity is shorter than the stated maturity.

Two-Step Mortgages

Akin to the idea of a balloon loan with a refinancing option for the borrower is a fixed-rate mortgage with a single rate reset at some point prior to maturity. Unlike a refinancing option, this rate reset occurs without specific action on the part of the borrower.

Unlike in balloon mortgages, the rate reset on the two-step mortgage does not consist of a repayment of the initial loan and the origination of a new one; thus, a 30-year two-step mortgage has a 30-year final maturity, rather than the shorter final maturity of a balloon mortgage. Essentially, then, the two-step mortgage is an adjustable-rate mortgage with a single reset.

Growing Equity Mortgages

A *growing equity mortgage* (GEM) is a fixed-rate mortgage whose monthly mortgage payments increase over time. The initial monthly mortgage payment is the same as for a level-payment mortgage. The higher monthly mortgage payments are applied to paying off the principal. As a result, the principal of a GEM is repaid faster. For example, a 30-year $100,000 GEM loan with a contract rate of 8.125% might call for an initial monthly payment of $742.50 (the same as a level-payment 8.125% 30-year mortgage loan). However, the GEM payment would gradually increase, and the GEM might be fully paid in only 15 years.

Tiered Payment Mortgages

Another mortgage design with a fixed rate and a monthly payment that graduates over time is the *tiered payment mortgage* (TPM). The initial monthly mortgage payments are below that of a traditional mortgage. There in no negative amortization because withdrawals are made from a buydown account to supplement the initial monthly payments to cover the shortfall of interest. The buydown account is established at the time the loan is originated by the borrower, lender, or a third party such as a relative or business associate.

CONVENTIONAL VERSUS INSURED MORTGAGES

When the lender makes the loan based on the credit of the borrower and on the collateral for the mortgage, the mortgage is said to be a *conventional mortgage*. The lender may require the borrower to obtain mortgage insurance to insure against default by the borrower. It is usually required by lenders on loans with a loan-to-value (LTV) ratio greater than 80%. The amount of insurance is based on the original LTV and the borrower's credit. The amount insured may decline as the LTV ratio declines. The cost of the insurance can be paid by the borrower upfront or on a monthly basis.

There are two forms of this insurance: insurance provided a government agency and private mortgage insurance. The federal agencies that provide this insurance to qualified borrowers are the Federal Housing Administration (FHA), the Veterans Administration (VA), and the Rural Housing Service (RHS). Private mortgage insurance can be obtained from a mortgage insurance company.

Another form of insurance may be required for mortgages on property that are located in geographical areas where the occurrence of natural disasters such as floods and earthquakes is higher than usual. This type of insurance is called *hazard insurance*.

CONFORMING VERSUS NONCONFORMING MORTGAGES

In the next three chapters we will discuss mortgage-backed securities issued by agencies of the U.S. government and private entities. In order for a loan to be included in a pool of loans backing an agency security, it must meet specified underwriting standards. These standards set forth the maximum size of the loan, the loan documentation required, the maximum loan-to-value ratio, and whether or not insurance is required.

If a loan satisfies the underwriting standards for inclusion as collateral for an agency mortgage-backed security, it is called a *conforming mortgage*. If a loan fails to satisfy the underwriting standards, it is called a *nonconforming mortgage*. Loans that fail to quality as a conforming mortgage because they exceed the maximum loan size are called *jumbo mortgages*. Loans that fail to qualify because of documentation are called either "no doc" or "low doc" mortgages, the former indicating that the lender did not require documentation to verify the borrower's income and the latter that there was only limited documentation to verify the borrower's income.

LOAN PURPOSE

There are also loans based on the purpose of the loan. Understanding the purpose of a loan can better help investors understand the potential prepayment behavior of borrowers with such loans that back a security.

Here are some examples. A loan to refinance an existing mortgage is called a *refinancing loan* or *refi loan*. When the loan is used to allow the borrower to withdraw equity from a home that has appreciated, it is called an *equity take-out loan*.

A loan used for financing a home purchased because the borrower was relocated by a corporation is called a *relocation loan* or *relo loan*. Freddie Mac, Fannie Mae, and several private originators have programs for relo loans and have securitized these loans. The loans are subsidized by corporate employers and must meet certain standards in order to qualify for an originator's relo loan program.

PREPAYMENT PENALTY MORTGAGES

Most mortgages have no prepayment penalty. That is, the borrower can prepay a loan in whole or in part at any time at par value. In 1996, mortgages with prepayment penalties were originated and in early 1997, Fannie Mae passthrough securities backed by prepayment penalty mortgages were issued. The purpose of the penalty is to deter prepayment when interest rates decline.

A prepayment penalty mortgage has the following structure. There is a period of time over which if the loan is prepaid in full or in excess of a certain amount of the outstanding balance, there is a prepayment penalty. This is referred to as the *penalty period*. During the penalty period, the borrower may prepay up to a specified amount of the outstanding balance without a penalty. The amount of the penalty is specified in terms of the number of months of interest that must be paid or a rate.

For example, in the first Fannie Mae passthroughs backed by prepayment penalty mortgages, a penalty is imposed if a loan is prepaid in the first five years. However, in the penalty period the borrower may prepay up to 20% of the outstanding balance each year without a penalty. The penalty is equal to six months of interest on the outstanding balance. For the prepayment penalty mortgages pooled by First Nationwide and Countrywide in 1997, the penalty period is three years and five years respectively. The prepayment penalty is $5/32$ on 7% securities and $9/32$ on 7.5% securities for the First Nationwide and $9/32$ on 7% securities and $13/32$ on 7.5% securities for Countrywide.

When prepayment penalty mortgages are securitized, it is important to understand that the prepayment penalty is paid to the issuer, not the investor. However, the penalty still discourages homeowners from prepaying when rates decline.

SUMMARY

In this chapter we surveyed the various types of mortgages that are have been pooled to create mortgage-backed securities. The various mortgage designs include (1) fixed-rate, level payment fully amortizing mortgages, (2) adjustable-rate mortgages, (3) balloon mortgages, (4) two-step mortgages, (5) growing equity mortgages, and (6) tiered payment mortgages. There are noninsured mortgages (called conventional mortgages) and insured mortgages. The latter are insured either by a government agency or a private entity. Conforming mortgages are those that satisfy the underwriting standards established by an agency for inclusion in a pool of mortgages that back a security. Nonconforming mortgages are those that fail one or more of the underwriting standards. Nonconforming mortgages include jumbo mortgages, no doc mortgages, and low doc mortgages. Mortgages are also categorized according to the purpose of the loan. Examples are refinancing loans, equity takeout loans, and relocation loans. Finally, in recent years, prepayment penalty mortgages have been originated.

Chapter 3

Passthroughs, Mortgage Strips, and Callable Passthroughs

Mortgage-backed securities are securities backed by a pool (collection) of mortgage loans. While any type of mortgage loans, residential or commercial, can be used as collateral for a mortgage-backed security, most are backed by residential mortgages. Mortgage-backed securities include the following securities: (1) mortgage passthrough securities, (2) collateralized mortgage obligations, and (3) stripped mortgage-backed securities. The latter two mortgage-backed securities are referred to as *derivative mortgage-backed securities* because they are created from mortgage passthrough securities. In this chapter we describe mortgage passthrough securities and stripped mortgage-backed securities. More specifically, we look at those securities either guaranteed by the full faith and credit of the U.S. government or guaranteed by a government sponsored enterprise. Such mortgage-backed securities are called *agency mortgage-backed securities*. In Chapter 5, we look at nonagency mortgage-backed securities.

MORTGAGE PASSTHROUGH SECURITIES

Investing in mortgages exposes an investor to default risk and prepayment risk. A more efficient way is to invest in a *mortgage passthrough security*. This is a security created when one or more holders of mortgages form a pool (collection) of mortgages and sell shares or participation certificates in the pool. A pool may consist of several thousand or only a few mortgages. When a mortgage is included in a pool of mortgages that is used as collateral for a mortgage passthrough security, the mortgage is said to be *securitized*.

The cash flows of a mortgage passthrough security depend on the cash flows of the underlying mortgages. As we explained in the previous chapter, the cash flows consist of monthly mortgage payments representing interest, the scheduled repayment of principal, and any prepayments.

Payments are made to security holders each month. Neither the amount nor the timing, however, of the cash flows from the pool of mortgages are identical to that of the cash flows passed through to investors. The monthly cash flows for a passthrough are less than the monthly cash flows of the underlying mortgages by an amount equal to servicing and other fees. The other fees are those charged by the issuer or guarantor of the passthrough for guaranteeing the issue.

21

The coupon rate on a passthrough, called the *passthrough coupon rate*, is less than the mortgage rate on the underlying pool of mortgage loans by an amount equal to the servicing fee and guarantee fee. The latter is a fee charged by an agency for providing one of the guarantees discussed later.

The timing of the cash flows is also different. The monthly mortgage payment is due from each mortgagor on the first day of each month, but there is a delay in passing through the corresponding monthly cash flow to the security holders. The length of the delay varies by the type of passthrough security.

Not all of the mortgages that are included in a pool of mortgages that are securitized have the same mortgage rate and the same maturity. Consequently, when describing a passthrough security, a weighted average coupon rate and a weighted average maturity are determined. A *weighted average coupon rate*, or WAC, is found by weighting the mortgage rate of each mortgage loan in the pool by the amount of the mortgage balance outstanding. A *weighted average maturity*, or WAM, is found by weighting the remaining number of months to maturity for each mortgage loan in the pool by the amount of the mortgage balance outstanding.

Features of Agency Passthroughs

Features of agency passthroughs vary not only by agency but also by program offered. The key features of a passthrough will have an impact on its investment characteristics (particularly its prepayment characteristics). These general features, summarized below and discussed further when we review the various agency programs, can be classified into five groups: (1) the type of guarantee, (2) the numbers of lenders whose mortgage loans are permitted in a pool, (3) the mortgage design of the loans, (4) the characteristics of the mortgage loans in a pool, and (5) the payment procedure.

Type of Guarantee

An agency can provide two types of guarantee. One type is the timely payment of both interest and principal, meaning the interest and principal will be paid when due, even if any of the mortgagors fail to make their monthly mortgage payments. Passthroughs with this type of guarantee are referred to as *fully modified passthroughs*. The second type guarantees both interest and principal payments; however, it only guarantees the timely payment of interest. The scheduled principal is passed through as it is collected with a guarantee that the scheduled payment will be made no later than a specified date. Passthroughs with this type of guarantee are called *modified passthroughs*.

Number of Lenders Permitted in a Pool

A pool may consist of mortgages originated by a single lender or multiple lenders. A single-lender pool may have mortgage loans concentrated in one geographical area or a few states. In multiple-lender pools, the underlying mortgage loans have greater geographical diversification of borrowers.

Mortgage Design of the Loans

Earlier we described different types of mortgage designs. Agency passthroughs have pools of loans with various mortgage designs.

Characteristics of the Mortgage Loans in the Pool

Not all mortgage loans are permitted in a pool that collateralizes a passthrough. The underwriting standards established by the agency specify the permissible loans. The key underwriting standards are summarized below.

Mortgage Loans Permitted in the Pool Mortgage loans can be classified as government-insured loans and conventional loans.

Maximum Size of a Loan For agency securities, the loan limits are reset annually.

Amount of Seasoning Permitted The seasoning of a mortgage loan refers to the time which has passed since the loan was originated.

Assumability of Mortgages If a mortgage loan may be taken over by another borrower, the loan is said to be assumable.

Maturity Programs are available with mortgage loans of different maturities. For example, a pool can have a stated maturity of 30 years, even though not all of the mortgage loans in the pool have a maturity of 30 years, since seasoned loans may be included.

Servicing Spread Permitted As explained earlier, for an individual mortgage loan the servicing spread is the difference between the coupon rate paid by the homeowner and the interest rate received by the investor. A maximum servicing spread permitted in an agency passthrough is specified.

Payment Procedure

Differences in payment procedures involve payment delays and the method of payment.

Payment Delays Payment delays for passthroughs occur for two reasons. First, monthly payments made by homeowners are made in arrears. That is, the payment for the funds borrowed in, say, March are due on the first of the month of April, the normal delay when investing in mortgage loans. When the payments are received by the trustee, they must be processed and the checks mailed to passthrough investors. The actual delay for passthrough investors — that is, the number of days that payment is delayed beyond the normal delay — varies with the agency and agency program. The "stated delay" of a passthrough is the normal delay plus the actual delay. If the payment is made on the 15th of the month, then the actual delay is 14 days, since the monthly payment would have been due on the first of the month. If the stated delay for a passthrough is 44 days, then the actual delay is 14 days.

Method of Payment By method of payment, we mean how many monthly checks an investor who owns several pools of an agency will receive. There can be either one check for all pools or multiple checks.

Types of Agency Mortgage Passthrough Securities

There are three types of agency passthrough securities. Each agency has different programs.

Government National Mortgage Association MBS

Government National Mortgage Association (nicknamed "Ginnie Mae") passthroughs are guaranteed by the full faith and credit of the U.S. government. For this reason, Ginnie Mae passthroughs are viewed as risk-free in terms of default risk, just like Treasury securities. The security guaranteed by Ginnie Mae is called a *mortgage-backed security* (MBS). Ginnie Mae MBSs are issued under one of two programs: GNMA I (established in 1970) and GNMA II (established in 1983).

Type of Guarantee All Ginnie Mae MBS are fully modified passthroughs.

Number of Lenders Permitted in a Pool Only single-lender pools are permitted under the GNMA I program; both single-lender and multiple-lender pools are allowed in the GNMA II program. Single-lender pools issued under the GNMA II program are called *custom pools*; multiple-lender pools are called *jumbo pools*.

Mortgage Design of the Loans Under the two programs, passthroughs with different types of mortgage designs are issued. The large majority of GNMA MBS are backed by single-family mortgages, where a single-family mortgage is a loan for a 1-to-4 family primary residence with a fixed-rate, level-payment mortgage. A Ginnie Mae MBS of this type is referred to as a "GNMA SF MBS." Exhibit 2 in Chapter 2 describes the various programs for ARMs.

Characteristics of the Mortgage Loans in the Pool The key underwriting standards for the mortgage loans are summarized below.

1. Mortgage Loans Permitted in the Pool Only mortgage loans insured or guaranteed by either the Federal Housing Administration, the Veterans Administration, or the Rural Housing Service can be included in a mortgage pool guaranteed by Ginnie Mae.

2. Maximum Size of a Loan The maximum loan size is set by Congress, based on the maximum amount that the FHA, VA, or RHS may guarantee. The maximum for a given loan varies with the region of the country and type of residential property.

3. Amount of Seasoning Permitted In both programs, only newly originated mortgage loans may be included in a pool. These are defined as mortgage loans that have been seasoned less than 24 months.

4. Assumability of Mortgages Assumable mortgages are permitted in the pool.

5. Maturity Within the single-family MBS, there are pools that consist of 30-year or 15-year mortgages that collateralize the security. The 15-year pools are commonly referred to as "midgets."

6. Servicing Spread In the GNMA I program, the servicing spread is 50 basis points; for the GNMA II program, the servicing spread may vary from 50 to 150 basis points.

Payment Procedure The stated delay for GNMA I and II programs are 45 and 50 days, respectively. Thus, corresponding actual delays are 14 and 19 days, respectively. The method of payment also differs between the two programs. In the GNMA I program, payments are made by the individual servicers. In the GNMA II program, payments from all pools owned by an investor are consolidated and paid in one check by the central paying agent.

Federal Home Loan Mortgage Corporation PC

The Federal Home Loan Mortgage Corporation (nicknamed "Freddie Mac") is a government sponsored enterprise that issues a passthrough security that is called a *participation certificate* (PC). Although a guarantee of Freddie Mac is not a guarantee by the U.S. government, most market participants view Freddie Mac PCs as similar, although not identical, in credit worthiness to Ginnie Mae passthroughs.

Freddie Mac has two programs from which it creates PCs: the Cash Program and the Guarantor/Swap Program. The underlying loans for both programs are conventional mortgages. In the cash program the mortgages that back the PC include individual conventional 1- to 4-family mortgage loans that Freddie Mac purchases from mortgage originators, pools, and then sells. Under the Guarantor/Swap Program, Freddie Mac allows originators to swap pooled mortgages for PCs backed by those mortgages. For example, a thrift may have $50 million of mortgages. It can swap these mortgages for a Freddie Mac PC whose underlying mortgage pool is the $50 million mortgage pool the thrift swapped for the PC. The PCs created under the first program are called *Cash PCs* or *Regular PCs*, under the second program they are called *Swap PCs*.

Type of Guarantee There are both modified passthroughs and fully modified passthroughs. Non-Gold PCs that have been issued as part of its Cash program and almost all that have been issued as part of the Guarantor/Swap program are modified passthroughs. There are a very small number of non-Gold PCs in the latter program that are fully modified passthroughs. All Gold PCs issued are fully modified passthroughs.

For modified PCs issued by Freddie Mac, the scheduled principal is passed through as it is collected, with Freddie Mac only guaranteeing that the scheduled payment will be made no later than one year after it is due.

Number of Lenders Permitted in a Pool There are only multiple-lender pools in the Cash Program. In the Guarantor/Swap program, there are both single-lender and multiple-lender pools.

Mortgage Design of the Loans There are pools with fixed-rate, level-payment, fully amortized mortgage loans, adjustable-rate mortgage loans, and balloon mortgage loans. A wide variety of ARM PCs are issued under both the Cash and Guarantor/Swap programs. (See Exhibit 2 in Chapter 2.)

Characteristics of the Mortgage Loans in the Pool The key underwriting standards for the mortgage loans are summarized below.

1. Mortgage Loans Permitted in the Pool The majority of PCs are backed by conventional mortgage loans. There are a small portion of PCs which are backed by FHA and VA guaranteed mortgage loans.

2. Maximum Size of a Loan The maximum loan size is set each year based on the annual percentage change in the average price of conventionally financed homes as determined by the Federal Home Loan Bank Board. The maximum loan for a 1-to-4 family residence depends on the number of units.

3. Amount of Seasoning Permitted There are no limits on seasoning for either program.

4. Assumability of Mortgages No assumable mortgages are permitted in a pool.

5. Maturity There are 30-year and 15-year Freddie Mac Regular and Swap PCs. The 15-year Regular PCs are called "gnomes" and Swap PCs are called "non-gnomes."

6. Net Interest Spread Permitted In general, the net interest spread can be 50 to 250 basis points for both programs.

Payment Procedure The stated delay and actual delay for non-Gold PCs issued as part of either program is 75 and 44 days, respectively. The Gold PCs have a shorter payment delay; the stated delay is 45 days, the actual delay 14 days. One monthly check is received in both programs for all pools an investor owns.

Federal National Mortgage Association MBS

The passthroughs issued by the Federal National Mortgage Association (nick-named "Fannie Mae") are called *mortgage-backed securities* (MBSs). Like a Freddie Mac PC, a Fannie Mae MBS is not the obligation of the U.S. government since Fannie Mae is a government sponsored enterprise. Fannie Mae also has a swap program similar to that of Freddie Mac, through which it issues most of its MBSs.

There are four standard MBS programs established by Fannie Mae, which we discuss below. In addition to its regular programs, Fannie Mae issues securities known as "boutique" securities. These are securities that are issued through negotiated transactions and not backed by one of the mortgage loan types in its regular program.

Type of Guarantee All Fannie Mae MBSs are fully modified passthroughs.

Number of Lenders Permitted in a Pool There are only multiple-lender pools in the Cash program. In this program Fannie Mae purchases mortgage loans from various lenders and then creates a pool to collateralize the MBS. In Fannie Mae's Guarantor/Swap program there are both single-lender and multiple-lender pools.

Mortgage Design of the Loans Three of the four standard programs have pools backed by mortgage loans that are fixed-rate, level-payment, fully amortized mortgages. The fourth standard program is a MBS collateralized by adjustable-rate mortgage loans. Exhibit 2 of the previous chapter describes the various ARMs programs.

Characteristics of the Mortgage Loans in the Pool The key underwriting standards for the mortgage loans are summarized below.

1. Mortgage Loans Permitted in the Pool Two of the four standard programs are backed by conventional mortgages. One is backed by FHA-insured or VA-guaranteed mortgages. Securities issued from the two programs backed by conventional mortgages are called *Conventional MBSs*. The MBSs that are backed by FHA-insured or VA-guaranteed mortgages are called *Government MBSs*.

2. Maximum Size of a Loan The maximum loan size is the same as for Freddie Mac PCs.

3. Amount of Seasoning Permitted There are no limits on seasoning.

4. Assumability of Mortgages No assumable mortgages are permitted in a pool.

5. Maturity The securities issued from the two programs backed by conventional mortgages are 30-year and 15-year MBS, commonly referred to as the *Conventional Long-Term* and *Conventional Intermediate-Term MBS*, respectively. The 15-year MBSs are also known as "dwarfs." The MBSs that are backed by 30-year FHA-insured or VA-guaranteed mortgages are called *Government Long-Term MBSs*.

6. Net Interest Spread Permitted In general, the net interest spread can be 50 to 250 basis points for both programs.

7. Payment Procedure The stated delay is 55 days and the actual delay 24 days.

Prepayment Conventions and Cash Flows

In order to value a passthrough security, it is necessary to project its cash flows. The difficulty is that the cash flows are unknown because of prepayments. The only way to project cash flows are to make some assumption about the prepayment rate over the life of the underlying mortgage pool. The prepayment rate is sometimes referred to as the *speed*. Two conventions have been used as a benchmark for prepayment rates — conditional prepayment rate and Public Securities Association prepayment benchmark.

Conditional Prepayment Rate

One convention for projecting prepayments and the cash flows of a passthrough assumes that some fraction of the remaining principal in the pool is prepaid each month for the remaining term of the mortgage. The prepayment rate assumed for a pool, called the *conditional prepayment rate* (CPR), is based on the characteristics of the pool (including its historical prepayment experience) and the current and expected future economic environment.

The CPR is an annual prepayment rate. To estimate monthly prepayments, the CPR must be converted into a monthly prepayment rate, commonly referred to as the *single-monthly mortality rate* (SMM). A formula can be used to determine the SMM for a given CPR:

$$SMM = 1 - (1 - CPR)^{1/12}$$

Suppose that the CPR used to estimate prepayments is 6%. The corresponding SMM is:

$$SMM = 1 - (1 - 0.06)^{1/12}$$
$$= 1 - (0.94)^{0.08333} = 0.005143$$

An SMM of $w\%$ means that approximately $w\%$ of the remaining mortgage balance at the beginning of the month, less the scheduled principal payment, will prepay that month. That is,

Prepayment for month t = SMM
   × (Beginning mortgage balance for month t
   − Scheduled principal payment for month t)

For example, suppose that an investor owns a passthrough in which the remaining mortgage balance at the beginning of some month is $290 million. Assuming that the SMM is 0.5143% and the scheduled principal payment is $3 million, the estimated prepayment for the month is:

$$0.005143 \times (\$290,000,000 - \$3,000,000) = \$1,476,041$$

Exhibit 1: Graphical Depiction of 100 PSA

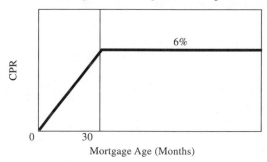

PSA Prepayment Benchmark

The Public Securities Association (PSA) prepayment benchmark is expressed as a monthly series of CPRs.[1] The PSA benchmark assumes that prepayment rates are low for newly originated mortgages and then will speed up as the mortgages become seasoned.

The PSA benchmark assumes the following prepayment rates for 30-year mortgages:

(1) a CPR of 0.2% for the first month, increased by 0.2% per year per month for the next 30 months when it reaches 6% per year, and

(2) a 6% CPR for the remaining years.

This benchmark, referred to as "100% PSA" or simply "100 PSA," is graphically depicted in Exhibit 1. Mathematically, 100 PSA can be expressed as follows:

if $t \le 30$ then CPR $= \dfrac{6\% \ t}{30}$

if $t > 30$ then CPR $= 6\%$

where t is the number of months since the mortgage originated.

Slower or faster speeds are then referred to as some percentage of PSA. For example, 50 PSA means one-half the CPR of the PSA benchmark prepayment rate; 150 PSA means 1.5 times the CPR of the PSA benchmark prepayment rate; 300 PSA means three times the CPR of the benchmark prepayment rate. A prepayment rate of 0 PSA means that no prepayments are assumed.

The CPR is converted to an SMM using the formula given above. For example, the SMMs for month 5, month 20, and months 31 through 360 assuming 100 PSA are calculated as follows:

---

[1] This benchmark is commonly referred to as a prepayment model, suggesting that it can be used to estimate prepayments. Characterization of this benchmark as a prepayment model is inappropriate. It is simply a market convention describing the behavior pattern of prepayments.

for month 5:

$$CPR = 6\% \ (5/30) = 1\% = 0.01$$
$$SMM = 1 - (1 - 0.01)^{1/12}$$
$$= 1 - (0.99)^{0.083333} = 0.000837$$

for month 20:

$$CPR = 6\% \ (20/30) = 4\% = 0.04$$
$$SMM = 1 - (1 - 0.04)^{1/12}$$
$$= 1 - (0.96)^{0.083333} = 0.003396$$

for months 31-360:

$$CPR = 6\%$$
$$SMM = 1 - (1 - 0.06)^{1/12}$$
$$= 1 - (0.94)^{0.083333} = 0.005143$$

The SMMs for month 5, month 20, and months 31 through 360 assuming 165 PSA are computed as follows:

for month 5:

$$CPR = 6\% \ (5/30) = 1\% = 0.01$$
$$165 \ PSA = 1.65 \ (0.01) = 0.0165$$
$$SMM = 1 - (1 - 0.0165)^{1/12}$$
$$= 1 - (0.9835)^{0.083333} = 0.001386$$

for month 20:

$$CPR = 6\% \ (20/30) = 4\% = 0.04$$
$$165 \ PSA = 1.65 \ (.04) = 0.066$$
$$SMM = 1 - (1 - 0.066)^{1/12}$$
$$= 1 - (0.934)^{0.083333} = 0.005674$$

for months 31-360:

$$CPR = 6\%$$
$$165 \ PSA = 1.65 \ (0.06) = 0.099$$
$$SMM = 1 - (1 - 0.099)^{1/12}$$
$$= 1 - (0.901)^{0.083333} = 0.007828$$

Notice that the SMM assuming 165 PSA is not just 1.65 times the SMM assuming 100 PSA. It is the CPR that is a multiple of the CPR assuming 100 PSA.

Illustration of Monthly Cash Flow Construction

We now show how to construct a monthly cash flow for a hypothetical passthrough given a PSA assumption. For the purpose of this illustration, the underlying mortgages for this hypothetical passthrough are assumed to be fixed-rate, level-payment, fully amortized mortgages with a weighted average coupon (WAC) rate of 8.125%. It will be assumed that the passthrough rate is 7.5% with a weighted average maturity (WAM) of 357 months.

Exhibit 2 shows the cash flow for selected months assuming 100 PSA. The cash flow is broken down into three components: (1) interest (based on the passthrough rate), (2) the regularly scheduled principal repayment, and (3) prepayments based on 100 PSA.

Let's walk through Exhibit 2 column by column.

Column 1: This is the month.

Column 2: This column gives the outstanding mortgage balance at the beginning of the month. It is equal to the outstanding balance at the beginning of the previous month reduced by the total principal payment in the previous month.

Column 3: This column shows the SMM for 100 PSA. Two things should be noted in this column. First, for month 1, the SMM is for a passthrough that has been seasoned three months. That is, the CPR is 0.8% for the first month. This is because the WAM is 357. Second, from month 27 on, the SMM is 0.00514 which corresponds to a CPR of 6%.

Column 4: The total monthly mortgage payment is shown in this column. Notice that the total monthly mortgage payment declines over time as prepayments reduce the mortgage balance outstanding. There is a formula to determine what the monthly mortgage balance will be for each month given prepayments.[2]

Column 5: The monthly interest paid to the passthrough investor is found in this column. This value is determined by multiplying the outstanding mortgage balance at the beginning of the month by the passthrough rate of 7.5% and dividing by 12.

Column 6: This column gives the regularly scheduled principal repayment. This is the difference between the total monthly mortgage payment [the amount shown in column (4)] and the gross coupon interest for the month. The gross coupon interest is 8.125% multiplied by the outstanding mortgage balance at the beginning of the month, then divided by 12.

Column 7: The prepayment for the month is reported in this column. The prepayment is found as follows:

SMM × (Beginning mortgage balance for month *t*
  − Scheduled principal payment for month *t*)

---

[2] The formula is presented in Chapter 20 of Frank J. Fabozzi, *Fixed Income Mathematics: Analytical and Statistical Techniques* (Chicago: Probus Publishing, 1993).

Exhibit 2: Monthly Cash Flow for a $400 Million Passthrough with a 7.5% Passthrough Rate, a WAC of 8.125%, and a WAM of 357 Months Assuming 100 PSA

(1)	(2)	(3)	(4)	(5)	(6)	(7)	(8)	(9)
Month	Outstanding Balance	SMM	Mortgage Payment	Net Interest	Scheduled Principal	Prepayment	Total Principal	Cash Flow
1	$400,000,000	0.00067	$2,975,868	$2,500,000	$267,535	$267,470	$535,005	$3,035,005
2	399,464,995	0.00084	2,973,877	2,496,656	269,166	334,198	603,364	3,100,020
3	398,861,631	0.00101	2,971,387	2,492,885	270,762	400,800	671,562	3,164,447
4	398,190,069	0.00117	2,968,399	2,488,688	272,321	467,243	739,564	3,228,252
5	397,450,505	0.00134	2,964,914	2,484,066	273,843	533,493	807,335	3,291,401
6	396,643,170	0.00151	2,960,931	2,479,020	275,327	599,514	874,841	3,353,860
7	395,768,329	0.00168	2,956,453	2,473,552	276,772	665,273	942,045	3,415,597
8	394,826,284	0.00185	2,951,480	2,467,664	278,177	730,736	1,008,913	3,476,577
9	393,817,371	0.00202	2,946,013	2,461,359	279,542	795,869	1,075,410	3,536,769
10	392,741,961	0.00219	2,940,056	2,454,637	280,865	860,637	1,141,502	3,596,140
11	391,600,459	0.00236	2,933,608	2,447,503	282,147	925,008	1,207,155	3,654,658
24	370,992,132	0.00462	2,806,607	2,318,701	294,681	1,710,908	2,005,589	4,324,290
25	368,986,543	0.00479	2,793,654	2,306,166	295,307	1,766,368	2,061,675	4,367,841
26	366,924,868	0.00497	2,780,270	2,293,280	295,883	1,820,970	2,116,852	4,410,133
27	364,808,016	0.00514	2,766,461	2,280,050	296,406	1,874,688	2,171,094	4,451,144
28	362,636,921	0.00514	2,752,233	2,266,481	296,879	1,863,519	2,160,398	4,426,879
29	360,476,523	0.00514	2,738,078	2,252,978	297,351	1,852,406	2,149,758	4,402,736
30	358,326,766	0.00514	2,723,996	2,239,542	297,825	1,841,347	2,139,173	4,378,715
100	231,249,776	0.00514	1,898,682	1,445,311	332,928	1,187,608	1,520,537	2,965,848
101	229,729,239	0.00514	1,888,917	1,435,808	333,459	1,179,785	1,513,244	2,949,052
102	228,215,995	0.00514	1,879,202	1,426,350	333,990	1,172,000	1,505,990	2,932,340
103	226,710,004	0.00514	1,869,538	1,416,938	334,522	1,164,252	1,498,774	2,915,712
200	109,791,339	0.00514	1,133,751	686,196	390,372	562,651	953,023	1,639,219
201	108,838,316	0.00514	1,127,920	680,239	390,994	557,746	948,740	1,628,980
202	107,889,576	0.00514	1,122,119	674,310	391,617	552,863	944,480	1,618,790
203	106,945,096	0.00514	1,116,348	668,407	392,241	548,003	940,243	1,608,650
300	32,383,611	0.00514	676,991	202,398	457,727	164,195	621,923	824,320
301	31,761,689	0.00514	673,510	198,511	458,457	160,993	619,449	817,960
302	31,142,239	0.00514	670,046	194,639	459,187	157,803	616,990	811,629
303	30,525,249	0.00514	666,600	190,783	459,918	154,626	614,545	805,328
353	2,524,037	0.00514	515,107	15,775	498,018	10,420	508,437	524,213
354	2,015,600	0.00514	512,458	12,597	498,811	7,801	506,612	519,209
355	1,508,988	0.00514	509,823	9,431	499,606	5,191	504,797	514,228
356	1,004,191	0.00514	507,201	6,276	500,401	2,591	502,992	509,269
357	501,199	0.00514	504,592	3,132	501,199	0	501,199	504,331

Note: Since the WAM is 357 months, the underlying mortgage pool is seasoned an average of three months. Therefore, the CPR for month 27 is 6%.

For example, in month 100, the beginning mortgage balance is $231,249,776, the scheduled principal payment is $332,298, and the SMM at 100 PSA is 0.00514301 (only 0.00514 is shown in the exhibit to save space). Therefore, the prepayment is:

$$0.00514301 \times (\$231,249,776 - \$332,928) = \$1,187,608.$$

Column 8: The total principal payment, which is the sum of columns (6) and (7), is shown in this column.

Column 9: The projected monthly cash flow for this passthrough is shown in this last column. The monthly cash flow is the sum of the interest paid to the passthrough investor [column (5)] and the total principal payments for the month [column (8)].

Exhibit 3 shows selected monthly cash flow for the same passthrough assuming 165 PSA.

Average Life Measure

The *average life* of a mortgage-backed security is the average time to receipt of principal payments (scheduled principal payments and projected prepayments), weighted by the amount of principal expected. Specifically, the average life is found by first calculating:

$1 \times$ (Projected principal received in month 1)
$2 \times$ (Projected principal received in month 2)
$3 \times$ (Projected principal received in month 3)
...
$$+ \quad \frac{T \times (\text{Projected principal received in month } T)}{\text{Weighted monthly average of principal received}}$$

where T is the last month that principal is expected to be received.
Then the average life is found as follows:

$$\text{Average life} = \frac{\text{Weighted monthly average of principal received}}{12(\text{Total principal to be received})}$$

The average life of a passthrough depends on the PSA prepayment assumption. To see this, the average life is shown below for different prepayment speeds for the passthrough we used to illustrate the cash flows for 100 PSA and 165 PSA in Exhibits 2 and 3:

PSA speed	50	100	165	200	300	400	500	600	700
Average life	15.11	11.66	8.76	7.68	5.63	4.44	3.68	3.16	2.78

A Closer Look at Prepayment Risk

An investor who owns passthrough securities does not know what the cash flows will be because that depends on prepayments. As we noted earlier, this risk is called prepayment risk.

Exhibit 3: Monthly Cash Flow for a $400 Million Passthrough with a 7.5% Passthrough Rate, a WAC of 8.125%, and a WAM of 357 Months Assuming 165 PSA

(1)	(2)	(3)	(4)	(5)	(6)	(7)	(8)	(9)
Month	Outstanding Balance	SMM	Mortgage Payment	Net Interest	Scheduled Principal	Prepayment	Total Principal	Cash Flow
1	$400,000,000	0.00111	$2,975,868	$2,500,000	$267,535	$442,389	$709,923	$3,209,923
2	399,290,077	0.00139	2,972,575	2,495,563	269,048	552,847	821,896	3,317,459
3	398,468,181	0.00167	2,968,456	2,490,426	270,495	663,065	933,560	3,423,986
4	397,534,621	0.00195	2,963,513	2,484,591	271,873	772,949	1,044,822	3,529,413
5	396,489,799	0.00223	2,957,747	2,478,061	273,181	882,405	1,155,586	3,633,647
6	395,334,213	0.00251	2,951,160	2,470,839	274,418	991,341	1,265,759	3,736,598
7	394,068,454	0.00279	2,943,755	2,462,928	275,583	1,099,664	1,375,246	3,838,174
8	392,693,208	0.00308	2,935,534	2,454,333	276,674	1,207,280	1,483,954	3,938,287
9	391,209,254	0.00336	2,926,503	2,445,058	277,690	1,314,099	1,591,789	4,036,847
10	389,617,464	0.00365	2,916,666	2,435,109	278,631	1,420,029	1,698,659	4,133,769
11	387,918,805	0.00393	2,906,028	2,424,493	279,494	1,524,979	1,804,473	4,228,965
24	356,711,789	0.00775	2,698,575	2,229,449	283,338	2,761,139	3,044,477	5,273,926
25	353,667,312	0.00805	2,677,670	2,210,421	283,047	2,843,593	3,126,640	5,337,061
26	350,540,672	0.00835	2,656,123	2,190,879	282,671	2,923,885	3,206,556	5,397,435
27	347,334,116	0.00865	2,633,950	2,170,838	282,209	3,001,955	3,284,164	5,455,002
28	344,049,952	0.00865	2,611,167	2,150,312	281,662	2,973,553	3,255,215	5,405,527
29	340,794,737	0.00865	2,588,581	2,129,967	281,116	2,945,400	3,226,516	5,356,483
30	337,568,221	0.00865	2,566,190	2,109,801	280,572	2,917,496	3,198,067	5,307,869
100	170,142,350	0.00865	1,396,958	1,063,390	244,953	1,469,591	1,714,544	2,777,933
101	168,427,806	0.00865	1,384,875	1,052,674	244,478	1,454,765	1,699,243	2,751,916
102	166,728,563	0.00865	1,372,896	1,042,054	244,004	1,440,071	1,684,075	2,726,128
103	165,044,489	0.00865	1,361,020	1,031,528	243,531	1,425,508	1,669,039	2,700,567
200	56,746,664	0.00865	585,990	354,667	201,767	489,106	690,874	1,045,540
201	56,055,790	0.00865	580,921	350,349	201,377	483,134	684,510	1,034,859
202	55,371,280	0.00865	575,896	346,070	200,986	477,216	678,202	1,024,273
203	54,693,077	0.00865	570,915	341,832	200,597	471,353	671,950	1,013,782
300	11,758,141	0.00865	245,808	73,488	166,196	100,269	266,465	339,953
301	11,491,677	0.00865	243,682	71,823	165,874	97,967	263,841	335,664
302	11,227,836	0.00865	241,574	70,174	165,552	95,687	261,240	331,414
303	10,966,596	0.00865	239,485	68,541	165,232	93,430	258,662	327,203
353	760,027	0.00865	155,107	4,750	149,961	5,277	155,238	159,988
354	604,789	0.00865	153,765	3,780	149,670	3,937	153,607	157,387
355	451,182	0.00865	152,435	2,820	149,380	2,611	151,991	154,811
356	299,191	0.00865	151,117	1,870	149,091	1,298	150,389	152,259
357	148,802	0.00865	149,809	930	148,802	0	148,802	149,732

Note: Since the WAM is 357 months, the underlying mortgage pool is seasoned an average of three months. Therefore, the CPR for month 27 is $1.65 \times 6\%$.

Contraction Risk and Extension Risk

To understand the significance of prepayment risk, suppose an investor buys a 10% coupon Ginnie Mae at a time when mortgage rates are 10%. Let's consider what will happen to prepayments if mortgage rates decline to, say, 6%. There will be two adverse consequences. First, a basic property of fixed income securities is that the price of an option-free bond will rise. But in the case of a passthrough security, the rise in price will not be as large as that of an option-free bond because a fall in interest rates will give the borrower an incentive to prepay the loan and refinance the debt at a lower rate. Thus, the upside price potential of a passthrough security is truncated because of prepayments. The second adverse consequence is that the cash flows must be reinvested at a lower rate. These two adverse consequences when mortgage rates decline are referred to as *contraction risk.*

Now let's look at what happens if mortgage rates rise to 15%. The price of the passthrough, like the price of any bond, will decline. But again it will decline more because the higher rates will tend to slow down the rate of prepayment, in effect increasing the amount invested at the coupon rate, which is lower than the market rate. Prepayments will slow down because homeowners will not refinance or partially prepay their mortgages when mortgage rates are higher than the contract rate of 10%. Of course this is just the time when investors want prepayments to speed up so that they can reinvest the prepayments at the higher market interest rate. This adverse consequence of rising mortgage rates is called *extension risk.*

Therefore, prepayment risk encompasses contraction risk and extension risk. Prepayment risk makes passthrough securities unattractive for certain individuals and financial institutions to hold for purposes of accomplishing their investment objectives. Some individuals and institutional investors are concerned with extension risk and others with contraction risk when they purchase a passthrough security. Is it possible to alter the cash flows of a passthrough so as to reduce the contraction risk and extension risk for institutional investors? This can be done, as we shall see in the next chapter.

Prepayments: Friend Or Foe?

The investor does not know precisely what the monthly prepayments will be when purchasing a passthrough security. A certain prepayment speed is assumed when a passthrough is purchased. Actual prepayments will usually differ from prepayments that were anticipated at the time of purchase.

Prepayments in excess or below the amount anticipated may be good or bad depending on the purchase price. If an investor purchases a passthrough at a premium above par value, then actual prepayments greater than anticipated prepayments will hurt the investor for two reasons. First, there will be a loss since only par is returned, and second, the proceeds must be reinvested at a lower rate. The opposite is true for an investor who purchases a passthrough at a discount. The investor realizes a gain (since par is received but less than par was paid) and the investor can reinvest the proceeds at a higher rate.

Trading and Settlement Procedures

Agency passthroughs are identified by a pool prefix and pool number provided by the agency. The prefix indicates the type of passthrough. For example, a pool prefix of 20 for a Freddie Mac PC means that the underlying pool consists of conventional mortgages with an original maturity of 15 years. A pool prefix of AR for a Ginnie Mae MBS means that the underlying pool consists of adjustable-rate mortgages. The pool number indicates the specific mortgages underlying the passthrough and the issuer of the passthrough.

There are specific rules established by the Public Securities Association for the trading and settlement of mortgage-backed securities. Our discussion here is limited to agency passthrough securities.

Many trades occur while a pool is still unspecified, and therefore no pool information is known at the time of the trade. This kind of trade is known as a "TBA" (to be announced) trade. In a TBA trade the two parties agree on the agency type, the agency program, the coupon rate, the face value, the price, and the settlement date. The actual pools underlying the agency passthrough are not specified in a TBA trade. However, this information is provided by the seller to the buyer before delivery, as explained below. There are trades where more specific requirements are established for the securities to be delivered. For example, a Freddie Mac Gold with a coupon rate of 8.5% and a WAC between 9.0% and 9.2%. There are also *specified pool trades* wherein the actual pool numbers to be delivered are specified.

Passthroughs are quoted in the same manner as U.S. Treasury coupon securities. A quote of 94-05 means 94 and 5/32nds of par value, or 94.15625% of par value. The price that the buyer pays the seller is the agreed upon sale price plus accrued interest. Given the par value, the dollar price (excluding accrued interest) is affected by the amount of the pool mortgage balance outstanding. The *pool factor* indicates the percentage of the initial mortgage balance still outstanding. So, a pool factor of 90 means that 90% of the original mortgage pool balance is outstanding. The pool factor is reported by the agency each month.

The dollar price paid for just the principal is found as follows given the agreed upon price, par value, and the month's pool factor provided by the agency:

Price × Par value × Pool factor

For example, if the parties agree to a price of 92 for $1 million par value for a passthrough with a pool factor of 85, then the dollar price paid by the buyer in addition to accrued interest is:

$0.92 \times \$1,000,000 \times 0.85 = \$782,000$

Trades settle according to a delivery schedule established by the PSA. This schedule is published quarterly by the PSA with information regarding delivery for the next six months. Each agency and program settles on a different day of the delivery month. There is also a distinction by coupon rate. Specifically, there are PSA settlement dates for the following:

- Freddie Mac Gold and 75-day, 30-year
  Fannie Mae 30-year

- All Ginnie Mae I and II 15-year
  Fannie Mae 15-year
  Freddie Mac Gold and 75-day, 15-year

- Ginnie Mae I and II coupons below 9.5%

- Fannie Mae Balloons
  Freddie Mac Gold and 75-day Balloons

- Ginnie Mae I and II coupons of 9.5% and greater
  All Ginnie Mae ARMs

By 3 p.m. eastern standard time two business days before the settlement date, the seller must furnish information to the buyer about pools that will be delivered. This is called the *48-hour rule*. The date that this information must be given is called the *notification date* or *call-out date*. Two parties can agree to depart from PSA guidelines and settle at any time.

Agency passthroughs are settled through electronic book-entry transfer rather than physical delivery. Freddie Mac and Fannie Mae securities are handled through the Fedwire (a system maintained by the Federal Reserve Bank). The electronic book-entry transfer systems used for Ginnie Mae securities are the Depository Trust Company and Participant Trust Company.

When an investor purchases, say, $1 million GNMA 8s on a TBA basis, the investor can receive up to three pools. Three pools can be delivered because the PSA has established guidelines for standards of delivery and settlement of mortgage-backed securities,[3] under which our hypothetical TBA trade permits three possible pools to be delivered. The option of what pools to deliver is left to the seller, as long as selection and delivery satisfy the PSA guidelines.

There are many seasoned issues of the same agency with the same coupon rate outstanding at a given point in time. For example, there are more than 30,000 pools of 30-year Ginnie Mae MBSs outstanding with a coupon rate of 9%. One passthrough may be backed by a pool of mortgage loans in which all the properties are located in California, while another may be backed by a pool of mortgage loans in which all the properties are in Minnesota. Yet another may be backed by a pool of mortgage loans in which the properties are from several regions of the country. So which pool are dealers referring to when they talk about Ginnie Mae 9s? They are not referring to any specific pool but instead to a generic security, despite the fact that the prepayment characteristics of passthroughs with

---

[3] Public Securities Association, *Uniform Practices for the Clearance and Settlement of Mortgage-Backed Securities*. More specifically, the requirement for good delivery permits a maximum of three pools per $1 million traded, or a maximum of four pools per $1 million for coupons of 12% or more.

underlying pools from different parts of the country are different. Thus, the projected prepayment rates for passthroughs reported by dealer firms are for generic passthroughs. A particular pool purchased may have a materially different prepayment speed from the generic. Moreover, when an investor purchases a passthrough without specifying a pool number, the seller can deliver the worst-paying pools as long as the pools delivered satisfy good delivery requirements.

TBA trades give another advantage to the seller. PSA delivery standards permit an under- or overdelivery tolerance of 1% per million traded. This means that if $1 million of par value is sold at par, the seller may deliver to the buyer passthroughs with a par value anywhere between $990,000 and $1,010,000. This delivery option is valuable. To understand why, suppose that interest rates decline between the trade date and the settlement date. The value of passthroughs will rise, and therefore it will be beneficial for the seller to deliver less than $1 million. The opposite is true if interest rates rise between the trade date and the settlement date: the seller will deliver $1,010,000. Investors need to recognize the valuable delivery options that are granted to the seller in a TBA trade, and that they can deny these options to the seller by engaging in a specified trade. The cost of such a trade, however, as measured by the bid-ask spread, will be larger than for a TBA trade, with the difference depending on the specific pool sought by the buyer.

STRIPPED MORTGAGE-BACKED SECURITIES

A mortgage passthrough security divides the cash flows from the underlying pool of mortgages on a pro rata basis to the security holders. A *stripped mortgage-backed security* is created by altering that distribution of principal and interest from a pro rata distribution to an unequal distribution. The result is that the securities created will have a price/yield relationship that is different from the price/yield relationship of the underlying passthrough security.

In the most common type of stripped mortgage-backed securities all the interest is allocated to one class (called the *interest only* or *IO* class) and all the principal to the other class (called the *principal only* or *PO* class). The IO class receives no principal payments.

The PO security is purchased at a substantial discount from par value. The return an investor realizes depends on the speed at which prepayments are made. The faster the prepayments, the higher the investor's return. For example, suppose there is a mortgage pool consisting of 30-year mortgages with $400 million in principal, and that investors can purchase POs backed by this mortgage pool for $175 million. The dollar return on this investment will be $225 million. How quickly that dollar return is recovered by PO investors determines the actual return that will be realized. In the extreme case, if all homeowners in the underlying mortgage pool decide to prepay their mortgage loans immediately, PO investors will realize the $225 million immediately. At the other extreme, if all homeowners decide to remain in their homes for 30 years and make no prepayments, the $225 million will be spread out over 30 years, which would result in a much lower return for PO investors.

Let's look at how the price of the PO would be expected to change as mortgage rates in the market change. When mortgage rates decline below the coupon rate, prepayments are expected to speed up, accelerating payments to the PO holder. Thus, the cash flows of a PO improve (in the sense that principal repayments are received earlier). The result is that the PO price will increase when mortgage rates decline. When mortgage rates rise above the coupon rate, prepayments are expected to slow down. The cash flows then deteriorate (in the sense that it takes longer to recover principal repayments). The price of a PO will fall when mortgage rates rise.

An IO has no par value. In contrast to the PO investor, the IO investor wants prepayments to be slow. The reason is that the IO investor receives interest only on the amount of the principal outstanding. When prepayments are made, less dollar interest will be received as the outstanding principal declines. In fact, if prepayments are too fast, the IO investor may not recover the amount paid for the IO. This is an important point since there have been reported losses by some investors who thought that since the IO was created from a passthrough either guaranteed by the U.S. government or government sponsored enterprise, there would be no loss. The guarantee only specifies that if there is a mortgage outstanding there is a guarantee that interest due will be paid.

Let's look at the expected price response of an IO to changes in mortgage rates. If mortgage rates decline below the coupon rate, prepayments are expected to accelerate. This would result in a deterioration of the expected cash flows for an IO. Typically there will be a decline in the price of an IO. If mortgage rates rise above the coupon rate, the expected cash flows improve and within a certain range of interest rates the price of an IO will increase. Thus, we see an interesting characteristic of an IO: its price tends to move in the same direction as the change in mortgage rates.

Both POs and IOs exhibit substantial price volatility when mortgage rates change. The greater price volatility of the IO and PO compared to the passthrough is due to the fact that the combined price volatility of the IO and PO must equal the price volatility of the passthrough.

An average life for a PO can be calculated based on some prepayment assumption. However, an IO receives no principal payments, so technically an average life cannot be computed. Instead, for an IO a "cash flow average life" is computed, using the projected interest payments in the average life formula instead of principal.

Trading and Settlement Procedures for Stripped Mortgage-Backed Securities

The trading and settlement procedures for stripped mortgage-backed securities are similar to those set by the Public Securities Association for agency passthroughs described in the previous section. The specifications are in the types of trades (TBA versus specified pool), calculations of the proceeds, and the settlement dates.

IOs and POs are extreme premium and discount securities and consequently are very sensitive to prepayments, which are driven by the specific characteristics (GWAC, WAM, geographic concentration, average loan size) of the underlying loans. The TBA delivery option on IOs and POs is of too great an economic value and this value is hard to quantify. Therefore, almost all secondary trades in IOs and POs are on a specified pool basis rather than on a TBA basis.

All IOs and POs are given a trust number. For instance, FNMA Trust 1 is a IO/PO trust backed by specific pools of FNMA 9% mortgages. FNMA Trust 2 is backed by FNMA 10% mortgages. FNMA Trust 23 is another IO/PO trust backed by FNMA 10% mortgages. The value of Trust 23 PO may be higher or lower than the value of Trust 2 PO depending on the perceived prepayment behavior of Trust 23 relative to that of Trust 2 based on the GWAM, WAM, and geographical concentration of the two specific trusts. (A more detailed discussion of collateral analysis is provided in Chapter 7.) Therefore, a portfolio manager must specify which trust he or she is buying.

Since the transactions are on a specified trust basis, they are also done based on the original face amount. For example, suppose a portfolio manager agrees to buy $10 million original face of Trust 23 PO for August settlement. At the time of the transaction, the August factor need not be known; however, there is no ambiguity in the amount to be delivered because the seller does not have any delivery option. The seller has to deliver $3 million current face amount if the August factor turns out to be 0.30 and the seller needs to deliver $2.5 million current face amount if the August factor turns out to be 0.25.

The total proceeds of a PO trade are calculated the same way as with a passthrough trade except that there is no accrued interest. For example, suppose a buyer and a seller agree to trade $10 million original face of Trust 23 PO at 75-08 for settlement on August 25. The proceeds for the trade are calculated as follows assuming an August trust factor of 0.25:

$$75.08 \times \$10,000,000 \times 0.25 = \$1,881,250$$

Price	Original face value	Pool factor	Proceeds

The market trades IOs based on notional principal. The proceeds include the price on the notional amount and the accrued interest. For example, suppose a buyer and a seller agree to trade $10 million original notional face of Trust 23 IO at 33-20 for settlement on August 25. The proceeds for the trade are calculated as follows assuming an August factor of 0.25:

$$(0.33625 + 0.10 \times 24 \text{ days}/360 \text{ days}) \times \$10,000,000 \times 0.25 = \$857,292$$

Price	coupon	days accrued interest	Orig. notional	Factor	Proceeds

Agency passthrough trades settle according to a delivery schedule established by the PSA. Stripped mortgage-backed securities trades follow the same delivery schedule according to their underlying mortgages. For example, suppose a trust is created by stripping FNMA 10% 30-year mortgages into a 7% class and a 13% class. The normal settlement date for both classes will be the same settlement date for premium (10%) FNMA 30-year passthroughs, even though the 7% class has a discounted coupon, because both classes are backed by FNMA 10% mortgages. Of course, these are only standard settlement dates and any other non-standard settlement dates can be agreed upon between the buyer and the seller. All IOs and POs settle though the Fedwire.

CALLABLE PASSTHROUGH CERTIFICATES

A fairly new innovation in the agency passthrough market is the *Callable Passthrough Certificates* (CPC). The program was started by Freddie Mac in June 1995. Since then, the issuance volume has grown substantially. As of May 1997, the cumulative issuance volume since the inception of the CPC program exceeded $13 billion. The CPC deals are identified by the Bloomberg ticker FCPC series C certificates. Each deal is labeled by a series number. As of May 1997, there have been about 50 series issued. Exhibit 4 shows the series, pricing dates, collateral, and volume of the existing CPC deals.

Structure

CPCs are structured passthrough securities comprised of pairs of classes, A and B, both collateralized by some eligible agency passthrough securities. Both Freddie Mac Gold-PCs and Ginnie Mae PCs are eligible collateral. Exhibit 5 provides a diagram of the structure of a CPC. The collateral is placed in a grantor trust from which classes A and B are issued. The holders of class A will receive 100% of the principal and interest from the underlying collateral. The holder of class B will not receive any payments of principal or interest, but will have the right to direct Freddie Mac to redeem the outstanding principal amount of class A, beginning on a specified date at a stated redemption price. The first specified call date is typically one year from the issue date and class A will then be callable on any subsequent principal and interest payment dates. In other words, class A is long the underlying collateral (therefore entitled to all principal and interest) and short a covered Bermudan call option exercisable one year out for the life of the passthrough securities.[4]

The redemption price is typically par plus accrued interest to the redemption date. Once the redemption is complete, the class B investor will then receive the underlying collateral and the subsequent principal and interest payments. In other words, class B is long a Bermudan call option on the underlying collateral. Since class A is equivalent to a covered call position, it has even more negative convexity than regular passthroughs but offers a higher potential yield. The yield advantage is typically 20 to 45 basis points depending on the collateral.

---

[4] A Bermudian call option, also called an Atlantic option and modified American call option, refers to an option in which the holder can exercise prior to the expiration date, but only on designated dates.

Exhibit 4: Callable Passthrough Certificate Issuance

Series	Pricing Date	Collateral	Original Balance ($000s)
2	Jun-95	GNMA	$35,000
3	Aug-95	Gold-PC	84,000
4	Aug-95	Gold-PC	100,000
5	Aug-95	Gold-PC	100,000
6	Sep-95	GNMA	25,000
8	Sep-95	Gold-PC	120,000
9	Sep-95	Gold-PC	61,000
10	Oct-95	GNMA	185,500
11	Oct-95	Gold-PC	50,000
12	Nov-95	GNMA	65,000
	1995 Subtotal		$825,500
13	Jan-96	GNMA	$94,000
14	Jan-96	Gold-PC	50,000
15	Feb-96	GNMA	60,000
16	Apr-96	GNMA	50,000
17	Jun-96	GNMA	45,000
18	Jun-96	Gold-PC	452,335
19	Jul-96	Gold-PC	100,000
20	Jul-96	Gold-PC	473,075
21	Aug-96	Gold-PC	150,000
22	Aug-96	Gold-PC	250,000
23	Aug-96	Gold-PC	615,500
24	Aug-96	Gold-PC	125,000
25	Aug-96	Gold-PC	250,000
26	Sep-96	Gold-PC	230,000
27	Sep-96	Gold-PC	200,000
28	Oct-96	Gold-PC	239,064
29	Nov-96	Gold-PC	37,000
30	Dec-96	Gold-PC	500,000
31	Dec-96	Gold-PC	487,500
	1996 Subtotal		4,408,474
32	Jan-97	Gold-PC	905,000
33	Jan-97	Gold-PC	225,000
34	Jan-97	Gold-PC	500,000
35	Feb-97	Gold-PC	483,400
36	Feb-97	Gold-PC	500,000
37	Feb-97	Gold-PC	394,969
38	Feb-97	Gold-PC	500,000
39	Feb-97	Gold-PC	522,788
40	Mar-97	Gold-PC	1,004,200
41	Mar-97	Gold-PC	450,000
42	Mar-97	Gold-PC	400,000
43	Mar-97	Gold-PC	625,000
44	Apr-97	Gold-PC	200,010
45	Apr-97	Gold-PC	350,000
46	Apr-97	Gold-PC	100,000
47	Apr-97	Gold-PC	225,000
48	Apr-97	Gold-PC	408,322
49	May-97	Gold-PC	300,000
50	May-97	Gold-PC	250,000
	1997 Subtotal		8,343,689
	Cumulative Total Since Inception		13,577,663

Exhibit 5: Structure of a Callable Passthrough Certificate

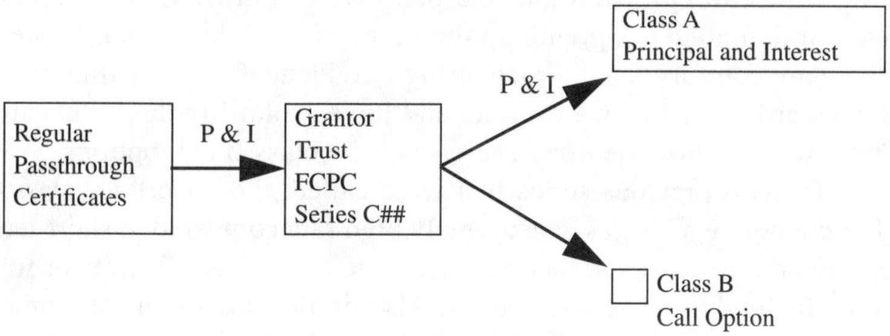

Exercise Process

The holder of class B has to notify Freddie Mac's Structured Finance Department during the preceding month of the intended call date. For example, if the class B investor intends to exercise the call on May 15 (the payment date), notification of Freddie Mac three days prior to the preceding month's record date (April 30) is required. The class B investor must then deposit with Freddie Mac the redemption amount and an exchange fee of $15,000. The redemption amount is the April balance of the collateral plus 14 days of accrued interest. Since the May factor won't be available until the fifth business day of May, the class B holder is over depositing the redemption amount. Any part of the redemption amount not used to redeem class A will be returned to the class B holder. The costs (exchange fee, interest cost on deposit, and the excess accrued interest) associated with the exercise of the call option depend on prepayments and the remaining balance of the deal.

Economics of the Call

The experience with CPCs as of mid 1997 is that only a few deals were actually called and only when the options were deep in the money. This is because all deals have a 1-year non-call protection. Most 1996 deals are just coming out of their non-call period and the 1997 deals are still call protected. Only a few 1995 deals and early 1996 deals were called. For example, both series 3 and 5 were collateralized by Gold 8s and were called when Gold 8s traded up to the 103s in early 1996. In other words, the call options were exercised only when the options were more than 3 points in the money. There are also costs associated with the exercise of the options as mentioned above. But the biggest cost is the time value of the option.

Basic option theory tells us that a simple call option on a non-dividend paying asset will never be exercised until expiration. That is because the option value has two components, the intrinsic value and the time value. The intrinsic value is the difference between the market value of the underlying collateral and the redemption price (strike price). If Gold 8s are trading at 103, and the redemption price is 100, the intrinsic value is 3% of the current balance. The time value is the option premium that prices in the probability that the future/forward price of the collateral will be higher than 103. The time value obviously depends on the remaining time to expiration and the perceived volatility. By exercising the option, the option holder is giving up the time value of the option. However with CPCs, there are contrary factors such as high dividends/coupons, diminishing balance, downward biased forward price, and lower volatility due to negative convexity[5] that would cause the early exercise of the class B call options.

In the two previous series that were called, the underlying passthroughs had an 8% coupon, which was an extremely high rate compared to short-term rates. The high coupon provides the income advantage to the class B investor for calling and owning the underlying passthroughs. Also, in the case of an extreme rally, the prepayment option moves into the money. The homeowners will start to refinance their mortgages, which will turn into prepayments on the underlying passthroughs. In other words, the notional balance of the call option will start to shrink. Even if the option premium continues to rise in a market rally, it may not rise fast enough to offset the paydown on the principal balance of the passthroughs.

The forward/future price of a high coupon fixed income security has a negative bias. In a positive yield curve environment, the cost of carrying that security by financing it at short-term rate is less than the coupon earned on that security. Therefore, the forward price must be lower than the spot price to create an arbitrage-free relationship. For example, the 1-year forward price of an 8% yielding bond in a 6% 1-year financing rate environment must be 2% lower than the spot price. This downward bias on the forward price of Gold 8s will erode the future time value of the option. Furthermore, the negative convexity of the Gold 8s will limit the upside price volatility even if the market continues to rally. Therefore, at a certain premium, the intrinsic value on the current balance may outweigh the time value of these long call options and thereby triggers the exercise.

---

[5] Negative convexity is discussed in Chapter 10.

Chapter 4

Agency Collateralized Mortgage Obligations

As explained in Chapter 2, by investing in a mortgage passthrough security a portfolio manager exposes a portfolio to prepayment risk. Furthermore, prepayment risk can be divided into extension risk and contraction risk. Some portfolio managers are concerned with extension risk and others with contraction risk when they invest in a passthrough. A portfolio manager may be willing to accept one form of prepayment risk but seek to avoid the other. For example, portfolio manager who seeks a short-term security is concerned with extension risk. A portfolio manager who seeks a long-term security, and wants to avoid reinvesting unexpected principal prepayments due to refinancing of mortgages should interest rates drop, is concerned with contraction risk.

By redirecting how the cash flows of passthrough securities are paid to different bond classes that are created, securities can be created that have different exposure to prepayment risk. When the cash flows of mortgage-related products are redistributed to different bond classes, the resulting securities are called *collateralized mortgage obligations* (CMOs). The creation of a CMO cannot eliminate prepayment risk, it can only redistribute the two forms of prepayment risk among different classes of bondholders.

The basic principle is that redirecting cash flows (interest and principal) to different bond classes, called *tranches*, mitigates different forms of prepayment risk. It is never possible to eliminate prepayment risk. If one tranche in a CMO structure has less prepayment risk than the mortgage passthrough securities that are collateral for the structure, then another tranche in the same structure has greater prepayment risk than the collateral.

In this chapter, we will discuss CMOs and the different types of tranches created. CMOs are also referred to as *paythroughs* or *multi-class passthroughs*. Because they are created so as to comply with a provision in the tax law called the Real Estate Mortgage Investment Conduit, or REMIC, they are also referred to as "REMICs." Throughout most of this chapter we refer to these structures as simply CMOs. A security structure in which collateral is carved into different bond classes is not uncommon. We will see similar paythrough or multi-class passthrough structures when we cover two mortgage-related products in the asset-backed securities market in Chapter 4.

ISSUERS OF AGENCY CMOS

Issuers of CMOs are the same three entities that issue agency passthrough securities: Freddie Mac, Fannie Mae, and Ginnie Mae. There has been little issuance of Ginnie Mae CMOs. However, Freddie Mac and Fannie Mae have used Ginnie Mae passthroughs as collateral for their own CMOs. CMOs issued by any of these entities are referred to as agency CMOs.

When an agency CMO is created it is structured so that even under the worst circumstances regarding prepayments, the interest and principal payments from the collateral will be sufficient to meet the interest obligation of each tranche and pay off the par value of each tranche.[1] Defaults are ignored because the agency that has issued the passthroughs used as collateral is expected to make up any deficiency. Thus, the credit risk of agency CMOs is minimal. However, as we noted in the previous chapter, the guarantee of a government sponsored enterprise does not carry the full faith and credit of the U.S. government. Fannie Mae and Freddie Mac CMOs created from Ginnie Mae passthroughs effectively carry the full faith and credit of the U.S. government.

CMO STRUCTURES

There is a wide-range of CMO structures. We review these structures below. Rather than just provide a definition, it is useful to see how the various types of CMOs are created. In an actual CMO structure, the information regarding the rules for distributing interest and principal to the bond classes is set forth in the prospectus.

Sequential-Pay Tranches

The first CMO was structured so that each class of bond would be retired sequentially. Such structures are referred to as *sequential-pay CMOs.*

To illustrate a sequential-pay CMO, we discuss FAF-01, a hypothetical deal made up to illustrate the basic features of the structure. The collateral for this hypothetical CMO is a hypothetical passthrough with a total par value of $400 million and the following characteristics: (1) the passthrough coupon rate is 7.5%, (2) the weighted average coupon (WAC) is 8.125%, and (3) the weighted average maturity (WAM) is 357 months. This is the same passthrough that we used in the previous chapter to describe the cash flows of a passthrough based on some PSA assumption.

From this $400 million of collateral, four bond classes or tranches are created. Their characteristics are summarized in Exhibit 1. The total par value of the four tranches is equal to the par value of the collateral (i.e., the passthrough

---

[1] There are CMO structures in which interest on a floating-rate tranche may not be sufficient to meet the interest as specified by the coupon formula. This has occurred in re-REMICs (discussed later in this chapter). In such cases, this is stated in the prospectus.

security). In this simple structure, the coupon rate is the same for each tranche and also the same as the collateral's coupon rate. There is no reason why this must be so, and, in fact, typically the coupon rate varies by tranche.

Now remember that a CMO is created by redistributing the cash flow — interest and principal — to the different tranches based on a set of payment rules. The payment rules at the bottom of Exhibit 1 set forth how the monthly cash flow from the passthrough (i.e., collateral) is to be distributed to the four tranches. There are separate rules for the payment of the coupon interest and the payment of principal, the principal being the total of the regularly scheduled principal payment and any prepayments.

In FAF-01, each tranche receives periodic coupon interest payments based on the amount of the outstanding balance. The disbursement of the principal, however, is made in a special way. A tranche is not entitled to receive principal until the entire principal of the tranche before it has been paid off. More specifically, tranche A receives all the principal payments until the entire principal amount owed to that tranche, $194,500,000, is paid off; then tranche B begins to receive principal and continues to do so until it is paid the entire $36,000,000. Tranche C then receives principal, and when it is paid off, tranche D starts receiving principal payments.

While the payment rules for the disbursement of the principal payments are known, the precise amount of the principal in each period is not. This will depend on the cash flow, and therefore principal payments, of the collateral, which depends on the actual prepayment rate of the collateral. An assumed PSA speed allows the monthly cash flow to be projected. Exhibit 3 in the previous chapter shows the monthly cash flow (interest, regularly scheduled principal repayment, and prepayments) assuming 165 PSA. Assuming that the collateral does prepay at 165 PSA, the cash flows available to all four tranches of FAF-01 will be precisely the cash flows shown in Exhibit 3 of the previous chapter.

Exhibit 1: FAF-01: A Hypothetical Four-Tranche Sequential-Pay Structure

Tranche	Par Amount	Coupon Rate (%)
A	$194,500,000	7.5
B	36,000,000	7.5
C	96,500,000	7.5
D	73,000,000	7.5
Total	$400,000,000	

Payment rules:

1. *For payment of periodic coupon interest:* Disburse periodic coupon interest to each tranche on the basis of the amount of principal outstanding at the beginning of the period.

2. *For disbursement of principal payments:* Disburse principal payments to tranche A until it is completely paid off. After tranche A is completely paid off, disburse principal payments to tranche B until it is completely paid off. After tranche B is completely paid off, disburse principal payments to tranche C until it is completely paid off. After tranche C is completely paid off, disburse principal payments to tranche D until it is completely paid off.

Exhibit 2: Monthly Cash Flow for Selected Months for FAF-01 Assuming 165 PSA

Month	Tranche A			Tranche B		
	Balance	Principal	Interest	Balance	Principal	Interest
1	194,500,000	709,923	1,215,625	36,000,000	0	225,000
2	193,790,077	821,896	1,211,188	36,000,000	0	225,000
3	192,968,181	933,560	1,206,051	36,000,000	0	225,000
4	192,034,621	1,044,822	1,200,216	36,000,000	0	225,000
5	190,989,799	1,155,586	1,193,686	36,000,000	0	225,000
6	189,834,213	1,265,759	1,186,464	36,000,000	0	225,000
7	188,568,454	1,375,246	1,178,553	36,000,000	0	225,000
8	187,193,208	1,483,954	1,169,958	36,000,000	0	225,000
9	185,709,254	1,591,789	1,160,683	36,000,000	0	225,000
10	184,117,464	1,698,659	1,150,734	36,000,000	0	225,000
11	182,418,805	1,804,473	1,140,118	36,000,000	0	225,000
12	180,614,332	1,909,139	1,128,840	36,000,000	0	225,000
75	12,893,479	2,143,974	80,584	36,000,000	0	225,000
76	10,749,504	2,124,935	67,184	36,000,000	0	225,000
77	8,624,569	2,106,062	53,904	36,000,000	0	225,000
78	6,518,507	2,087,353	40,741	36,000,000	0	225,000
79	4,431,154	2,068,807	27,695	36,000,000	0	225,000
80	2,362,347	2,050,422	14,765	36,000,000	0	225,000
81	311,926	311,926	1,950	36,000,000	1,720,271	225,000
82	0	0	0	34,279,729	2,014,130	214,248
83	0	0	0	32,265,599	1,996,221	201,660
84	0	0	0	30,269,378	1,978,468	189,184
85	0	0	0	28,290,911	1,960,869	176,818
95	0	0	0	9,449,331	1,793,089	59,058
96	0	0	0	7,656,242	1,777,104	47,852
97	0	0	0	5,879,138	1,761,258	36,745
98	0	0	0	4,117,880	1,745,550	25,737
99	0	0	0	2,372,329	1,729,979	14,827
100	0	0	0	642,350	642,350	4,015
101	0	0	0	0	0	0
102	0	0	0	0	0	0
103	0	0	0	0	0	0
104	0	0	0	0	0	0
105	0	0	0	0	0	0

To demonstrate how the payment rules for FAF-01 work, Exhibit 2 shows the cash flow for selected months assuming the collateral prepays at 165 PSA. For each tranche, the exhibit shows: (1) the balance at the end of the month, (2) the principal paid down (regularly scheduled principal repayment plus prepayments), and (3) interest. In month 1, the cash flow for the collateral consists of a principal payment of $709,923 and interest of $2.5 million (0.075 times $400 million divided by 12). The interest payment is distributed to the four tranches based on the amount of the par value outstanding. So, for example, tranche A receives $1,215,625 (0.075 times $194,500,000 divided by 12) of the $2.5 million. The principal, however, is all distributed to tranche A. Therefore, the cash flow for tranche A in month 1 is $1,925,548.

The principal balance at the end of month 1 for tranche A is $193,790,076 (the original principal balance of $194,500,000 less the principal payment of $709,923). No principal payment is distributed to the three other tranches because there is still a principal balance outstanding for tranche A. This will be true for months 2 through 80.

Exhibit 2 (Concluded)

Month	Tranche C			Tranche D		
	Balance	Principal	Interest	Balance	Principal	Interest
1	96,500,000	0	603,125	73,000,000	0	456,250
2	96,500,000	0	603,125	73,000,000	0	456,250
3	96,500,000	0	603,125	73,000,000	0	456,250
4	96,500,000	0	603,125	73,000,000	0	456,250
5	96,500,000	0	603,125	73,000,000	0	456,250
6	96,500,000	0	603,125	73,000,000	0	456,250
7	96,500,000	0	603,125	73,000,000	0	456,250
8	96,500,000	0	603,125	73,000,000	0	456,250
9	96,500,000	0	603,125	73,000,000	0	456,250
10	96,500,000	0	603,125	73,000,000	0	456,250
11	96,500,000	0	603,125	73,000,000	0	456,250
12	96,500,000	0	603,125	73,000,000	0	456,250
95	96,500,000	0	603,125	73,000,000	0	456,250
96	96,500,000	0	603,125	73,000,000	0	456,250
97	96,500,000	0	603,125	73,000,000	0	456,250
98	96,500,000	0	603,125	73,000,000	0	456,250
99	96,500,000	0	603,125	73,000,000	0	456,250
100	96,500,000	1,072,194	603,125	73,000,000	0	456,250
101	95,427,806	1,699,243	596,424	73,000,000	0	456,250
102	93,728,563	1,684,075	585,804	73,000,000	0	456,250
103	92,044,489	1,669,039	575,278	73,000,000	0	456,250
104	90,375,450	1,654,134	564,847	73,000,000	0	456,250
105	88,721,315	1,639,359	554,508	73,000,000	0	456,250
175	3,260,287	869,602	20,377	73,000,000	0	456,250
176	2,390,685	861,673	14,942	73,000,000	0	456,250
177	1,529,013	853,813	9,556	73,000,000	0	456,250
178	675,199	675,199	4,220	73,000,000	170,824	456,250
179	0	0	0	72,829,176	838,300	455,182
180	0	0	0	71,990,876	830,646	449,943
181	0	0	0	71,160,230	823,058	444,751
182	0	0	0	70,337,173	815,536	439,607
183	0	0	0	69,521,637	808,081	434,510
184	0	0	0	68,713,556	800,690	429,460
185	0	0	0	67,912,866	793,365	424,455
350	0	0	0	1,235,674	160,220	7,723
351	0	0	0	1,075,454	158,544	6,722
352	0	0	0	916,910	156,883	5,731
353	0	0	0	760,027	155,238	4,750
354	0	0	0	604,789	153,607	3,780
355	0	0	0	451,182	151,991	2,820
356	0	0	0	299,191	150,389	1,870
357	0	0	0	148,802	148,802	930

Exhibit 3: Average Life for the Collateral and the Four Tranches of FAF-01

Prepayment speed (PSA)	Average life for				
	Collateral	Tranche A	Tranche B	Tranche C	Tranche D
50	15.11	7.48	15.98	21.02	27.24
100	11.66	4.90	10.86	15.78	24.58
165	8.76	3.48	7.49	11.19	20.27
200	7.68	3.05	6.42	9.60	18.11
300	5.63	2.32	4.64	6.81	13.36
400	4.44	1.94	3.70	5.31	10.34
500	3.68	1.69	3.12	4.38	8.35
600	3.16	1.51	2.74	3.75	6.96
700	2.78	1.38	2.47	3.30	5.95

After month 81, the principal balance will be zero for tranche A. For the collateral the cash flow in month 81 is \$3,318,521, consisting of a principal payment of \$2,032,196 and interest of \$1,286,325. At the beginning of month 81 (end of month 80), the principal balance for tranche A is \$311,926. Therefore, \$311,926 of the \$2,032,196 of the principal payment from the collateral will be disbursed to tranche A. After this payment is made, no additional principal payments are made to this tranche as the principal balance is zero. The remaining principal payment from the collateral, \$1,720,271, is disbursed to tranche B. According to the assumed prepayment speed of 165 PSA, tranche B then begins receiving principal payments in month 81.

Exhibit 2 shows that tranche B is fully paid off by month 100, when tranche C begins to receive principal payments. Tranche C is not fully paid off until month 178, at which time tranche D begins receiving the remaining principal payments. The maturity (i.e., the time until the principal is fully paid off) for these four tranches assuming 165 PSA is 81 months for tranche A, 100 months for tranche B, 178 months for tranche C, and 357 months for tranche D.

The *principal pay down window* for a tranche is the time period between the beginning and the ending of the principal payments to that tranche. So, for example, for tranche A, the principal pay down window would be month 1 to month 81 assuming 165 PSA. For tranche B it is from month 81 to month 100. The window is also specified in terms of the length of the time from the beginning of the principal pay down window to the end of the principal pay down window. For tranche A, the window would be stated as 81 months, for tranche B 20 months. In confirmation of trades involving CMOs, the principal pay down window is specified in terms of the initial month that principal is expected to be received to the final month that principal is expected to be received.

Let's look at what has been accomplished by creating the CMO. First, in the previous chapter we saw that the average life of the passthrough is 8.76 years, assuming a prepayment speed of 165 PSA. Exhibit 3 reports the average life of the collateral and the four tranches assuming different prepayment speeds. Notice that the four tranches have average lives that are both shorter and longer than the collateral thereby attracting investors who have a preference for an average life different from that of the collateral.

There is still a major problem: there is considerable variability of the average life for the tranches. We'll see how this can be tackled later on. However, there is some protection provided for each tranche against prepayment risk. This is because prioritizing the distribution of principal (i.e., establishing the payment rules for principal) effectively protects the shorter-term tranche A in this structure against extension risk. This protection must come from somewhere — it comes from the three other tranches. Similarly, tranches C and D provide protection against extension risk for tranche B. At the same time, tranches C and D benefit because they are provided protection against contraction risk, the protection coming from tranches A and B.

Accrual Tranches

In FAF-01, the payment rules for interest provide for all tranches to be paid interest each month. In many sequential-pay CMO structures, at least one tranche does not receive current interest. Instead, the interest for that tranche would accrue and be added to the principal balance. Such a bond class is commonly referred to as an accrual tranche or a Z bond (because the bond is similar to a zero-coupon bond). The interest that would have been paid to the accrual bond class is then used to speed up pay down of the principal balance of earlier bond classes.

To see this, consider FAF-02, a hypothetical CMO structure with the same collateral as FAF-01 and with four tranches, each with a coupon rate of 7.5%. The difference is in the last tranche, Z, which is an accrual tranche. The structure for FAF-02 is shown in Exhibit 4.

Exhibit 4: FAF-02: A Hypothetical Four-Tranche Sequential-Pay Structure with an Accrual Bond Class

Tranche	Par Amount	Coupon rate (%)
A	$194,500,000	7.5
B	36,000,000	7.5
C	96,500,000	7.5
Z (Accrual)	73,000,000	7.5
Total	$400,000,000	

Payment rules:

1. *For payment of periodic coupon interest:* Disburse periodic coupon interest to tranches A, B, and C on the basis of the amount of principal outstanding at the beginning of the period. For tranche Z, accrue the interest based on the principal plus accrued interest in the previous period. The interest for tranche Z is to be paid to the earlier tranches as a principal paydown.

2. *For disbursement of principal payments:* Disburse principal payments to tranche A until it is completely paid off. After tranche A is completely paid off, disburse principal payments to tranche B until it is completely paid off. After tranche B is completely paid off, disburse principal payments to tranche C until it is completely paid off. After tranche C is completely paid off, disburse principal payments to tranche Z until the original principal balance plus accrued interest is completely paid off.

Exhibit 5: Monthly Cash Flow for Selected Months for Tranches A and B of FAF-02 Assuming 165 PSA

Month	Tranche A			Tranche B		
	Balance	Principal	Interest	Balance	Principal	Interest
1	194,500,000	1,150,965	972,500	36,000,000	0	195,000
2	193,349,035	1,265,602	966,745	36,000,000	0	195,000
3	192,083,433	1,379,947	960,417	36,000,000	0	195,000
4	190,703,486	1,493,906	953,517	36,000,000	0	195,000
5	189,209,581	1,607,383	946,048	36,000,000	0	195,000
6	187,602,197	1,720,286	938,011	36,000,000	0	195,000
7	185,881,911	1,832,519	929,410	36,000,000	0	195,000
8	184,049,392	1,943,990	920,247	36,000,000	0	195,000
9	182,105,402	2,054,604	910,527	36,000,000	0	195,000
10	180,050,798	2,164,271	900,254	36,000,000	0	195,000
11	177,886,528	2,272,897	889,433	36,000,000	0	195,000
12	175,613,631	2,380,393	878,068	36,000,000	0	195,000
60	16,303,583	3,079,699	81,518	36,000,000	0	195,000
61	13,223,884	3,061,796	66,119	36,000,000	0	195,000
62	10,162,088	3,044,105	50,810	36,000,000	0	195,000
63	7,117,983	3,026,624	35,590	36,000,000	0	195,000
64	4,091,359	3,009,352	20,457	36,000,000	0	195,000
65	1,082,007	1,082,007	5,410	36,000,000	1,910,280	195,000
66	0	0	0	34,089,720	2,975,428	184,653
67	0	0	0	31,114,292	2,958,773	168,536
68	0	0	0	28,155,519	2,942,321	152,509
69	0	0	0	25,213,198	2,926,071	136,571
70	0	0	0	22,287,128	2,910,020	120,722
71	0	0	0	19,377,107	2,894,169	104,959
72	0	0	0	16,482,938	2,878,515	89,283
73	0	0	0	13,604,423	2,863,057	73,691
74	0	0	0	10,741,366	2,847,794	58,182
75	0	0	0	7,893,572	2,832,724	42,757
76	0	0	0	5,060,849	2,817,846	27,413
77	0	0	0	2,243,003	2,243,003	12,150
78	0	0	0	0	0	0
79	0	0	0	0	0	0
80	0	0	0	0	0	0

Exhibit 5 shows the cash flow for selected months for tranches A and B. Let's look at month 1 and compare it to month 1 in Exhibit 2. Both cash flows are based on 165 PSA. The principal payment from the collateral is $709,923. In FAF-01, this is the principal paydown for tranche A. In FAF-02, the interest for tranche Z, $456,250, is not paid to that tranche but instead is used to pay down the principal of tranche A. So, the principal payment to tranche A in Exhibit 5 is $1,166,173, the collateral's principal payment of $709,923 plus the interest of $456,250 that was diverted from tranche Z.

The expected final maturity for tranches A, B, and C has shortened as a result of the inclusion of tranche Z. The final payout for tranche A is 64 months rather than 81 months; for tranche B it is 77 months rather than 100 months; and for tranche C it is 112 months rather than 178 months.

The average lives for tranches A, B, and C are shorter in FAF-02 compared to FAF-01 because of the inclusion of the accrual bond. For example, at 165 PSA, the average lives are as follows:

Structure	Tranche A	Tranche B	Tranche C
FAF-02	2.90	5.86	7.87
FAF-01	3.48	7.49	11.19

The reason for the shortening of the non-accrual tranches is that the interest that would be paid to the accrual tranche is being allocated to the other tranches. Tranche Z in FAF-02 will have a longer average life than tranche D in FAF-01.

Thus, shorter term tranches and a longer term tranche are created by including an accrual bond. The accrual bond has appeal to investors who are concerned with reinvestment risk. Since there are no coupon payments to reinvest, reinvestment risk is eliminated until all the other tranches are paid off.

Different Versions of Accrual Tranches

Different versions of accrual tranches or Z bonds can be created. A CMO deal structure can have additional principal paydown priority on top of the sequential structure. For example, some kind of trigger event can cause the paydown priority to change. The trigger event can be based on the level of interest rate, a certain level on an index, time, or prepayment speed.

Using FAF-02 as an example, under normal condition, the principal paydown sequence is tranche A, B, C, and then lastly Z. In other words, the Z tranche has the last priority. However, if on any month that the prepayment speed exceeds a trigger level, say 275 PSA, the Z bond "jumps" in front of all other tranches and takes on the first priority to become the first tranche to be paid down. This type of Z bond is commonly called a *jump Z*. Another example of a jump Z is one that jumps if and when 6-month LIBOR drops below 5%.

The "jump" can be either permanent or temporary. The "jump" is said to be permanent if the trigger event has to be triggered only once for the jump Z to jump and take on first priority. An example would be if on any month that the prepayment rate exceeds 275 PSA, the jump Z jumps and takes on the first priority that month and subsequently every month until it is paid off entirely, regardless of future prepayment speeds. This type of jump Z is known as a *sticky jump Z*. In other words, once it jumps to the front, it also sticks to the front. A *non-sticky jump Z* would jump only on those months that the jump condition is triggered. On any month that the jump is not triggered, it reverts back to the last priority and accrues interest.

A Z bond is normally last in paydown priority and therefore has long average life. When the jump event occurs, the average life of a jump Z shortens dramatically and the average lives of other tranches would lengthen. The average life profile of a typical jump Z with jump speed of 275 PSA would look as follows:

Exhibit 6: FAF-03: A Hypothetical Five-Tranche Sequential-Pay Structure with Floater, Inverse Floater, and Accrual Bond Classes

Tranche	Par amount	Coupon rate
A	$194,500,000	7.50%
B	36,000,000	7.50%
FL	72,375,000	1-mo. LIBOR + 0.50
IFL	24,125,000	$28.50 - 3 \times (1\text{-mo. LIBOR})$
Z (Accrual)	73,000,000	7.50%
Total	$400,000,000	

Payment rules:

1. *For payment of periodic coupon interest:* Disburse periodic coupon interest to tranches A, B, FL, and IFL on the basis of the amount of principal outstanding at the beginning of the period. For tranche Z, accrue the interest based on the principal plus accrued interest in the previous period. The interest for tranche Z is to be paid to the earlier tranches as a principal paydown. The maximum coupon rate for FL is 10%; the minimum coupon rate for IFL is 0%.

2. *For disbursement of principal payments:* Disburse principal payments to tranche A until it is completely paid off. After tranche A is completely paid off, disburse principal payments to tranche B until it is completely paid off. After tranche B is completely paid off, disburse principal payments to tranches FL and IFL until they are completely paid off. The principal payments between tranches FL and IFL should be made in the following way: 75% to tranche FL and 25% to tranche IFL. After tranches FL and IFL are completely paid off, disburse principal payments to tranche Z until the original principal balance plus accrued interest is completely paid off.

PSA	100	200	275	280	300	400	500
Average Life	20.1	15.1	9.6	0.8	0.7	0.6	0.5

Floating-Rate Tranches

A floating-rate tranche can be created from a fixed-rate tranche by creating a floater and an inverse floater. We will illustrate the creation of a floating-rate and an inverse floating-rate tranche using the hypothetical CMO structure FAF-02, which is a four tranche sequential-pay structure with an accrual bond. We can select any of the tranches from which to create a floating-rate and an inverse floating-rate tranche. In fact, we can create these two securities for more than one of the four tranches or for only a portion of one tranche.

In this case, we created a floater and an inverse floater from tranche C. The par value for this tranche is $96.5 million, and we create two tranches that have a combined par value of $96.5 million. We refer to this CMO structure with a floater and an inverse floater as FAF-03. It has five tranches, designated A, B, FL, IFL, and Z, where FL is the floating-rate tranche and IFL is the inverse floating-rate tranche. Exhibit 6 describes FAF-03. Any reference rate can be used to create a floater and the corresponding inverse floater. The reference rate selected for setting the coupon rate for FL and IFL in FAF-03 is 1-month LIBOR. As in the case of the floater, the principal paydown of an inverse floater will be a proportionate amount of the principal paydown of tranche C.

The amount of the par value of the floating-rate tranche will be some portion of the $96.5 million. There are an infinite number of ways to cut up the $96.5 million between the floater and inverse floater, and final partitioning will be driven by the demands of investors. In the FAF-03 structure, we made the floater from $72,375,000 or 75% of the $96.5 million. The coupon rate on the floater is set at 1-month LIBOR plus 50 basis points. So, for example, if LIBOR is 3.75% at the coupon reset date, the coupon rate on the floater is 3.75% + 0.5%, or 4.25%. There is a cap on the coupon rate for the floater (discussed later).

Unlike a floating-rate note whose principal is unchanged over the life of the instrument, the floater's principal balance declines over time as principal repayments are made. The principal payments to the floater are determined by the principal payments from the tranche from which the floater is created. In our CMO structure, this is tranche C.

Since the floater's par value is $72,375,000 of the $96.5 million, the balance is the inverse floater. Assuming that 1-month LIBOR is the reference rate, the coupon reset formula for an inverse floater takes the following form:

$$K - L \times (\text{1-month LIBOR})$$

In FAF-03, K is set at 28.50% and L at 3. Thus, if 1-month LIBOR is 3.75%, the coupon rate for the month is:

$$28.50\% - 3 \times (3.75\%) = 17.25\%$$

K is the cap or maximum coupon rate for the inverse floater. In FAF-03, the cap for the inverse floater is 28.50%.

The L or *multiple* in the coupon reset formula for the inverse floater is called the *coupon leverage*. The higher the coupon leverage, the more the inverse floater's coupon rate changes for a given change in 1-month LIBOR. For example, a coupon leverage of 3 means that a 1-basis point change in 1-month LIBOR will change the coupon rate on the inverse floater by 3 basis points.

Because 1-month LIBOR is always positive, the coupon rate paid to the floating-rate tranche cannot be negative. If there are no restrictions placed on the coupon rate for the inverse floater, however, it is possible for the coupon rate for that tranche to be negative. To prevent this, a floor, or minimum, can be placed on the coupon rate. In many structures, the floor is set at zero. Once a floor is set for the inverse floater, a cap or ceiling is imposed on the floater. In FAF-03, a floor of zero is set for the inverse floater. The floor results in a cap or maximum coupon rate for the floater of 10%.

Superfloaters

A *superfloater* is a floating-rate CMO whose coupon rate is a multiple of a reference rate. A superfloater takes the same form as an inverse floater, except that the superfloater's coupon rate increases with the reference rate. The formula is as follows, assuming that the reference rate is 1-month LIBOR:

Exhibit 7: FAF-04: A Hypothetical Five-Tranche Sequential-Pay Structure with Superfloater, Inverse Superfloater, and Accrual Bond Classes

Tranche	Par amount	Coupon rate (%)
A	$194,500,000	7.50
B	36,000,000	7.50
SFL	60,312,500	3 × (1-month LIBOR) − 16.5
ISFL	36,187,500	47.5 − 5 × (1-month LIBOR)
Z (Accrual)	73,000,000	7.50
Total	$400,000,000	

Payment rules:

1. *For payment of periodic coupon interest*: Disburse periodic coupon interest to tranches A, B, SFL, and ISFL on the basis of the amount of principal outstanding at the beginning of the period. For tranche Z, accrue the interest based on the principal plus accrued interest in the previous period. The interest for tranche Z is to be paid to the earlier tranches as a principal paydown. The minimum (floor) coupon rate for SFL is 6%, and the maximum (cap) is 12%. The minimum (floor) coupon rate for ISFL is 0%, and the maximum (cap) is 10%.

2. *For disbursement of principal payments*: Disburse principal payments to tranche A until it is completely paid off. After tranche A is completely paid off, disburse principal payments to tranche B until it is completely paid off. After tranche B is completely paid off, disburse principal payments to tranches SFL and ISFL until they are completely paid off. The principal payments between tranches SFL and ISFL should be made in the following way: 62.5% to tranche SFL and 37.5% to tranche ISFL. After tranches SFL and ISFL are completely paid off, disburse principal payments to tranche Z until the original principal balance plus accrued interest is completely paid off.

$$C \times (\text{1-month LIBOR}) - M$$

where C is the coupon leverage and M is a constant.

For example, if C is 3 and M is 16.5%, then the formula for the coupon rate for the superfloater is:

$$3 \times (\text{1-month LIBOR}) - 16.5\%$$

If 1-month LIBOR is 8%, for example, then the superfloater's coupon rate for the month is

$$3 \times 8\% - 16.5\% = 7.5\%$$

There must be a floor on the coupon rate to prevent it from becoming negative. As with the conventional floater, an inverse floater is needed so that the collateral can support the interest payments regardless of the level of 1-month LIBOR.

To illustrate a superfloater, let's consider once again FAF-02. From tranche C, we created a floater and an inverse floater, described as FAF-03. In FAF-04 we create a superfloater and inverse superfloater from tranche C. Exhibit 7 summarizes this CMO structure. The superfloater (labeled tranche SFL in the structure) is created from 62.5% of the $96.5 million of tranche C, and the inverse superfloater (labeled tranche ISFL) is created from the balance. The coupon rate and restrictions on the superfloater and inverse superfloater are summarized below:

Tranche	Coupon	Floor	Cap
Superfloater	$3 \times (1\text{-mo. LIBOR}) - 16.5$	6%	12%
Inverse superfloater	$47.5 - 5 \times (1\text{-mo. LIBOR})$	0%	10%

Exhibit 8 gives the coupon rate for the superfloater and inverse superfloater for a range of rates for 1-month LIBOR. Notice that there are two critical levels for LIBOR where the restrictions on the superfloater and inverse superfloater will take effect. If LIBOR is 7.5% or less, the superfloater's coupon rate reaches its floor (6%) while the inverse superfloater's coupon rate realizes its cap (10%). Thus, LIBOR of 7.5% is referred to as the strike rate for the superfloater, since for any LIBOR level below 7.5%, the coupon rate is 6%. It is referred to as the *strike rate* as it is nothing more than an interest rate floor. In such agreements, the buyer of the floor is guaranteed a minimum interest rate, and that minimum rate is the strike rate. Thus, the buyer of a superfloater has effectively purchased an interest rate floor. Viewed from the perspective of the buyer of the inverse superfloater, the 7.5% is effectively the strike rate on an interest rate cap sold.

Exhibit 8: Coupon Rate for Superfloater (SFL) and Inverse Superfloater (ISFL) in FAF-04 Structure at Different Levels of LIBOR

1-Month LIBOR (%)	Superfloater (%)	Inverse Superfloater (%)
1.00	6.00	10.00
2.00	6.00	10.00
3.00	6.00	10.00
4.00	6.00	10.00
5.00	6.00	10.00
6.00	6.00	10.00
7.00	6.00	10.00
7.25	5.25	11.25
7.50	6.00	10.00
7.75	6.75	8.75
8.00	7.50	7.50
8.25	8.25	6.25
8.50	9.00	5.00
8.75	9.75	3.75
9.00	10.50	2.50
9.25	11.25	1.25
9.50	12.00	0.00
11.00	12.00	0.00
12.00	12.00	0.00
13.00	12.00	0.00

Exhibit 9: FAF-05: A Hypothetical Six-Tranche Sequential-Pay Structure with a Floater, Inverse Floater, PO, IO, and Accrual Bond Classes

Tranche	Par amount	Coupon rate (%)
A	$194,500,000	7.50
IO	0	*
PO	36,000,000	0
FL	72,375,000	1-month LIBOR + 0.50
IFL	24,125,000	28.50 − 3 × (1-month LIBOR)
Z (Accrual)	73,000,000	7.50
Total	$400,000,000	

* Interest equal to 7.5% times the balance outstanding for the PO tranche.

Payment rules:

1. *For payment of periodic coupon interest:* Disburse periodic coupon interest to tranches A, B, FL, and IFL on the basis of the amount of principal outstanding at the beginning of the period. Disburse periodic coupon interest to tranche IO based on the amount of principal outstanding at the beginning of the period for tranche PO. For tranche Z, accrue the interest based on the principal plus accrued interest in the previous period. The interest for tranche Z is to be paid to the earlier tranches as a principal paydown. The maximum coupon rate for FL is 10%; the minimum coupon rate for IFL is 0%.

2. *For disbursement of principal payments:* Disburse principal payments to tranche A until it is completely paid off. After tranche A is completely paid off, disburse principal payments to tranche PO until it is completely paid off. After tranche PO is completely paid off, disburse principal payments to tranches FL and IFL until they are completely paid off. The principal payments between tranches FL and IFL should be made in the following way: 75% to tranche FL and 25% to tranche IFL. After tranches FL and IFL are completely paid off, disburse principal payments to tranche Z until the original principal balance plus accrued interest is completely paid off.

The other critical LIBOR level is 9.5%. At that level, the superfloater reaches its cap (12%) and forgoes any upside potential should LIBOR rise above 9.5%. At 9.5%, the inverse superfloater reaches its floor (0%). Thus, 9.5% is also a strike rate. In this case, the buyer of the superfloater has effectively sold an interest rate cap. Viewed from the perspective of the buyer of the inverse super-floater, the 9.5% is effectively the strike rate on an interest rate floor purchased.

Between these two strike rates, the coupon rates for the superfloater and inverse superfloater change according to their respective formula. Because of the two strike rates that create a lower and upper tier for the coupon rates, this type of superfloater is referred to as a *two-tier index bond*, or TTIB.

IO Inverse Floater

CMO structures can be created so that a tranche can receive only the principal or only the interest. For example, consider FAF-04. Suppose that tranche B in this structure is divided into two tranches, a principal-only tranche and an interest-only tranche. We will call this structure FAF-05, described in Exhibit 9.

In the calculation of the average life for a tranche, only the principal received is considered. Since an IO does not return principal, an average life cannot be calculated. Instead, a *cash flow average life* can be computed by using cash flow in lieu of principal in the average life formula. Obviously, the cash flow is just the interest.

Exhibit 10: FAF-06: A Three-Tranche Structure with a Floater, Inverse IO Floater, and PO

Tranche	Par amount	Coupon rate (%)
FL	$300,000,000	1-month LIBOR + 0.50
IIO	0	*
PO	100,000,000	0
Total	$400,000,000	

* Interest equal to:

$[28.50\% - 3 \times (1\text{-month LIBOR})] \times$ PO balance outstanding.

Payment rules:

1. *For payment of periodic coupon interest:* Disburse periodic coupon interest to tranche FL determined by the specified formula and on the basis of the amount of principal outstanding at the beginning of the period. Disburse periodic coupon interest to tranche IIO using the IIO specified formula and according to the amount of principal outstanding at the beginning of the period for tranche PO. The maximum coupon rate for FL is 10%; the minimum coupon rate for IIO is 0%.

2. *For disbursement of principal payments:* Disburse principal payments to tranche FL and tranche PO on the following basis: for each principal payment of $1, distribute $0.75 to tranche FL and $0.25 to tranche PO.

To illustrate other types of CMO structures including a PO or an IO, consider FAF-06 shown in Exhibit 10. This is a three-tranche structure using the $400 million, 7.5% coupon, 357 WAM collateral. Tranche F is a floater with a coupon rate of 1-month LIBOR plus 50 basis points; its par value is $300 million. There is a 10% cap on tranche F. The balance of the collateral, $100 million, is used to create the remaining two tranches. There is a PO tranche, and there is a tranche denoted IIO, which is a bond class that receives only interest (i.e., an IO tranche) based on the outstanding balance of the PO tranche. Rather than a fixed coupon rate, the interest is based on a formula where the coupon rate changes inversely with 1-month LIBOR (i.e., it is an inverse floater). The formula is the same as for FAF-04, $28.5\% - 3 \times (1\text{-month LIBOR})$. This bond class is referred to as an *inverse IO* (IIO).

The principal payment from the collateral is distributed to the floater and PO tranches on the basis of their par value relative to the total par value of the collateral, $400 million. Thus, for each $100 of principal payment from the collateral, $75 is distributed to the floater and $25 to the PO. The average life for the floater and the PO is the same as the tranche from which these two tranches were created.

Planned Amortization Class Tranches

A *planned amortization class* (PAC) bond is one in which a schedule of principal payments is set forth in the prospectus. The PAC bondholders have priority over all other bond classes in the structure with respect to the receipt of the scheduled principal payments. While there is no assurance that the principal payments will be actually realized so as to satisfy the schedule, a PAC bond is structured so that if prepayment speeds are within a certain range, the collateral will throw off sufficient principal to meet the schedule of principal payments.

The greater certainty of the cash flow for the PAC bonds comes at the expense of the non-PAC classes, called the *support* or *companion bonds*. It is these tranches that absorb the prepayment risk. Because PAC bonds have protection against both extension risk and contraction risk, they are said to provide two-sided prepayment protection.

To illustrate how to create a PAC bond, we will use as collateral the $400 million passthrough with a coupon rate of 7.5%, an 8.125% WAC, and a WAM of 357 months. From this collateral a PAC bond with a par value of $243.8 million will be created. The second column of Exhibit 11 shows the principal payment (regularly scheduled principal repayment plus prepayments) for selected months assuming a prepayment speed of 90 PSA, and the next column shows the principal payments for selected months assuming that the passthrough prepays at 300 PSA.

The last column of Exhibit 11 gives the minimum principal payment if the collateral speed is 90 PSA or 300 PSA for months 1 to 349. (After month 349, the outstanding principal balance will be paid off if the prepayment speed is between 90 PSA and 300 PSA.) For example, in the first month, the principal payment would be $508,169.52 if the collateral prepays at 90 PSA and $1,075,931.20 if the collateral prepays at 300 PSA. Thus, the minimum principal payment is $508,169.52, as reported in the last column of Exhibit 11. In month 103, the minimum principal payment is also the amount if the prepayment speed is 90 PSA, $1,446,761, compared to $1,458,618.04 for 300 PSA. In month 104, however, a prepayment speed of 300 PSA would produce a principal payment of $1,433,539.23, which is less than the principal payment of $1,440,825.55 assuming 90 PSA. So, $1,433,539.23 is reported in the last column of Exhibit 11. In fact, from month 104 on the minimum principal payment is the one that would result assuming a prepayment speed of 300 PSA.

Actually, if the collateral prepays at any speed between 90 PSA and 300 PSA, the minimum principal payment would be the amount reported in the last column of Exhibit 11. For example, if we had included principal payment figures assuming a prepayment speed of 200 PSA, the minimum principal payment would not change: from month 11 through month 103, the minimum principal payment is that generated from 90 PSA, but from month 104 on, the minimum principal payment is that generated from 300 PSA.

This characteristic of the collateral allows for the creation of a PAC bond, assuming that the collateral prepays over its life at a constant speed between 90 PSA and 300 PSA. A schedule of principal repayments that the PAC bondholders are entitled to receive before any other tranche in the CMO structure is specified. The monthly schedule of principal repayments is as specified in the last column of Exhibit 11, which shows the minimum principal payment. While there is no assurance that the collateral will prepay at a constant rate between these two speeds, a PAC bond can be structured assuming that it will.

Exhibit 11: Monthly Principal Payment for $400 Million Par 7.5% Coupon Passthrough with an 8.125% WAC and a 357 WAM Assuming Prepayment Rates of 90 PSA and 300 PSA

Month	At 90% PSA	At 300% PSA	Minimum principal payment PAC schedule
1	$508,169.52	$1,075,931.20	$508,169.52
2	569,843.43	1,279,412.11	569,843.43
3	631,377.11	1,482,194.45	631,377.11
4	692,741.89	1,683,966.17	692,741.89
5	753,909.12	1,884,414.62	753,909.12
6	814,850.22	2,083,227.31	814,850.22
7	875,536.68	2,280,092.68	875,536.68
8	935,940.10	2,474,700.92	935,940.10
9	996,032.19	2,666,744.77	996,032.19
10	1,055,784.82	2,855,920.32	1,055,784.82
11	1,115,170.01	3,041,927.81	1,115,170.01
12	1,174,160.00	3,224,472.44	1,174,160.00
13	1,232,727.22	3,403,265.17	1,232,727.22
14	1,290,844.32	3,578,023.49	1,290,844.32
15	1,348,484.24	3,748,472.23	1,348,484.24
16	1,405,620.17	3,914,344.26	1,405,620.17
17	1,462,225.60	4,075,381.29	1,462,225.60
18	1,518,274.36	4,231,334.57	1,518,274.36
101	1,458,719.34	1,510,072.17	1,458,719.34
102	1,452,725.55	1,484,126.59	1,452,725.55
103	1,446,761.00	1,458,618.04	1,446,761.00
104	1,440,825.55	1,433,539.23	1,433,539.23
105	1,434,919.07	1,408,883.01	1,408,883.01
211	949,482.58	213,309.00	213,309.00
212	946,033.34	209,409.09	209,409.09
213	942,601.99	205,577.05	205,577.05
346	618,684.59	13,269.17	13,269.17
347	617,071.58	12,944.51	12,944.51
348	615,468.65	12,626.21	12,626.21
349	613,875.77	12,314.16	3,432.32
350	612,292.88	12,008.25	0
351	610,719.96	11,708.38	0
352	609,156.96	11,414.42	0
353	607,603.84	11,126.28	0
354	606,060.57	10,843.85	0
355	604,527.09	10,567.02	0
356	603,003.38	10,295.70	0
357	601,489.39	10,029.78	0

Exhibit 12: FAF-07 CMO Structure with One PAC Bond and One Support Bond

Tranche	Par amount	Coupon rate (%)
P (PAC)	$243,800,000	7.5
S (Support)	156,200,000	7.5
Total	$400,000,000	

Payment rules:

1. *For payment of periodic coupon interest:* Disburse periodic coupon interest to each tranche on the basis of the amount of principal outstanding at the beginning of the period.

2. *For disbursement of principal payments:* Disburse principal payments to tranche P based on its schedule of principal repayments. Tranche P has priority with respect to current and future principal payments to satisfy the schedule. Any excess principal payments in a month over the amount necessary to satisfy the schedule for tranche P are paid to tranche S. When tranche S is completely paid off, all principal payments are to be made to tranche P regardless of the schedule.

Exhibit 13: Average Life for PAC Bond and Support Bond in FAF-07 Assuming Various Prepayment Speeds

Prepayment rate (PSA)	PAC Bond (P)	Support Bond (S)
0	15.97	27.26
50	9.44	24.00
90	7.26	18.56
100	7.26	18.56
150	7.26	12.57
165	7.26	11.16
200	7.26	8.38
250	7.26	5.37
300	7.26	3.13
350	6.56	2.51
400	5.92	2.17
450	5.38	1.94
500	4.93	1.77
700	3.70	1.37

Exhibit 12 shows a CMO structure, FAF-07, created from the $400 million 7.5% coupon passthrough with a WAC of 8.125% and a WAM of 357 months. There are just two tranches in this structure: a 7.5% coupon PAC bond created assuming 90 to 300 PSA with a par value of $243.8 million, and a support bond with a par value of $156.2 million. The two speeds used to create a PAC bond are called the *initial PAC collars* (or *initial PAC bands*). For FAF-07, 90 PSA is the lower collar and 300 PSA the upper collar.

Exhibit 13 reports the average life for the PAC bond and the support bond in FAF-07 assuming various actual prepayment speeds. Notice that between 90 PSA and 300 PSA, the average life for the PAC bond is stable at 7.26 years. However, at slower or faster PSA speeds the schedule is broken and the average life changes, lengthening when the prepayment speed is less than 90 PSA and short-ening when it is greater than 300 PSA. Even so, there is much greater variability for the average life of the support bond.

Creating a Series of PAC Bonds

Most CMO PAC structures have more than one class of PAC bonds. Exhibit 14 shows six PAC bonds created from the single PAC bond in FAF-07. We will refer to this CMO structure as FAF-08. Information about this CMO structure is pro-vided in Exhibit 14. The total par value of the six PAC bonds is equal to $243.8 million, which is the amount of the single PAC bond in FAF-07.

Exhibit 15 shows the average life for the six PAC bonds and the support bond in FAF-08 at various prepayment speeds. From a PAC bond in FAF-07 with an average life of 7.26, we have created six PAC bonds with an average life as short as 2.58 years (P-A) and as long as 16.92 years (P-F) if prepayments stay within 90 PSA and 300 PSA.

As expected, the average lives are stable if the prepayment speed is between 90 PSA and 300 PSA. Notice that even outside this range the average life is stable for several of the PAC bonds. For example, PAC P-A is stable even if pre-payment speeds are as high as 400 PSA. For the PAC P-B, the average life does not vary when prepayments are between 90 PSA and 350 PSA. Why is it that the shorter the PAC, the more protection it has against faster prepayments?

Exhibit 14: FAF-08 CMO Structure with Six PAC Bonds and One Support Bond

Tranche	Par amount	Coupon rate (%)
P-A	$85,000,000	7.5
P-B	8,000,000	7.5
P-C	35,000,000	7.5
P-D	45,000,000	7.5
P-E	40,000,000	7.5
P-F	30,800,000	7.5
S	156,200,000	7.5
Total	$400,000,000	

Payment rules:
1. *For payment of periodic coupon interest:* Disburse periodic coupon interest to each tranche on the basis of the amount of principal outstanding at the beginning of the period.
2. *For disbursement of principal payments:* Disburse principal payments to tranches P-A to P-F based on their respective schedules of principal repayments. Tranche P-A has priority with respect to current and future principal payments to satisfy the schedule. Any excess principal payments in a month over the amount necessary to satisfy the schedule for tranche P-A are paid to tranche S. Once tranche P-A is com-pletely paid off, tranche P-B has priority, then tranche P-C, etc. When tranche S is completely paid off, all principal payments are to be made to the remaining PAC tranches in order of priority regardless of the schedule.

Exhibit 15: Average Life for PAC Bond and Support Bond in FAF-08 Assuming Various Prepayment Speeds

Prepayment rate (PSA)	PAC Bonds					
	P-A	P-B	P-C	P-D	P-E	P-F
0	8.46	14.61	16.49	19.41	21.91	23.76
50	3.58	6.82	8.36	11.30	14.50	18.20
90	2.58	4.72	5.78	7.89	10.83	16.92
100	2.58	4.72	5.78	7.89	10.83	16.92
150	2.58	4.72	5.78	7.89	10.83	16.92
165	2.58	4.72	5.78	7.89	10.83	16.92
200	2.58	4.72	5.78	7.89	10.83	16.92
250	2.58	4.72	5.78	7.89	10.83	16.92
300	2.58	4.72	5.78	7.89	10.83	16.92
350	2.58	4.72	5.94	6.95	9.24	14.91
400	2.57	4.37	4.91	6.17	8.33	13.21
450	2.50	3.97	4.44	5.56	7.45	11.81
500	2.40	3.65	4.07	5.06	6.74	10.65
700	2.06	2.82	3.10	3.75	4.88	7.51

To understand why this is so, remember that there are $156.2 million in support bonds that are protecting the $85 million of PAC P-A. Thus, even if prepayments are faster than the initial upper collar, there may be sufficient support bonds to assure the satisfaction of the schedule. In fact, as can been from Exhibit 15, even if prepayments are at 400 PSA over the life of the collateral, the average life is unchanged.

Now consider PAC P-B. The support bonds are providing protection for both the $85 million of PAC P-A and $93 million of PAC P-B. As can be seen from Exhibit 15, prepayments could be 350 PSA and the average life is still unchanged. From Exhibit 15 it can be seen that the degree of protection against extension risk increases the shorter the PAC. Thus, while the initial collar may be 90 to 300 PSA, the effective collar is wider for the shorter PAC tranches.

Effective Collars and Actual Prepayments

As we have emphasized, the creation of a mortgage-backed security cannot make prepayment risk disappear. This is true for both a passthrough and a CMO. Thus, the reduction in prepayment risk (both extension risk and contraction risk) that a PAC bond offers must come from somewhere.

Where does the prepayment protection come from? It comes from the support bonds. It is the support bonds that forego principal payments if the collateral prepayments are slow; support bonds do not receive any principal until the PAC bonds receive the scheduled principal repayment. This reduces the risk that the PAC bonds will extend. Similarly, it is the support bonds that absorb any principal payments in excess of the scheduled principal payments that are made. This reduces the contraction risk of the PAC bonds. Thus, the key to the prepayment protection offered by a PAC bond is the amount of support bonds outstanding. If the support bonds are paid off quickly because of faster-than-expected prepayments, then there is no longer any protection for the PAC bonds. In fact, in FAF-08, if the support bond is paid off, the structure is effectively reduced to a sequential-pay CMO. In such cases, the schedule is unlikely to be maintained, and the structure is referred to as a *busted PAC*.

The support bonds can be thought of as bodyguards for the PAC bondholders. When the bullets fly — i.e., prepayments occur — it is the bodyguards that get killed first. The bodyguards are there to absorb the bullets. Once all the bodyguards are killed off (i.e., the support bonds paid off with faster-than-expected prepayments), the PAC bonds must fend for themselves: they are exposed to all the bullets.

With the bodyguard metaphor for the support bonds in mind, let's consider two questions asked by CMO buyers:

1. Will the schedule of principal repayments be satisfied if prepayments are faster than the initial upper collar?
2. Will the schedule of principal repayments be satisfied as long as prepayments stay within the initial collar?

Let's address the first question. The initial upper collar for FAF-07 is 300 PSA. Suppose that actual prepayments are 500 PSA for seven consecutive months. Will this disrupt the schedule of principal repayments? The answer is: it depends!

There are two pieces of information we will need to answer this question. First, when does the 500 PSA occur? Second, what has been the actual prepayment experience up to the time that prepayments are 500 PSA? For example, suppose six years from now is when the prepayments reach 500 PSA, and also suppose that for the past six years the actual prepayment speed has been 90 PSA every month. What this means is that there are more bodyguards (i.e., support bonds) around than was expected when the PAC was structured at the initial collar. In establishing the schedule of principal repayments, it was assumed that the bodyguards would be killed off at 300 PSA. But the actual prepayment experience results in them being killed off at only 90 PSA. Thus, six years from now when the 500 PSA is assumed to occur, there are more bodyguards than expected. Thus, a 500 PSA for seven consecutive months may have no effect on the ability of the schedule of principal repayments to be met.

In contrast, suppose that the actual prepayment experience for the first six years is 300 PSA (the upper collar of the initial PAC collar). In this case, there are no extra bodyguards around. As a result, any prepayment speeds faster than 300 PSA, such as 500 PSA in our example, jeopardize satisfaction of the principal repayment schedule and increase contraction risk. This does not mean that the schedule will be "busted" — the term used in the CMO market when a PAC schedule is broken. What it does mean is that the prepayment protection is reduced.

Exhibit 16: Average Life Two Years from Now for PAC Bond of FAF-07 Assuming Prepayments of 300 PSA

PSA from Year 2 on	Average Life
95	6.43
105	6.11
115	6.01
120	6.00
125	6.00
300	6.00
305	5.62

It should be clear from these observations that the initial collars are not particularly useful in assessing the prepayment protection for a seasoned PAC bond. This is most important to understand, as it is common for CMO buyers to compare prepayment protection of PACs in different CMO structures, and conclude that the greater protection is offered by the one with the wider initial collars. This approach is inadequate because it is actual prepayment experience that determines the degree of prepayment protection going forward, as well as the expected future prepayment behavior of the collateral.

The way to determine this protection is to calculate the effective collar for a PAC bond. An *effective collar* for a PAC is the lower and the upper PSA that can occur in the future and still allow maintenance of the schedule of principal repayments.

The effective collar changes every month. An extended period over which actual prepayments are below the upper range of the initial PAC collar will result in an increase in the upper range of the effective collar. This is because there will be more bodyguards around than anticipated. An extended period of prepayments slower than the lower range of the initial PAC collar will raise the lower range of the effective collar. This is because it will take faster prepayments to make up the shortfall of the scheduled principal payments not made plus the scheduled future principal payments.

The PAC schedule may not be satisfied even if the actual prepayments never fall outside of the initial collar. This may seem surprising since our previous analysis indicated that the average life would not change if prepayments are at either extreme of the initial collar. However, recall that all of our previous analysis has been based on a single PSA speed for the life of the structure.

If we vary the PSA speed over time rather than keep it constant over the life of the CMO, we can see what happens to the effective collar if the prepayments are at the initial upper collar for a certain number of months. Exhibit 16 shows the average life two years from now for the PAC bond in FAF-07 assuming that prepayments are 300 PSA for the first 24 months. Notice that the average life is stable at six years if the prepayments for the following months are between 115 PSA and 300 PSA. That is, the effective PAC collar is no longer the initial collar.

Instead, the lower collar has shifted upward. This means that the protection from year 2 on is for 115 to 300 PSA, a narrower band than initially, even though the earlier prepayments did not exceed the initial upper collar.

Providing Greater Prepayment Protection for PACs

There are two ways to provide greater protection for PAC bonds: lockouts and reverse PAC structures. One obvious way to provide greater protection for PAC bonds is to issue fewer PAC bonds relative to support bonds. In FAF-08, for example, rather than creating the six PAC bonds with a total par value of $243.8 million, we could use only $158.8 million of the $400 million of collateral to create these bonds by reducing the amount of each of the six PAC bonds. An alternative is not to issue one of the PAC bonds, typically the shorter-term one. For example, suppose that we create only the last five of the six PAC bonds in FAF-08. The $85 million for PAC P-A is then used to create more support bonds. Such a CMO structure with no principal payments to a PAC bond in the earlier years is referred to as a *lockout structure*.

A lockout structure provides greater prepayment protection to all PAC bonds in the CMO structure. One way to provide greater prepayment protection to only some PAC bonds is to alter the principal payment rules for distributing principal once all the support bonds have been paid off.

In FAF-08, for example, once the support bond in this structure is paid off, the structure effectively becomes a sequential-pay structure. For PAC P-A this means that while there is protection against extension risk, as this tranche receives principal payments before the other five PAC bonds, there is no protection against contraction. To provide greater protection to PAC P-A, the payment rules set forth in the prospectus can specify that after all support bonds have been paid off any principal payments in excess of the scheduled amount will be paid to the last PAC bond, P-F in FAF-08. Thus, PAC P-F is exposed to greater contraction risk, which provides the other five PAC bonds with more protection against contraction risk. The principal payment rules would also specify that once the support bonds and PAC P-F bond are paid off, then all principal payments in excess of the scheduled amount to earlier tranches are to be paid to the next-to-the-last PAC bond, PAC P-E in our example.

A CMO structure requiring any excess principal payments to be made to the longer PAC bonds after all support bonds are paid off is called a *reverse PAC structure*.

Other PAC Tranches

Earlier we described how the collateral can be used to create a CMO structure with accrual bonds and floater and inverse floater bonds. These same types of bond classes can be created from a PAC bond. The difference between the bond classes described and those created from a PAC bond is simply the prepayment protection offered by the PAC structure.

Exhibit 17: FAF-09 CMO Structure with One TAC Bond and One Support Bond

Tranche	Par amount	Coupon rate (%)
T (TAC)	$350,000,000	7.50
S (Support)	50,000,000	7.50
Total	$400,000,000	

Payment rules:

1. *For payment of periodic coupon interest:* Disburse periodic coupon interest to each tranche based on the amount of principal outstanding at the beginning of the period.

2. *For disbursement of principal payments*: Disburse principal payments to tranche T based on its schedule of principal repayments. Tranche T has priority with respect to current and future principal payments to satisfy the schedule. Any excess principal payments in a month over the amount necessary to satisfy the schedule for tranche T are paid to tranche S. When tranche S is completely paid off, all principal payments are to be made to tranche T regardless of the schedule.

Targeted Amortization Class Bonds

A *targeted amortization class*, or TAC, bond resembles a PAC bond in that both have a schedule of principal repayment. The difference between a PAC bond and a TAC bond is that the former has a wide PSA range over which the schedule of principal repayment is protected against contraction risk and extension risk. A TAC bond, in contrast, has a single PSA rate from which the schedule of principal repayment is protected. As a result, the prepayment protection afforded the TAC bond is less than that for a PAC bond. As we shall see, the creation of a bond with a schedule of principal repayments based on a single prepayment rate results in protection against contraction risk but not extension risk. Thus, while PAC bonds are said to have two-sided prepayment protection, TAC bonds have one-sided prepayment protection. Such a bond is acceptable to institutional investors who are not overly concerned with some extension risk but greatly concerned with contraction risk.

As an example of a CMO structure with a TAC bond, consider FAF-09, which has one TAC bond and one support bond. The collateral for this structure is the same $400 million passthrough that we have used throughout this chapter. The par value for the TAC bond is $350 of the $400 million, and the par value for the support bond is $50 million. The TAC bond schedule is generated for a prepayment rate of 165 PSA. The average life at this speed is 6.86 years. Exhibit 17 summarizes the structure of FAF-09.

The TAC bond is designed to have protection against contraction risk but not extension risk. To see this, let's look at four scenarios for the prepayment speeds for the collateral:

> *Scenario 1*: The collateral pays at exactly 165 PSA for its entire life.
> *Scenario 2*: The collateral pays at less than 165 PSA for its entire life.
> *Scenario 3*: The collateral pays faster than 165 PSA but slower than approximately 235 PSA for its entire life.

Exhibit 18: Average Life for the TAC Bond in FAF-09 for Various Assumed Prepayment Rates

Prepayment Rate (PSA)	TAC Bond	Support Bond
0	19.14	29.06
50	13.28	28.07
90	10.21	26.56
100	9.62	26.07
150	7.36	23.15
165	6.86	22.21
200	7.00	12.58
220	7.15	7.39
230	7.27	4.67
235	7.36	3.07
250	7.10	2.43
300	6.21	1.71
350	5.49	1.40
400	4.92	1.21
450	4.46	1.08
500	4.08	0.98
700	3.08	0.73

Scenario 4: The collateral pays faster than approximately 235 PSA for its entire life.

Exhibit 18 reports the average life for the TAC bond and the support bond for these scenarios.

Scenario 1: In this scenario, the schedule of principal repayments will be met because the TAC bond was created assuming a prepayment rate of 165 PSA. The average life is 6.86 years.

Scenario 2: The principal payments from the collateral will not be sufficient to satisfy the schedule in the earlier years. Usually, the principal payments in later years will be sufficient to make up the shortfall and to get back on schedule. In FAF-09, for example, there would be a shortfall in the principal payments from months 1 to 273 if the collateral prepays at 100 PSA. As can be seen from Exhibit 18, the average life of the TAC bond extends to 9.62 years at 100 PSA. The extension is greater at slower speeds.

Scenario 3: If the prepayment speed is greater than 165 PSA but less than 235 PSA, the schedule of principal repayments can be satisfied until all the support bonds are paid off. At that time, the principal payments available from the remaining collateral will be insufficient to meet the schedule of principal repayments for a period of time. After that time, however, the principal payments from the remaining collateral will be sufficient to meet the schedule of principal repayments for the TAC bond. As can be seen in Exhibit 18, the average life assuming various prepayment rates between 165 PSA and 235 PSA reported in Exhibit 18 indicates that the extension could be as long as 7.36 years.

Scenario 4: If the prepayment speed is greater than 236 PSA over the life of the collateral, the average life will shorten. The average life would shorten from 6.86 years assuming 165 PSA to 3.08 years if the collateral speed is 700 PSA.

These scenarios clearly indicate how, assuming a constant PSA speed over the life of the collateral, the TAC bond is protected against contraction risk but exposed to extension risk.

As in the case of PAC bonds where the effective collar changes each month depending on the actual prepayment experience, the PSA rate at which the TAC bond is protected also changes each month when the actual prepayment experience is different from the initial PSA rate used to create the TAC bond. It is possible for there to be a narrow collar for the TAC bond. To understand why, once again consider what happens to the support bonds when prepayments are slower than the 165 PSA rate used to create the TAC bond in FAF-09. There are more bodyguards — the support bonds — than would exist if the prepayment speed is 165 PSA. It is therefore possible that the prepayments can be slightly slower or faster than 165 PSA and still meet the schedule of principal repayments.

Reverse TAC Bond Structures

Some portfolio managers are interested in protection against extension risk but are willing to accept contraction risk. This is the opposite protection from that sought by the buyers of TAC bonds. The structures created to provide such protection are referred to as *reverse TAC bonds*.

For example, a reverse TAC structure can be created by splitting the collateral as follows: $250 million to create the reverse TAC tranche and $150 million for the support bond. The principal repayment schedule is generated assuming a prepayment speed of 90 PSA. The average life assuming 90 PSA is 6.85 years.

TAC Bonds as Support Bonds

TAC bonds in a CMO structure were used quite differently in earlier deals. Today TAC and reverse TAC bonds are created from support bonds and thereby provide support for PAC bonds.

Very Accurately Determined Maturity Bonds

Accrual or Z-bonds have been used in CMO structures as support for bonds called *very accurately determined maturity* (VADM) or guaranteed final maturity bonds. In this case, the interest accruing (i.e., not being paid out) on a Z bond is used to pay the interest and principal on a VADM bond. This effectively provides protection against extension risk even if prepayments slow down, since the interest accruing on the Z bond will be sufficient to pay off the scheduled principal and interest on the VADM bond. Thus, the maximum final maturity can be determined with a high degree of certainty. However, if prepayments are high, resulting in the supporting Z bond being paid off faster, a VADM bond can shorten.

A VADM is similar in character to a reverse TAC. For structures with similar collateral, however, a VADM bond offers greater protection against extension risk. Moreover, most VADMs will not shorten significantly if prepayments speed up. Thus, they offer greater protection against contraction risk compared to a reverse TAC with the same underlying collateral. Compared to PACs, VADM bonds have greater absolute protection against extension risk, and while VADM bonds do not have as much protection against contraction risk, the structures that have included these bonds are such that contraction risk is generally not significant.

As an illustration of a plain vanilla CMO structure with a VADM, consider FAF-10 in Exhibit 19. The speed assumed is 165 PSA. There are four tranches, V, B, C, and Z. The interest accruing to the Z-bond, or accrual bond, is used to pay down tranche V, the VADM bond. Exhibit 20 shows the outstanding balance for the first 31 months assuming 165 PSA. The final maturity is in month 30. The maximum extension can be determined by finding the mortgage balance assuming no prepayment (i.e., 0 PSA). The final maturity in this case would be 83 months.

Exhibit 21 shows a VADM created from a PAC structure. There are five tranches in this structure FAF-11: V, B, C, Z, and S. Tranches V, B, C, and Z are the PAC bonds, and tranche S is the support bond. The VADM bond is tranche V, and the accrual bond from which the interest will be used to pay down the VADM is tranche Z. The PAC bonds are created with a PAC band of 90 to 300 PSA. The corresponding mortgage balances for selected months for each PAC tranche if the prepayment speed is between 90 and 300 PSA are shown in Exhibit 22. The final maturity for the VADM can be seen to be seven years (84 months).

Exhibit 19: FAF-10 CMO Sequential-Pay Structure with a VADM Tranche

Tranche	Par amount	Coupon rate (%)
V (VADM)	$77,000,000	7.5
B	88,000,000	7.5
C	165,000,000	7.5
Z (Accrual)	70,000,000	7.5
Total	$400,000,000	

Payment rules:

1. *For payment of periodic coupon interest:* Disburse periodic coupon interest to tranches V, B, and C based on the amount of principal outstanding at the beginning of the period. The interest earned by tranche Z is to be paid to tranche V as a paydown of principal and accrued as interest to tranche Z.

2. *For disbursement of principal payments:* Disburse principal payments to tranche V until it is completely paid off. The interest from tranche Z is to be paid to tranche V as a paydown of principal. After tranche V is completely paid off, disburse principal payments to tranche B until it is completely paid off. After tranche B is completely paid off, disburse principal payments to tranche C until it is completely paid off. After tranche C is completely paid off, disburse principal payments to tranche Z until the original mortgage balance plus accrued interest is completely paid off.

Exhibit 20: Mortgage Balance for Months 1-31 for FAF-10 Assuming 165 PSA

Month	Tranche			
	V (VADM)	B	C	Z (Accrual)
1	77,000,000	88,000,000	165,000,000	70,000,000
2	75,852,577	88,000,000	165,000,000	70,437,500
3	74,590,446	88,000,000	165,000,000	70,877,734
4	73,213,901	88,000,000	165,000,000	71,320,720
5	71,723,325	88,000,000	165,000,000	71,766,475
6	70,119,198	88,000,000	165,000,000	72,215,015
7	68,402,095	88,000,000	165,000,000	72,666,359
8	66,572,684	88,000,000	165,000,000	73,120,524
9	64,631,727	88,000,000	165,000,000	73,577,527
10	62,580,078	88,000,000	165,000,000	74,037,387
11	60,418,685	88,000,000	165,000,000	74,500,120
12	58,148,586	88,000,000	165,000,000	74,965,746
27	12,024,369	88,000,000	165,000,000	82,309,747
28	8,225,769	88,000,000	165,000,000	82,824,183
29	4,452,903	88,000,000	165,000,000	83,341,834
30	705,500	88,000,000	165,000,000	83,862,721
31	0	84,983,291	165,000,000	84,386,863

Exhibit 21: FAF-11 CMO PAC Structure with a VADM

Tranche	Par amount	Coupon rate (%)
V (VADM)	$75,000,000	7.5
B	92,800,000	7.5
C	10,000,000	7.5
Z (Accrual)	66,000,000	7.5
S	156,200,000	7.5
Total	$400,000,000	

Payment rules:

1. *For payment of periodic coupon interest:* Disburse periodic coupon interest to tranches V, B, C, and S on the basis of the amount of principal outstanding at the beginning of the period. The interest earned by tranche Z is to be paid to tranche V as a paydown of principal and accrued as interest to tranche Z.

2. *For disbursement of principal payments:* Disburse principal payments to tranches V, B, C, and Z based on their respective schedules of principal repayments. Tranches V, B, C, and Z have priority with respect to current and future principal payments to satisfy the schedule. Any excess principal payments in a month over the amount necessary to satisfy the schedule for tranche V are paid to tranche S. Once tranche V is completely paid off, tranche B has priority, then tranche C, etc. When tranche S is completely paid off, all principal payments are to be made to the remaining classes with a schedule in order of priority regardless of the schedule.

Exhibit 23 shows the same information assuming no prepayments (i.e., 0 PSA). As can be seen from this exhibit, the VADM has a final maturity of seven years if no prepayments are made. If the prepayment speed is outside the upper PAC band, the VADM's final maturity will be less than seven years. The average life for all five tranches assuming a wide range of prepayment scenarios is shown in Exhibit 24. Note the stability of the average life of the VADM bond.

Exhibit 22: Mortgage Balance for Selected Months for FAF-11 Assuming 90 to 300 PSA

Month	Tranche			
	V (VADM)	B	C	Z (Accrual)
1	75,000,000	92,800,000	10,000,000	66,000,000
2	74,319,965	92,559,365	10,000,000	66,412,500
3	73,635,541	92,258,868	10,000,000	66,827,578
4	72,946,698	91,898,661	10,000,000	67,245,250
5	72,253,409	91,478,925	10,000,000	67,665,533
6	71,555,645	90,999,871	10,000,000	68,088,443
7	70,853,377	90,461,736	10,000,000	68,513,996
8	70,146,575	89,864,789	10,000,000	68,942,208
9	69,435,211	89,209,324	10,000,000	69,373,097
10	68,719,255	88,495,666	10,000,000	69,806,679
11	67,998,676	87,724,168	10,000,000	70,242,971
12	67,273,447	86,895,209	10,000,000	70,681,989
71	15,059,365	4,060,751	10,000,000	102,083,716
72	13,992,276	2,837,012	10,000,000	102,721,740
73	12,918,294	1,623,114	10,000,000	103,363,750
74	11,837,374	419,042	10,000,000	104,009,774
75	10,749,472	0	9,224,783	104,659,835
76	9,654,543	0	8,040,323	105,313,959
77	8,552,541	0	6,865,651	105,972,171
78	7,443,420	0	5,700,752	106,634,497
79	6,327,135	0	4,545,615	107,300,963
80	5,203,639	0	3,400,228	107,971,594
81	4,072,884	0	2,264,578	108,646,416
82	2,934,825	0	1,138,655	109,325,456
83	1,789,415	0	22,447	110,008,740
84	636,604	0	0	109,612,237
85	0	0	0	108,683,625
86	0	0	0	107,124,919
87	0	0	0	105,572,694
345	0	0	0	55,873
346	0	0	0	42,272
347	0	0	0	29,003
348	0	0	0	16,059
349	0	0	0	3,432
350	0	0	0	0

Exhibit 23: Mortgage Balance for Selected Months for FAF-11 Assuming No Prepayments (0 PSA)

Month		Tranche		
	V (VADM)	B	C	Z (Accrual)
1	75,000,000	92,800,000	10,000,000	66,000,000
2	74,319,965	92,800,000	10,000,000	66,412,500
3	73,635,541	92,800,000	10,000,000	66,827,578
4	72,946,698	92,800,000	10,000,000	67,245,250
5	72,253,409	92,800,000	10,000,000	67,665,533
6	71,555,645	92,800,000	10,000,000	68,088,443
7	70,853,377	92,800,000	10,000,000	68,513,996
8	70,146,575	92,800,000	10,000,000	68,942,208
9	69,435,211	92,800,000	10,000,000	69,373,097
10	68,719,255	92,800,000	10,000,000	69,806,679
11	67,998,676	92,800,000	10,000,000	70,242,971
12	67,273,447	92,800,000	10,000,000	70,681,989
80	5,203,639	92,800,000	10,000,000	107,971,594
81	4,072,884	92,800,000	10,000,000	108,646,416
82	2,934,825	92,800,000	10,000,000	109,325,456
83	1,789,415	92,800,000	10,000,000	110,008,740
84	636,604	92,800,000	10,000,000	110,696,295
85	0	92,276,346	10,000,000	111,388,147
86	0	91,108,593	10,000,000	112,084,323
146	0	5,302,864	10,000,000	162,891,520
147	0	3,573,053	10,000,000	163,909,592
148	0	1,832,059	10,000,000	164,934,027
149	0	79,811	10,000,000	165,964,864
150	0	0	8,316,236	167,002,145
151	0	0	6,541,260	168,045,908
152	0	0	4,754,809	169,096,195
153	0	0	2,956,810	170,153,046
154	0	0	1,147,188	171,216,503
155	0	0	0	171,612,472
156	0	0	0	170,856,168
157	0	0	0	170,094,742
158	0	0	0	169,328,161
346	0	0	0	42,272
347	0	0	0	29,003
348	0	0	0	16,059
349	0	0	0	3,432
350	0	0	0	0

Exhibit 24: Average Life of Each Tranche of FAF-11 Assuming 0 to 700 PSA

PSA	Average Life				
	V	B	C	Z	S
0	3.83	9.88	12.61	19.52	27.26
50	3.83	5.10	8.59	13.80	24.00
90	3.83	3.35	6.51	11.54	20.06
100	3.83	3.35	6.51	11.54	18.56
150	3.83	3.35	6.51	11.54	12.57
165	3.83	3.35	6.51	11.54	11.16
200	3.83	3.35	6.51	11.54	8.38
250	3.83	3.35	6.51	11.54	5.37
300	3.83	3.35	6.51	11.54	3.13
350	3.60	3.41	6.26	10.27	2.51
400	3.26	3.39	5.70	9.24	2.17
450	2.98	3.30	5.24	8.38	1.94
500	2.74	3.19	4.85	7.65	1.77
700	2.16	2.71	3.76	5.64	1.37

Notional IOs

In our previous illustrations, we used a CMO structure in which all the tranches have the same coupon rate (7.5%) and that coupon rate is the same as the collateral. In practice, the same coupon rate would not be given to each tranche. Instead, the coupon rate would depend on the term structure of interest rates and the average life of the tranche, among other things.

In the earlier CMO deals, all of the excess interest between the coupon rate on the tranches and the coupon interest on the collateral was paid to an equity class referred to as the *CMO residual*. This is no longer the practice today. Instead, a tranche is created that receives the excess coupon interest. This tranche is called a *notional interest-only class*, or *notional IO*.

To see how a notional IO is created, consider the CMO structure shown in Exhibit 25, FAF-12. This is the same structure as FAF-02 except that the coupon rate varies by tranche and there is a class denoted "IO" which is the class of interest to us.

Notice that for this structure the par amount for the IO class is shown as $52,566,667 and the coupon rate is 7.5%. Since this is an IO class there is no par amount. The amount shown is the amount upon which the interest payments will be determined, not the amount that will be paid to the holder of this bond. Therefore, it is called a *notional amount*.

Let's look at how the notional amount is determined. Consider first tranche A. The par value is $194.5 million and the coupon rate is 6%. Since the collateral's coupon rate is 7.5%, the excess interest is 150 basis points (1.5%). Therefore, an IO with a 1.5% coupon rate and a notional amount of $194.5 million can be created from tranche A. But this is equivalent to an IO with a notional amount of $38.9 million and a coupon rate of 7.5%. Mathematically, this notional amount is found as follows:

$$\text{Notional amount for 7.5\% IO} = \frac{\text{Tranches par value} \times \text{Excess interest}}{0.075}$$

Exhibit 25: FAF-12: A Hypothetical Five Tranche Sequential-Pay with an Accrual Tranche, and an Interest-Only Tranche

Tranche	Par amount	Coupon rate (%)
A	$194,500,000	6.00
B	36,000,000	6.50
C	96,500,000	7.00
Z	73,000,000	7.25
IO	52,566,667 (Notional)	7.50
Total	$400,000,000	

Payment rules:

1. *For payment of periodic coupon interest:* Disburse periodic coupon interest to tranches A, B, and C on the basis of the amount of principal outstanding at the beginning of the period. For tranche Z, accrue the interest based on the principal plus accrued interest in the previous period. The interest for tranche Z is to be paid to the earlier tranches as a principal pay down. Disburse periodic interest to the IO tranche based on the notional amount at the beginning of the period.

2. *For disbursement of principal payments:* Disburse principal payments to tranche A until it is completely paid off. After tranche A is completely paid off, disburse principal payments to tranche B until it is completely paid off. After tranche B is completely paid off, disburse principal payments to tranche C until it is completely paid off. After tranche C is completely paid off, disburse principal payments to tranche Z until the original principal balance plus accrued interest is completely paid off.

3. *No principal is to be paid to the IO tranche:* The notional amount of the IO tranche declines based on the principal payments to all other tranches.

---

where

Excess interest = Collateral coupon rate − Tranche coupon rate

For example, for tranche A:

Excess interest = 0.075 − 0.060 = 0.015

Tranche's par value = $194,500,000

$$\text{Notional amount for 7.5\% IO} = \frac{\$194,500,000 \times 0.015}{0.075} = \$38,900,000$$

Similarly, from tranche B with a par value of $36 million, the excess interest is 100 basis points (1%) and therefore an IO with a coupon rate of 1% and a notional amount of $36 million can be created. But this is equivalent to creating an IO with a notional amount of $4.8 million and a coupon rate of 7.5%. This procedure is shown below for all four tranches:

Tranche	Par amount	Excess interest (%)	Notional amount for a 7.5% coupon rate IO
A	$194,500,000	1.50	$38,900,000
B	36,000,000	1.00	4,800,000
C	96,500,000	0.50	6,433,333
Z	73,000,000	0.25	2,433,334
Notional amount for 7.5% IO			$52,566,667

Exhibit 26: FAF-13 CMO Structure with a PAC I Bond, a PAC II Bond, and a Support Bond Class without a Principal Repayment Schedule

Initial PAC collar for the PAC I: 90 PSA to 300 PSA
Initial PAC collar for the PAC II: 100 PSA to 225 PSA

Tranche	Par amount ($)	Coupon rate (%)
P-I (PAC I)	$243,800,000	7.50
P-II (PAC II)	50,330,000	7.50
S	105,870,000	7.50
Total	$400,000,000	

Payment rules:

1. *For payment of periodic coupon interest:* Disburse periodic coupon interest to each tranche based on the amount of principal outstanding at the beginning of the period.

2. *For disbursement of principal payments:* Disburse principal payments to tranche P-I based on its schedule of principal repayments. Tranche P-I has priority with respect to current and future principal payments to satisfy the schedule. Any excess principal payments in a month over the amount necessary to satisfy the schedule for tranche P-I are paid to tranches P-II and S. Priority is given to tranche P-II to satisfy its schedule of principal repayments. Any excess principal payments in a month are paid to tranche S. When tranche S is completely paid off its original balance, then any excess is to be paid to tranche P-II regardless of its schedule. After tranche P-II is completely paid off its original mortgage balance, any excess is paid to tranche P-I regardless of its schedule.

Support Bonds

The support bonds — or bodyguards — are the bonds that provide prepayment protection for the PAC tranches. *Consequently, support tranches expose investors to the greatest level of prepayment risk.* Because of this, investors must be particularly careful in assessing the cash flow characteristics of support bonds to reduce the likelihood of adverse portfolio consequences due to prepayments.

The support bond typically is divided into different bond classes. All the bond classes we have discussed earlier are available, including sequential-pay support bond classes, floater and inverse floater support bond classes, and accrual support bond classes.

The support bond can even be partitioned so as to create support bond classes with a schedule of principal payments. That is, support bond classes that are PAC bonds can be created. In a structure with a PAC bond and a support bond with a PAC schedule of principal payments, the former is called a *PAC I bond* or *Level I PAC bond* and the latter a *PAC II bond* or *Level II PAC bond*. While PAC II bonds have greater prepayment protection than the support bond classes without a schedule of principal repayments, the prepayment protection is less than that provided PAC I bonds.

To illustrate this, the CMO structure shown in Exhibit 26 was created, FAF-13, for the par amounts shown. There is the same PAC bond as in FAF-07 with an initial PAC collar of 90 PSA to 300 PSA. That tranche is now labeled P-I, and it is called a PAC I. The support bond in FAF-07 has been split into a support bond with a schedule, labeled P-II, and a support bond without a schedule, labeled S. P-II is a PAC II bond that was created with an initial PAC collar of 100 PSA to 225 PSA.

Exhibit 27: Average Life for FAF-13 for Various Assumed Prepayment Rates

Prepayment rate	Average life			
	PAC I bond	PAC II bond	Bond S	Support bond in FAF-04
0	15.973	25.44	28.13	27.26
50	9.44	20.32	25.77	24.00
90	7.26	15.69	22.14	20.06
100	7.26	13.77	20.84	18.56
150	7.26	13.77	12.00	12.57
165	7.26	13.77	9.91	11.16
200	7.26	13.77	5.82	8.38
225	7.26	13.77	3.42	6.75
250	7.26	10.75	2.81	5.37
300	7.26	5.07	2.20	3.13
350	6.56	3.85	1.88	2.51
400	5.92	3.24	1.66	2.17
450	5.38	2.85	1.51	1.94
500	4.93	2.58	1.39	1.77
700	3.70	1.99	1.08	1.37

Exhibit 27 indicates the average life for all the bond classes in FAF-13 under various prepayment scenarios. Also shown in the exhibit is the average life for the support bond in FAF-07. The PAC I enjoys the same prepayment protection in the structure with a PAC II as it does in the structure without a PAC II. The PAC II has considerably more average life variability than the PAC I but less variability than the support bond class S. Comparison of the support bond class S in FAF-13 with the support bond in FAF-07 shows that the presence of a PAC II increases the average life variability. Now the support bond class is providing protection for not only a PAC I but also a support bond with a schedule.

There is more that can be done with the PAC II bond. A series of PAC IIs can be created just as we did with the PACs in FAF-08. PAC IIs can also be used to create any other type of bond class, such as a PAC II inverse floater or accrual bond, for example.

The support bond without a principal repayment schedule can be used to create any type of bond class. In fact, a portion of the non-PAC II support bond can be given a schedule of principal repayments. This bond class would be called a PAC III bond or a Level III PAC bond. While it provides protection against prepayments for the PAC I and PAC II bonds and is therefore subject to considerable prepayment risk, such a bond class has greater protection than the support bond class without a schedule of principal repayments.

RE-REMICS

In most cases, the underlying collateral of a CMO structure is in the form of a fixed-rate mortgage passthroughs. In general, any mortgage asset can be used as collateral for a CMO structure. Since 1992, a good number of CMO deals were created whose underlying collateral is tranches from existing CMO structures. These deals are called *re-REMICs* because they use parts of previously issued REMICs to create another REMIC.

The purpose of a re-REMIC is to take advantage of pricing discrepancy by altering the existing structures of the CMO collateral. More than a billion dollars of notional face of IOette to Trust IO re-REMICs were done in 1992 when IOettes traded at 500 to 1,000 basis points cheap to Trust IOs. Floater/inverse floater and floater/inverse IO to fixed-rate re-REMICs were most common in 1994 and 1995 when CMO derivatives traded at 20% discount to their recombination value after a major hedge fund that invested in CMOs failed in early 1994. "Kitchen sink" re-REMICs were invented when CMO dealers had a huge inventory of CMO derivatives such as IOs, POs, inverses, and support bonds. They used re-REMICs to create a product that had better investment characteristics than the individual REMIC pieces from which they were created. Complex floater re-REMIC was invented when the market had no demand for low cap floaters.

IOette to IO Re-REMIC

IOettes are stripped mortgage-backed securities with a huge coupon, e.g. 900%. IOettes are economically IOs with a tiny bit of principal. A 900% coupon IOette is economically equivalent to combining 100 parts of a 9% notional IO with 1 part of a PO. They normally traded around 50 to 100 basis points cheap to trust IOs due to liquidity and accounting issues given the large coupon. Due to the unprecedented prepayments in 1992 given the extreme rally in the market and the historically steep yield curve, the liquidity premium on prepayment sensitive derivatives were amplified several times. IOettes traded at 500 to 1,000 basis points cheap to IOs. Wall Street dealers then stripped out the principal from these IOettes to re-create trust IOs and POs. For example, a $100 million of IOettes with a 900% coupon can be stripped into a $10 billion notional amount of 9% IOs and $100 million of POs. The new IOs immediately tightened in spreads because they looked and behaved like regular trust IOs. The POs traded even better in a fast prepayment environment. This is a classic example of a re-REMIC taking advantage of the pricing discrepancy of two economically equivalent, but structurally different securities.

Floater/Inverse Floater to Fixed-Rate Re-REMIC

The 1994 bear market in the fixed-income sector and the major setback in the CMO market in early 1994 also created another re-REMIC arbitrage opportunity — the floater/inverse floater to fixed-rate re-REMIC arbitrage. The creation of a floater and inverse floater from a fixed-rate tranche was illustrated earlier in this chapter and the re-REMIC process is essentially the reverse of that. Inverse floaters historically traded near their "creation value."[2] During the bear market of 1994 and especially after the liquidation of a major hedge fund's portfolio, there was little demand for and a lot of supply of long duration and leveraged securities such as inverse floaters. Inverse floaters traded at 15% to 20% below their creation value. Consequently, Wall Street dealers and other sophisticated investors bought up the floater/inverse floater pairs to recombine them back into fixed-rate re-REMIC tranches. The re-REMIC fixed-rate tranches created were 25 to 40 basis points cheaper than generic fixed-rate CMO tranches with similar characteristics.

Kitchen Sink Re-REMIC

The supply and demand imbalance also posed big concern for CMO dealers with huge derivative inventory. They wanted to reduce the size of their inventory but were unwilling to "dump" more securities into the already depressed market. They had to transform their existing inventory into something that was more sellable into the market. In the 1994 rising rate environment, high cap floaters were in demand. Therefore, the dealers packaged the whatever "leftover" derivatives (inverse floaters, inverse IOs, POs, support bonds, and Z-bonds) in their inventory and utilized the cash flows to re-issue high cap floaters in a re-REMIC form; hence the name "kitchen sink."[3] A typical kitchen sink floater had a 200 basis points margin over LIBOR and a 11% cap. It was also overcollateralized, meaning $100 million of leftover derivatives were used to collateralize $85 million of floater. The $15 million residual piece was typically kept by the dealer.

Complex Floater Re-REMIC

The bear market of 1994 also depressed the prices of low cap floaters. Normally, floaters are defensive securities because of their floating-rate coupons. However, in a rapidly rising rate and steep yield curve environment, coupled with the average life extensions in the CMO floaters, the short out-of-the-money caps suddenly became long at-the-money caps. This caused the low cap floaters to depreciate in price like long duration securities. This also caused the demand for low cap floaters to dry up. CMO dealers with large inventory of low cap floaters again used the re-REMIC machine to transform the low cap floaters into higher cap floaters. The result of the re-REMIC was a residual piece with a complex floating-rate coupon formula.

MODIFIABLE AND COMBINABLE REMIC

While the re-REMIC arbitrage can be used to promote pricing efficiency, it is not without cost. There are fixed costs associated with the issuance of REMIC deals.

---

[2] See **Chapter XX**.

[3] Some dealers used their inventory plus tranches purchased from other dealers or clients to create structures that were more attractive to investors.

These costs may or may not be significant depending on the size of the deal. An investor may find that the fixed costs may erode most of the arbitrage profit of combining small pieces of floaters and inverses. In early 1996, Freddie Mac started the *Modifiable and Combinable REMIC* (MACR) program to further promote the liquidity of REMIC tranches. MACR is essentially the same as the re-REMIC process but more flexible and cost efficient.

MACR Structure

REMICs with the MACR feature allow investors to reconfigure their holdings of particular REMIC tranches into new tranches backed by the same cash flows without the expense and complication of a re-REMIC. At the inception of a new REMIC, the structuring underwriter creates the basic REMIC structure to be issued, and defines additional classes, known as MACR classes, which are creatable from the underlying set of REMIC tranches. All MACR structural options must be defined at the outset of the new REMIC. The MACR classes and the regular REMIC classes all share the same Freddie Mac series number.

There are currently four main types of reconfigurations available in REMICs with the MACR feature:

1. Combining PAC and support tranches into plain vanilla tranches.
2. Combining several narrow window sequential tranches into a single wide window tranche.
3. Splitting coupons to form discount and premium classes.
4. Creating fixed-rate bonds from floater/inverse combinations.

A REMIC with the MACR feature can be illustrated by the following example. Consider the following hypothetical REMIC structure:

Class	Principal Amount	Type	Coupon	Average Life (yrs)
A	$20,000,000	PAC Fixed	8%	1
B	$20,000,000	PAC Fixed	8%	3
C	$20,000,000	PAC Fixed	8%	5
F	$30,000,000	Support Floater	6%	10
S	$10,000,000	Support Inverse	14%	10

Note that classes A, B, and C are fixed coupon PAC classes of different sequential average lives. The 8% fixed-rate support bond has been structured into a floater (F) and a three times leverage inverse (S). The prospectus of a REMIC with the MACR feature will have an appendix showing all available pre-determined combinations at issuance. The MACR appendix which shows the available combinations will look like the following:

Multiclass Securities			
Class	Orig. Prin.	A.L.	Coupon
Combination 1			
A	20,000,000	1	8%
B	20,000,000	3	8%
C	20,000,000	5	8%
Combination 2			
F	30,000,000	10	6%
S	10,000,000	10	14%
Combination 3			
B	20,000,000	3	8%

MACR Certificates			
Class	Orig. Prin.	A.L.	Coupon
D	60,000,000	3	8%
L	40,000,000	10	8%
PB	20,000,000	3	7%
PI	20,000,000	notional	1%

As illustrated by the appendix, the holder of classes A, B, and C can deliver all three classes to Freddie Mac and exchange them for a wide window PAC having the same cash flows as the three classes combined. The holder of the inverse/floater pair (F and S) can exchange them for a fixed-rate tranche backed by the same cash flows. The holder of class B can create a discount coupon and a notional IO.

Cost, Flexibility and Liquidity Benefits

Before the MACR program, all these reconfigurations have to be done through a re-REMIC which can be costly and time consuming. An MACR exchange can take place in as little as two days at a cost of 1 tick or $2,000, whichever is greater. Cost is not the only benefit. The exchange option lasts for the life of the deal and is reversible as long as the tranches are still outstanding (not paid off yet). Perhaps, the biggest benefit is the improvement in liquidity. For example, an investor in a sequential class REMIC could only get a bid on a sequential, and could only sell the bond to a sequential buyer. With MACR, the investor can get competitive bids from a PAC buyer, a support buyer, or even a floater/inverse buyer on the reconfigured MACR certificates. The holder of the 8% PAC bond can obtain competitive bids from a discount PAC buyer and a PAC IO buyer.

The liquidity is also supported by the information available. All classes, both REMIC and MACR, are posted on Bloomberg for investors' reference and analysis. Factors are updated monthly for all potential classes, whether they are currently existing or not. All exchanges, REMIC to MACR or vice versa, will be posted to Bloomberg the following day.

Chapter 5

Credit-Sensitive Mortgage-Backed Securities

In the previous two chapters we looked at agency mortgage-backed securities in which the underlying mortgages are 1- to 4-single family residential mortgages. The mortgage-backed securities market includes other types of securities. These securities are called *nonagency mortgage-backed securities* (referred to as nonagency securities hereafter). Other mortgage-backed products that are separately classified in the industry as asset-backed securities are home equity loan-backed securities and manufactured housing-backed securities. Since all of these securities expose an investor to credit risk, these securities are sometimes referred to as *credit-sensitive mortgage-backed securities*. In this chapter we discuss these products.

NONAGENCY MORTGAGE-BACKED SECURITIES

The underlying loans for agency securities are those that conform to the underwriting standards of the agency issuing or guaranteeing the issue. That is, only conforming loans are included in pools that are collateral for an agency mortgage-backed security. The three main underwriting standards deal with (1) the maximum loan-to-value ratio, (2) the maximum payment-to-income ratio, and (3) the maximum loan amount. A nonconforming mortgage loan is one that does not conform to the underwriting standards established by any of the agencies.

Typically, the loans for a nonagency security are nonconforming mortgage loans that fail to qualify for inclusion because the amount of the loan exceeds the limit established by the agencies. Such loans are referred to as *jumbo loans*. Jumbo loans do not necessarily have greater credit risk than conforming mortgages. For example, a $300,000 mortgage loan sought by an individual with an annual income of $500,000 seeking to purchase a single family house with a value of $1 million would be classified as a jumbo loan since the amount of the mortgage exceeds the limit currently established for a conforming mortgage. The individual's income can easily accommodate the monthly mortgage payments assuming that there are no other significant debt obligations outstanding. Moreover, the lender's risk exposure is minimal since it has lent $300,000 backed by collateral of $1 million.

Loans that fail to qualify because of the first two underwriting standards expose the lender to greater credit risk. In general, lenders classify borrowers by credit quality. Borrowers are classified as A borrowers, B borrowers, C borrowers, and D borrowers. A borrowers are those that are viewed as having the best credit record. Such borrowers are referred to as *prime borrowers*. Borrowers rated below A are viewed as *subprime borrowers*. Unfortunately, there is no industry-wide classification system for prime and subprime borrowers. Several definitions based on the borrower's credit history are given later in this chapter.

An *Alternative A* mortgage is a loan to an A-rated borrower but there is some underwriting standard that the borrower fails. For example, the loan could fail to qualify for inclusion in an agency pool because the property is non-owner occupied, the property could be a second home, or the documentation is not complete.

Issuers of Nonagency Securities

Nonagency securities are issued by private entities. These entities can be classified as mortgage conduits, commercial bank- and S&L-related entities, and investment banking firm-related entities. A mortgage conduit is an entity that specializes in originating and/or acquiring mortgages. A mortgage conduit will temporarily warehouse the mortgages until it has a sufficient number of mortgages to either sell them in the secondary market or use them as collateral for the issuance of a security backed by those mortgages.

The major mortgage conduits that have issued nonagency securities include Prudential Home Mortgage Securities Co., Residential Funding Corporation, GE Mortgage Capital Services, Saxon Mortgage Securities Corporation, Countrywide Mortgage Backed Securities, Ryland Mortgage Securities Corporation, and Capstead Mortgage Corporation Securities. The major bank-related issuers are Chase Mortgage Finance Company, Citicorp Mortgage Securities Inc., First Bank System, Marine Midland Bank, and Fleet Mortgage Securities Inc. S&Ls that have issued these securities are Home Owners Federal S&L Association and Coast S&L. The Resolution Trust Corporation (RTC) was a major issuer of nonagency securities.

Roles of Trustee and Servicer

To create a nonagency security, the collateral loans are delivered to a trustee. In turn, the trustee puts the collateral loans into a bankruptcy remote trust for the benefit of the securityholders. This is an important legal vehicle for any type of asset securitization because it means that if the seller of the collateral becomes bankrupt, its creditors cannot look to the collateral for satisfaction of the seller's obligations.

As with an agency mortgage-backed security, the servicer is responsible for the collection of interest and principal, which is passed along to the trustee. The servicer also handles delinquencies and foreclosures. Typically, there will be a master servicer and subservicers. As we describe nonagency securities below, the important role played by servicers will be seen. In fact, in assessing the credit risk of a nonagency security, rating companies look carefully at the quality of the servicers.

Differences Between Agency and Nonagency Securities

Nonagency securities can be either passthroughs or CMOs. In the agency market, CMOs are created from pools of passthrough securities. In the nonagency market, a CMO can be created from either a pool of passthroughs or unsecuritized mortgage loans. It is uncommon for nonconforming mortgage loans to be securitized as passthroughs and then the passthroughs carved up to create a CMO. Instead, in the nonagency market a CMO is typically carved out of mortgage loans that have not been securitized as passthroughs. Since a mortgage loan is commonly referred to as a whole loan, nonagency CMOs are commonly referred to as *whole-loan CMOs*.

The major differences between agency and nonagency securities have to do with guarantees, dispersion of the characteristics of the underlying collateral, servicer advances, compensating interest, and clean-up calls. We discuss each below.

Guarantees

With a nonagency security there is no explicit or implicit government guarantee of payment of interest and principal as there is with an agency security. The absence of any such guarantee means that the investor in a nonagency security is exposed to credit risk.

The nationally recognized statistical rating organizations rate nonagency securities. Later in this chapter we will discuss the factors that the rating agencies consider when assigning a rating. As with corporate bond ratings, an issue's rating can be upgraded or downgraded. It is interesting to note that the worst year for the downgrading of nonagency securities was 1992. In that year, Moody's downgraded 3.7% issues. In stark contrast, in the investment grade sector of the corporate bond market, 36.3% of the issues it rated were downgraded.

Dispersion of Characteristics of Underlying Collateral

While both agency and nonagency securities are backed by 1- to 4-single family residential mortgages, the underlying loans for nonagency securities will typically be more heterogeneous with respect to coupon rate and maturity of the individual loans. For example, a nonagency security might include both 15-year and 30-year mortgages in the same mortgage pool. The greater dispersion of the coupon rate means that it is more difficult to predict prepayments due to refinancing based on the pool's weighted average coupon.

Servicer Advances

When there is a delinquency by the homeowner, the investor in a nonagency security may or may not be affected. This depends on whether a servicer is required to make advances. Thus, the financial capacity of the servicer to make advances is critical. Typically, a back-up servicer is used just in case the master servicer cannot meet its obligation with respect to advances. The servicer recovers advances when delinquent payments are made or the property is foreclosed and proceeds received.

There are different forms of advancing: (1) mandatory advancing, (2) optional advancing, and (3) limited advancing. The strongest form from the investor's perspective is mandatory advancing wherein failure to advance by a servicer is an event of default. However, a servicer need not advance if it can show that there is not a strong likelihood of recovery of the amount advanced when the property is ultimately disposed of. In an optional or a voluntary advancing, the servicer is not legally obligated to advance so that failure to do so is not an event of default. In a limited advancing the issuer is obligated to advance, but the amount it must advance is limited.

Compensating Interest

An additional factor to consider which is unique to nonagency securities is *compensating interest*. Mortgage passthroughs and CMOs pay principal and interest on a monthly basis. While homeowners may prepay their mortgage on any day throughout the month, the agencies guarantee and pay investors a full month of interest as if all the prepayments occur on the last day of the month. This guarantee does not apply to nonagency securities. If a homeowner pays off a mortgage on the tenth day of the month, he will stop paying interest for the rest of the month. Because of the payment delay (for example, 25 days), the investor will receive full principal but only 10 days of interest on the 25th of the following month.

This phenomenon is known as payment interest shortfall or *compensating interest* and is handled differently by different issuers. Some issuers will only pay up to a specified amount and some will not pay at all. Actually, it is the servicers who will pay any compensating interest. The servicer obtains the shortfall in interest from the servicing spread. The shortfall that will be made up to the investor may be limited to the entire servicing spread or part of the servicing spread. Thus, while an investor has protection against the loss of a full month's interest, the protection is limited.

For a nonagency security in which there is compensating interest, typically prepayments of the entire outstanding balance are covered. Curtailments (i.e., partial prepayments) are not covered.

In an agency CMO and nonagency CMO, the interest is paid to each tranche on the basis of the distribution rules for interest. In a nonagency CMO, as explained below there are tranches within credit classes. When there is a shortfall in the full month's interest, typically the shortfall is prorated among the credit classes based on the outstanding principal balance. Then, for each tranche within a credit class, the shortfall is prorated based on the interest that would be due.

In a nonagency CMO structure, the economic value of compensating interest depends on the level of prepayment and the types of CMO tranches. Generally, the faster the prepayments and the greater the coupon for the tranche, the higher the economic value of compensating interest.

Clean-Up Call Provisions

All nonagency CMO structures are issued with "clean-up" call provisions. The clean-up call provides the servicers or the residual holders (typically the issuers) the right, but not the obligation, to call all the outstanding tranches of the CMO structure when the CMO balance is paid down to a certain percentage of the original principal balance. The servicer typically finds it more costly than the servicing fee to service the CMO when the balance is paid down to a small amount. For example, suppose a $100 million CMO was originally issued with a 10% clean-up call. When the entire CMO balance is paid down to $10 million or less, the servicer can exercise the call to pay off all outstanding tranches regardless of the percentage balance of the individual tranches.

The call provision, when exercised, shortens the principal paydown window and the average life of the back-end tranches of a CMO. This provision is not unique to nonagency CMO structures. It is mandatory, however, for all nonagency CMO structures while agency CMOs may or may not have clean-up calls. Typically, Freddie Mac CMOs have 1% clean-up calls and Fannie Mae CMOs do not have clean-up calls.

How Rating Agencies View Credit Risk[1]

In this section we review the approach that the four commercial rating agencies take in evaluating the loss potential of defaults of the underlying mortgages. Rating agencies need to evaluate the magnitude of potential loss of a pool of loans to determine the amount of credit support the issuer needs to achieve the desired credit rating. Their approaches consist of four parts: (1) frequency of default; (2) severity of loss given default; (3) pool characteristics or the structure of the pool; and, (4) credit enhancement or the structure of the security.

Frequency of Default

There is ample evidence suggesting that most homeowners default relatively early in the life of the mortgage. Exhibit 1 shows the effect of seasoning assumed by two rating agencies and the Public Securities Association. These seasoning curves are based on default experience of so-called prime loans — a 30-year fixed-rate mortgage with a 75% to 80% LTV that is fully documented for the purchase of an owner-occupied single-family detached house. These characteristics describe the most common mortgage type generally associated with the lowest default rates. Loans with almost any other characteristic generally are assumed to have a greater frequency of default.

Loan-to-Value Ratio/Seasoning A mortgage's loan-to-value (LTV) ratio is the single most important determinant of its likelihood of default and therefore the amount of required credit enhancement. Rating agencies treat loans with LTVs above 80% as a negative factor. The rationale is straightforward. Homeowners with large amounts of equity in their properties are unlikely to default. They will either try to protect this equity by remaining current, or if they fail, sell the house or refinance it to unlock the equity. In any case, the lender is protected by the buyer's self-interest.

---

[1] This section is adapted from Douglas L. Bendt, Chuck Ramsey, and Frank J. Fabozzi, "The Rating Agencies' Approach: New Evidence," Chapter 6 in Frank J. Fabozzi, Chuck Ramsey, and Frank Ramirez (eds.), *Whole-Loan CMOs* (New Hope, PA: Frank J. Fabozzi Associates, 1995).

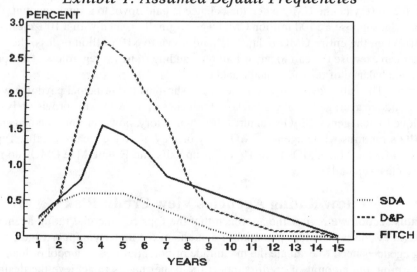

Exhibit 1: Assumed Default Frequencies

On the other hand, if the borrower has little or no equity in the property, the value of the default option is much greater. This argument is consistent with the long-held view that default rates for FHA/VA loans are much higher than for conventional loans.

Until recently, rating agencies considered the LTV only at the time of origination. Seasoning was an unalloyed good — if a loan did not default in the first three to four years, it deserved credit for making it past the hump. And many loans did not default because they were prepaid.

Declines in housing prices in some regions of the country, increased volume of seasoned product, and greater emphasis on surveillance have made the *current LTV* rather the original LTV the focus of attention. Current LTV is the ratio of the loan amount to the current (estimated) market value of the property. Seasoning now is as likely to be a negative for a pool as it is to be a plus. It is little comfort to own a pool of original 80% LTV mortgages from California originated in 1990 because many of the borrowers may owe more than their houses are worth; their LTVs may exceed 100%. Moreover, the prepayment option has been taken away for these borrowers.

Mortgage Term Amortization increases the equity a homeowner has in a property, which reduces the likelihood of default. Because amortization schedules for terms less than 30 years accumulate equity faster, all the rating agencies view this as a positive factor.

Mortgage Type Fixed-rate mortgages are considered "prime" because both the borrower and the lender know the monthly payment and amortization schedule with certainty. Presumably, the loan was underwritten considering this payment stream and the borrower's current income.

Both lender and borrower are uncertain about the future payment schedule for adjustable-rate mortgages (ARMs). Because most ARMs have lower initial ("teaser") rates, underwriting usually is done to ensure that the borrower will be able to meet the monthly payment assuming the rate adjusts up to the fully indexed rate at the first reset date. Beyond that first date, however, there is uncertainty both about the future stream of payments and the borrower's ability to meet higher payments. Future payment schedules for balloon mortgages are known, but uncertainty about borrowers' income still exists. All non-fixed-rate mortgages are viewed as a negative by the rating agencies.

Transaction Type Mortgages taken out for cash-out refinancings are considered riskier than mortgages taken out for purchases, chiefly because the homeowner is reducing the equity in the home. In addition, the fact that the homeowner is taking out cash may be an indication of need, which could indicate shakier finances, and the homeowner's monthly payment will increase. On the other hand, a no-cash refinancing — in which the rate is reduced — lowers the monthly payment and speeds the rate of amortization, so there are no penalties for such mortgages in the view of rating agencies.

Documentation "Full" documentation generally means that the borrower has supplied income, employment, and asset verification sufficient to meet Fannie Mae/Freddie Mac underwriting standards. "Low," "alternative," or "reduced" documentation means at least one form was not supplied, perhaps, for example, because the borrower is self-employed. In this case, because the income stream is likely to be more volatile, the borrower is more likely to default.

"No" documentation loans generally are made as "hard money" loans; that is, the value of the collateral is the most important criterion in the lending decision. Typically, lenders require larger down payments for these types of loans.

Occupancy Status Property owners obviously have a greater vested interest in not defaulting on a mortgage on a house in which they live. Thus, mortgages for second homes or rental property are a negative factor.

Property Type Generally, single-family detached houses are the most desirable properties because they are larger, more private, and include more land. Moreover, the supply of condominiums or townhouses is more likely to become overbuilt in a local area with the addition of a single large project, potentially increasing the volatility of prices and the length of time needed to sell a property.

Mortgage Size/House Price As noted earlier in this chapter, most mortgages that are used in nonagency securities have loan balances that exceed the agency conforming limits. The rating agencies make the strong presumption that higher-valued properties with larger mortgages are much riskier.

Creditworthiness of the Borrower Although loan originators place a great deal of emphasis on borrowers' credit histories, these data are not available to the rating agencies. The Fair Credit Reporting Act restricts access to such information to parties involved in a credit extension decision. As a result, the agencies use credit proxies such as the debt-to-income ratio, the mortgage coupon rate, past delinquencies or seasoned loans, or originators' scores from credit scoring models.

Severity of Loss

In the case of default, foreclosure, and ultimate property sale, lenders incur two costs: (1) direct foreclosure costs and (2) market decline. These costs may be mitigated to the extent there is equity in the property, i.e., lower LTVs will reduce the severity of loss.

Direct Foreclosure Costs Once a lender begins the foreclosure process — often as soon as a borrower becomes 60 days delinquent — it begins to incur significant direct costs. The direct foreclosure costs include unpaid interest, property taxes, management fees, and legal fees. Unpaid interest results because the lender stops accruing interest on the mortgage as income, instead adding it to the unpaid balance of the loan. Thus direct foreclosure costs include the coupon rate of the mortgage per year.

Property taxes are a foreclosure cost because the lender becomes responsible for paying taxes to preserve its first lien position. This cost can be up to 2% or more of the house price annually. Management fees are incurred because the property must be maintained so as to preserve its value for sale. The cost can average 6% of the house price annually. Legal fees are a variable cost.

Market Decline When a house is sold out of foreclosure, the lender is unlikely to obtain market value. Potential buyers know that the seller is distressed and know the size of the mortgage on the property. One common bidding strategy is to bid for the amount of the outstanding mortgage, figuring it is the seller's obligation to cover the out of pocket costs. The price received on a foreclosure sale depends greatly on local economic conditions and future housing prices, both of which are unknown at the time a rating agency is evaluating a loan. The range of assumed losses is 25% to 45%.

Pool Characteristics

Rating agencies draw upon general portfolio theory that diversification reduces risk and concentration increases risk. They typically consider two characteristics of the overall pool composition in setting credit enhancement levels: (1) size of the pool and (2) geographic composition/location.

Pool Size Pools with fewer than 300 loans are penalized by three of the four rating agencies, while larger pools are viewed positively. The rationale is that smaller pools are not sufficiently diversified to take account of (unspecified) desirable statistical properties.

Geography The first kind of geographic consideration is again a question of diversification: "too many" loans concentrated in a single zip code or small local area. For example, a lender might finance an entire subdivision, townhouse development, or condominium project that might be exposed to a common, special risk such as a single plant closing or an environmental hazard.

      The second kind of geographic consideration is generally broader in scope, such as a pool with a high concentration in Southern California that is exposed to risks not of a single plant but of a single industry. In special cases such as Boeing in Seattle, the risk is both industry-specific and company-specific.

Quality of the Seller/Servicer

Underwriting standards are not established by any government agency or the rating companies. Each financial institution or loan originator establishes it own underwriting standards. In many cases the servicer is the seller or originator of the loans used as the collateral.

      Duff & Phelps reviews the following when evaluating servicers: (1) servicing history, (2) experience, (3) originations, (4) servicing capabilities, (5) human resources, (6) financial condition, and (6) growth/competition/business environment. Based on its analysis, Duff & Phelps determines whether the servicer is acceptable or unacceptable. The latter are not rated. Acceptable servicers are rated within one of the following four categories:

> *S-A1* Highest quality servicing capabilities and strong financial condition.
> *S-A2* Above-average servicing capability and financial condition.
> *S-A3* Average servicing capability and below investment grade financial condition. A master servicer and structural enhancements may be required for an investment grade structured financing.
> *S-A4* Average servicing capability, but severely limited operating history. Financial condition is volatile. A master servicer and structural enhancements will be required for an investment grade structured financing.

      The rating companies may require a backup servicer if there is a concern about the ability of a servicer to perform.

Calculating Credit Enhancement Levels

Pool characteristic risks are cumulative; that is, if a loan has two or more adverse characteristics, the factors are multiplied to determine the relative degree of the frequency of default. Then one calculates an expected loss equal to the discounted probability of default times the expected loss severity. After performing these calculations on a loan-by-loan basis, the overall pool characteristics are taken into account.

Credit enhancement levels are determined relative to a specific rating desired for a security. Specifically, an investor in a triple A rated security expects to have "minimal," that is to say, virtually no chance of losing any principal due to defaults. For example, Standard & Poor's requires credit enhancement equal to four times expected losses to obtain a triple A rating.

Lower-rated securities require less credit enhancement for four reasons. First, the loss coverage ratio is lower. Second, some of the factors may be less stringent. Third, the base case frequency of default may be lower. And fourth, the severity of loss may be less.

Credit Enhancements

Typically a double A or triple A rating is sought for the most senior tranche in a nonagency security. The amount of credit enhancement necessary depends on rating agency requirements. There are two general types of credit enhancement structures: external and internal. We describe each type below.

External Credit Enhancements

External credit enhancements come in the form of third-party guarantees that provide for first loss protection against losses up to a specified level, for example, 10%. The most common forms of external credit enhancements are (1) a corporate guarantee, (2) a letter of credit, (3) pool insurance, and (4) bond insurance.

Pool insurance policies cover losses resulting from defaults and foreclosures. Policies are typically written for a dollar amount of coverage that continues in force throughout the life of the pool. However, some policies are written so that the dollar amount of coverage declines as the pool seasons as long as two conditions are met: (1) the credit performance is better than expected and (2) the rating agencies that rated the issue approve. The three major providers of pool insurance are GEMICO, PMI Mortgage Insurance Corp., and United Guarantee Insurance. Since only defaults and foreclosures are covered, additional insurance must be obtained to cover losses resulting from bankruptcy (i.e., court mandated modification of mortgage debt — "cramdown"), fraud arising in the origination process, and special hazards (i.e., losses resulting from events not covered by a standard homeowner's insurance policy).

Bond insurance provides the same function as in municipal bond structures. The major insurers are FGIC, AMBAC, and MBIA. Typically, bond insurance is not used as the primary protection but to supplement other forms of credit enhancement.

A nonagency security with external credit support is subject to the credit risk of the third-party guarantor. Should the third-party guarantor be downgraded, the issue itself could be subject to downgrade even if the structure is performing as expected. This is based on the "weak link" test followed by rating agencies.

According to this test, when evaluating a proposed structure, credit quality of the issue is only as good as the weakest link in credit enhancement regardless of the quality of underlying loans. For example, in the early 1990s, mortgage-backed securities issued by Citibank Mortgage Securities Inc. were downgraded when Citibank, the third-party guarantor, was downgraded. This is the chief disadvantage of third-party guarantees. Therefore, it is imperative that investors monitor the third-party guarantor as well as the collateral.

External credit enhancements do not materially alter the cash flow characteristics of a CMO structure except in the form of prepayment. In case of a default resulting in net losses within the guarantee level, investors will receive the principal amount as if a prepayment has occurred. If the net losses exceed the guarantee level, investors will realize a shortfall in the cash flows.

Internal Credit Enhancements

Internal credit enhancements come in more complicated forms than external credit enhancements and may alter the cash flow characteristics of the loans even in the absence of default. The most common forms of internal credit enhancements are reserve funds and senior/subordinated structures.

Reserve Funds Reserve funds come in two forms, cash reserve funds and excess servicing spread. *Cash reserve funds* are straight deposits of cash generated from issuance proceeds. In this case, part of the underwriting profits from the deal are deposited into a hypothecated fund which typically invests in money market instruments. Cash reserve funds are typically used in conjunction with letters of credit or other kinds of external credit enhancements.

Excess servicing spread accounts involve the allocation of excess spread or cash into a separate reserve account after paying out the net coupon, servicing fee, and all other expenses on a monthly basis. For example, suppose that the gross weighted average coupon (gross WAC) is 7.75%, the servicing and other fees are 0.25%, and the net weighted average coupon (net WAC) is 7.25%. This means that there is excess servicing of 0.25%. The amount in the reserve account will gradually increase and can be used to pay for possible future losses.

The excess spread is analogous to the guarantee fee paid to the issuer of an agency mortgage-backed security except that this is a form of self-insurance. This form of credit enhancement relies on the assumption that defaults occur infrequently in the very early life of the loans but gradually increase in the following two to five years. This assumption is consistent with the PSA's Standard Default Assumption (SDA) curve described later in this chapter.

Senior/Subordinated Structure The most widely used internal credit support structure is by far the *senior/subordinated structure*. Today a typical structure will have a senior bond and several junior bonds. The junior bonds represent the subordinated bonds of the structure. The issuer will seek a triple A or double A rating for the senior bond. The junior bonds will have lower ratings — investment grade and non-investment grade. Typically, the most junior bond — called the *first loss piece* — will not be rated.

Exhibit 2 shows a hypothetical $200 million structure with a senior bond representing 92.25% of the deal and five junior bonds representing 7.75% of the deal. Note that all that has been done in this structure is credit tranching. The senior or any of the junior bonds can then be carved up to create CMO tranches.

The first loss piece in this hypothetical deal is bond X5. The subordination level in this hypothetical structure is 7.75%. The junior classes will absorb all losses up to $15.5 million and the senior class will start to experience losses thereafter. So, if there is a $10 million loss, no loss will be realized by the senior bond. If, instead, there is a $20 million loss, the senior bond will experience a loss of $4.5 million ($20 million minus $15.5 million) or a 2.4% loss ($4.5/$184.5).

In the case where the loss is $10, the first loss piece (bond X5), bond X4, and bond X3 absorb $9.5 million. These bonds will realize a loss experience of 100%. Bond X2 will realize a loss of $0.5 million, thereby having a loss experience of 25% ($0.5/$2.0). Bond X1 will not realize any loss. If the loss is $20 million, all junior bonds will have a loss experience of 100%.

The junior bonds obviously would require a yield premium to take on the greater credit risk exposure relative to the senior bond. This setup is another form of self-insurance wherein investors in the senior bond are giving up yield spread to the investors in the junior classes. This form of credit enhancement still does not affect cash flow characteristics of the senior class except in the form of prepayment. To the extent that losses are within the subordination level, investors in the senior bond will receive principal as if a prepayment has occurred.

Almost all existing senior/subordinated structures also incorporate a shifting interest structure. A *shifting interest structure* redirects prepayments disproportionally from the subordinated classes to the senior class according to a specified schedule. An example of such a schedule would be as follows:

Exhibit 2: Hypothetical $200 Million Senior/Subordinated Structure

Bond	Rating	Amount ($ in millions)	Percent of deal(%)
Senior	AAA	$184.50	92.25
Junior			
X1	AA	4.00	2.00
X2	A	2.00	1.00
X3	BBB	3.00	1.50
X4	BB	4.00	2.00
X5*	Not rated	2.50	1.25

* First loss piece.

Months	Percentage of prepayments directed to senior class
1-60	100%
61-72	70%
73-84	60%
85-96	40%
97-108	20%
109+	pro rata

The rationale for the shifting interest structure is to have enough insurance outstanding to cover future losses. Because of the shifting interest structure, the subordination amount may actually grow in time especially in a low default and fast prepayment environment. This is sometimes referred to as "riding up the credit curve." Using the same example of our previous $200 million deal with 7.75% initial subordination and assuming a cumulative paydown (prepayments at 165 PSA and regular repayments) of $40 million by year 3, the subordination will actually increase to 10.7% [$15.5/($184.50 − $40)] without any net losses. Even if the subordinated classes have experienced some losses, say, $1 million, the subordination will still increase to 9.3% [($15.5 − $1)/($184.50 − $40)].

While the shifting interest structure is beneficial to the senior bond from a credit standpoint, it does alter the cash flow characteristics of the senior bond even in the absence of defaults. A 7.75% subordination with the shifting interest structure will shorten the average life of the senior bond to 8.41 assuming 165 PSA and no defaults. The size of the subordination also matters. Larger subordinated bonds result in the redirecting of a higher proportion of prepayments to the senior bond, thereby shortening the average life even further.

It may be counter-intuitive that the size of the subordination should affect the average life and cash flows of the senior bond more than the credit quality. The reason is that the size of the subordination is already factored into the rating. Rating agencies typically requires more subordination for lower credit quality loans to obtain a triple A rating and less subordination for better credit quality loans. From a credit standpoint, the investor may be indifferent between a 5% subordination on a package of good quality loans and a 10% subordination on a package of lower quality loans as long as the rating agency gives them the same rating. However, the quality of the underlying loans will determine the default rate and therefore the timing of the cash flows.

WAC Interest-Only and Principal-Only Securities

In Chapter 3 we explained how in an agency CMO a notional interest-only tranche can be created. This is done by stripping the excess interest between the coupon rate of the passthrough securities that is the collateral for the CMO and the coupon rate for a particular tranche. In the case of stripped mortgage-backed securities discussed in Chapter 2, we explained how principal-only and interest-only securities can be created.

Exhibit 3: Description of Collateral Used to Create a WAC IO and WAC PO

Remittance rate: 9%
Collateral description: $200 million, 30-year nonconforming mortgages

Dispersion of collateral:

Coupon rate (%)	Par amount
8	$40,000,000
9	90,000,000
10	70,000,000

Because of the wide dispersion of the coupon rates on the underlying mortgages for a nonagency security, a different type of IO and PO security can be created. This is done by the issuer first establishing the rate that it wants to pay on the issue. This is called the *remittance rate*. Then from all underlying mortgages with a coupon rate that is in excess of the remittance rate, the excess interest is stripped off to create an IO security. This IO security is called a *WAC IO*. A principal-only security is created from the underlying mortgages for which the coupon rate is less than the remittance rate. The resulting PO security is called a *WAC PO*.

To illustrate this, consider the $200 million 30-year pool described in Exhibit 3 that is going to be used as collateral for a nonagency security. Suppose that the issuer determines that to sell the security a remittance rate of 9% will be required. Of the $200 million in collateral, there is $110 million whose coupon rate is different from the remittance rate. There is $70 million whose coupon rate is above the remittance rate. Since the coupon rate is 10% and the remittance rate is 9%, a WAC IO can be created from the 100 basis points excess interest of the $70 million of mortgages with a 10% coupon rate.

There is $40 million with a coupon rate of 8% which is less than the remittance rate. The issuer can calculate the amount of par value of the $40 million that is needed to generate a 9% coupon. The interest generated from the $40 million of the 8% coupon portion of the collateral is $3.2 million ($40 million times 8%). The amount of par value from the $40 million of the 8% coupon needed to create a 9% coupon is $35.6 ($3.2 million divided by 9%). The difference of $4.4 million between the $40 million par value of 8% coupon collateral and $35.6 of par value needed to create a 9% remittance rate is the par amount for a WAC PO.

PSA Standard Default Assumption Benchmark

With the increase in nonagency security issuance, a standardized benchmark for default rates has been introduced by the Public Securities Association. The PSA standard default assumption (SDA) benchmark gives the annual default rate for a mortgage pool as a function of the seasoning of the mortgages. The PSA SDA benchmark, or 100 SDA, specifies the following:

1. the default rate in month 1 is 0.02% and increases by 0.02% up to month 30 so that in month 30 the default rate is 0.60%;
2. from month 30 to month 60, the default rate remains at 0.60%;
3. from month 61 to month 120, the default rate declines from 0.60% to 0.03%;
4. from month 120 on, the default rate remains constant at 0.03%.

This pattern is consistent with the default data reported in Exhibit 1. As with the PSA prepayment benchmark, multiples of the benchmark are found by multiplying the default rate by the assumed multiple. A 0 SDA means that no defaults are assumed.

Illustrations

Let's look at two nonagency security deals: Prudential Home Mortgage Securities Company, Inc. Mortgage Pass-Through Certificates, Series 1991-3 and the Tryon Mortgage Funding, Inc. Mortgage Pass-Through Certificates, Series 1996-1.

Pru-Home Series 1991-3

The Prudential Home Mortgage Securities Company, Inc. Mortgage Pass-Through Certificates, Series 1991-3 (hereafter Pru-Home Series 1991-3) was a $164.5 million offering. The servicer is The Prudential Home Mortgage Company (PHMC).

The underlying mortgage loans consisted of approximately 542 fixed-rate conventional mortgages for 1- to 4-single family residential properties. The loans are fully amortizing loans. All the loans have a first lien on the mortgaged property. The prospectus provides information about the 542 loans. Specifically, the prospectus provides tables disclosing the distribution of the 542 loans with respect to: (1) mortgage rates; (2) remaining months to stated maturity; (3) years since origination; (4) original loan-to-value ratios; (5) original mortgage loan principal balances; (6) types of mortgaged-properties; (6) geographical concentration of mortgage properties; (7) originators of the mortgage loans; and, (8) purposes of the loans. The distribution is provided in terms of the number of loans and as a percentage of the aggregate principal balance.

As of March 1, 1991 (the cut-off date for the certificates), the unpaid principal balance of a loan was not less than $177,373 and not greater than $995,319. The average mortgage loan amount was $328,141. The remaining term of the 542 loans ranged from 136 months (one loan) to 180 months (two loans). The weighted average remaining term of the loans was 174 months (14.5 years). The dispersion of the loans around 174 months was not substantial. Therefore, while one major difference between agency and nonagency securities that we cited earlier was that there may be a substantial dispersion in the maturity of the loans, this is not the case in this deal.

The mortgage rates on the 542 loans ranged from 9.25% (two loans, 0.24% of the aggregate principal balance) to 11.375% (one loan, 0.54% of the aggregate principal balance). The weighted average mortgage rate was approximately 10.198%. The servicing fee is 25 basis points so that the net weighted average mortgage rate was 9.948%.

There were underlying loans with a loan-to-value ratio (at origination) equal to 50% or less (62 loans, 12.7% of the aggregate principal balance). There were 26 loans (3.62% of the aggregate principal balance) with an LTV greater than 80%; there were no loans with an LTV greater than 90%.

While all the mortgaged properties were 1- to 4-single family housing units, they were broken down into: (1) single-family detached units; (2) 2- to 4-family units; (3) condominiums (high rise and low rise); (4) planned unit developments; and, (5) townhouses. The bulk of the loans (495, 91.64% of the aggregate principal balance) were for single-family detached units.

Of the 542 loans, 196 (39.23% of the aggregate principal balance) were for properties located in California. The following states had properties that represented about 10% of the aggregate principal balance: New Jersey, New York, and Texas. There was no more than 1.91% in any one zip code.

About half the loans (in number and as a percent of the aggregate principal balance) were originated by PHMC or it affiliates. The purpose of the loans was categorized as purchase, rate/term refinance, or equity take out refinance. The majority of the loans (352, 64.15% of the aggregate principal balance) were for purchase.

The prospectus also provides information on the delinquency, foreclosure, and loss experience on the loans included in PHMC's mortgage loan servicing portfolio. The information was broken down in terms of the loans originated by PHMC or its affiliates and those acquired by PHMC or its affiliates.

There are two certificate classes in this deal: Class A and Class B. Class A is the senior class and Class B is the subordinated class. Class A is tranched into eight subclasses. The initial principal balance and passthrough rate for the first six subclasses are:

Subclass Designation	Initial Subclass Principal Balance	Passthrough Rate (%)
Class A-1	$27,974,000	8.00
Class A-2	52,423,000	8.55
Class A-3	27,098,000	8.90
Class A-4	31,300,000	9.00
Class A-5	25,657,000	9.00
Class A-6	1,000	9.00

Class A-7 had an initial principal balance of only $50,000. The distribution rule for available funds for Class A-7 as stated in the prospectus is:

Interest will accrue on the Class A-7 Certificates each month in an amount equal to the sum of (i) the product of $\frac{1}{12}$th of 1.00% and the Subclass Principal Balance of the Class A-1 Certificates, (ii) the product of $\frac{1}{12}$th of 0.45% and the Subclass Principal Balance of the Class A-2 Certificates, (iii) the product of $\frac{1}{12}$th of 0.10% and the Subclass Principal Balance of the Class A-3 Certificates, and (iv) the product of 9.00% and the Subclass Principal Balance of the Class A-7 Certificates.

Thus, Class A-7 is an interest-only bond class. It has a 9% coupon rate based on its nominal (not notional) principal balance of $50,000 and the excess interest between 9% and the passthrough rate paid to Classes A-1, A-2, and A-3. The prospectus notes that the effective interest rate of Class A-7 is 1,094.483%.

The Class A-6 Certificate and the Class A-LR Certificates represent the residual. The Class A-8 Certificate and the Class A-LR Certificate were not offered for sale. They were held by the seller.

The rule for the distribution of principal repayments (regularly scheduled payments plus prepayments) among the subclasses of Class A as set forth in the prospectus (pages S-21 and S-22) is as follows:

> *first*, approximately 99.907960% to the Class A-1 Certificates and approximately 0.092040% to the Class A-7 Certificates, concurrently, until the Subclass Principal Balance of the Class A-1 Certificates have been reduced to zero;
> *second*, approximately 99.958561% to the Class A-2 Certificates and approximately 0.041439% to the Class A-7 Certificates, concurrently, until the Subclass Principal Balance of the Class A-2 Certificates have been reduced to zero;
> *third*, approximately 99.990788% to the Class A-3 Certificates and approximately 0.009212% to the Class A-7 Certificates, concurrently, until the Subclass Principal Balances of the Class A-3 Certificates and Class A-7 Certificates have been reduced to zero;
> *fourth*, to the Class A-4 Certificates until the Subclass Principal Balance thereof has been reduced to zero;
> *fifth*, to the Class A-5 Certificates until the Subclass Principal Balance thereof has been reduced to zero; and,
> *sixth*, to the Class A-6 Certificates until the Subclass Principal Balance thereof has been reduced to zero.

Consequently, the Class A certificates of Pru-Home Series 1991-3 are structured as a sequential-pay CMO.

With respect to periodic advancing, the prospectus specifies that (pages S-22 and S-23):

> ... the Servicer will be obligated to advance on or before the related Distribution Date for the benefit of the holders of the Series 1991-3 Certificates an amount in cash equal to all delinquent payments of principal and interest due on each Mortgage

Loan ...., but only to the extent that such amounts will be recoverable by it from liquidation proceeds or other recoveries in respect of the related Mortgage Loan.

Thus, advances are mandatory. Furthermore, if Moody's determines at some future time that the ability of the servicer (PHMC) is impaired, a reserve fund must be established by the servicer.

Tryon Mortgage Funding Series 1996-1

The initial aggregate balance for the certificates sold for the Tryon Mortgage Funding, Inc. Mortgage Pass-Through Certificates, Series 1996-1 was $115,493,259. The underlying mortgage loans consist of approximately 3,309 loans with an aggregate principal balance of $122,865,169. The mortgaged properties are 1- to 4-single family residential properties. Approximately 75% of the loans were fully amortizing loans; the other 25% were balloon loans. All the loans have a first lien on the mortgaged property.

The prospectus provides similar information about the loans as the PHMS Series 1991-3. As of the cut-off date for the certificates, the unpaid principal balance of a loan ranged from $3,252 to $456,187 with the average being $37,160. For the balloon mortgages, the balloon payments ranged from $2,591 to $331,121, with the average being $43,548. The remaining term of the 3,309 loans ranged from 1-12 months (60 loans, 2.48% of the aggregate principal balance) to 685-696 months (one loan). The weighted average remaining term of the loans was 145.7 months (12.14 years). The dispersion of the loans around 145.7 months was substantial, a characteristic that we noted for nonagency securities.

Similarly, there was considerable dispersion in the mortgage rates. The weighted average mortgage rate was approximately 9.615%. Twenty of the 3,909 loans had a mortgage rate of 6% or less (less than 1% of the aggregate principal balance); there were 23 loans that had a mortgage rate greater than 13% (less than 1% of the aggregate principal balance).

There was considerable dispersion in the LTV. The large majority of the loans had an 80% or lower LTV (3,196 loans, 74.15% of the aggregate principal balance). There were 28 loans with an LTV greater than 100% (less than 1% of the aggregate principal balance). The average LTV was 67.4%.

While all the mortgaged properties were 1- to 4-single family housing units, there were manufactured housing units included. We will discuss these properties later in this chapter. About 5% of the loans were secured by manufactured housing units. Of the 3,909 loans, 679 (18.82% of the aggregate principal balance) were for properties located in Texas. There were 580 loans (16.98% of the aggregate principal balance) from Washington and 332 loans (12.3% of the aggregate principal balance) from California.

The sellers of the mortgages from which the loan pool was created were Metropolitan Mortgage & Securities Co., Inc., Summit Securities Inc., Western

United Life Assurance Company, and Old Standard Life Insurance Company. The master servicer is Spokane Mortgage Co. The delinquency and foreclosure experience for the loans serviced by Spokane Mortgage Co. were reported.

The certificates offered were designated Class A-1, Class A-2, Class A-3, Class A-4, Class B-1, and Class B-2. The first four classes were the senior classes and the last two the subordinate classes. All of the classes had a fixed rate. Summary information about each offered class and its rating is provided below:

Class	Initial Class Balance	Passthrough Rate (%)	Rating	
			Moody's	Duff & Phelps
A-1	$46,688,764	6.35	Aaa	AAA
A-2	20,887,079	7.30	Aaa	AAA
A-3	12,286,517	7.55	Aaa	AAA
A-4	27,030,337	7.70	Aaa	AAA
B-1	4,484,579	7.75	Aa2	AA
B-2	4,115,983	7.90	A	A

Notice that both of the subordinated classes, Class B-1 and Class B-2, received an investment grade rating.

There were classes that were not offered but were part of the structure: Class B-3, Class B-4, and Class R. Class B-3 ($2,395,871 approximate initial class balance and passthrough rate of 8.25%) and Class B-4 ($675,758 approximate initial class balance and passthrough rate of 8.25%) provided limited credit support for the offered certificates. Class R is the residual.

The priority for the distribution of available funds to the classes is as follows: (1) interest to each senior class, (2) principal to each senior class, (3) interest and then principal to Class B-1 and Class B-2, (4) interest to Class B-3, (5) interest to Class B-4, and (6) interest to the residual.

The offered certificates are to be paid off sequentially. That is, for the senior classes, Class A-1's principal balance is to be paid off first, followed by Class A-2, etc. For the two offered subordinate classes, first Class B-1 receives principal and once it is paid off, Class B-2 receives principal. The certificates not offered are not entitled to a distribution of principal until the entire balance of all the offered certificates is paid off.

As for advances, the prospectus states (page S-32):

> ... the Master Servicer will be required to advance prior to each Distribution Date from its own funds or funds in the Collection Account that do not constitute Available Funds for such Distribution Date, an amount equal to the aggregate of payments of principal and interest ...

Advances are therefore mandatory. The prospectus further states that advances with respect to delinquencies need only be made by the servicer "to the extent that such Advances are, in its judgement, reasonably recoverable from future payments and collections or insurance payments or proceeds from liquidation of the related Mortgage Loan." For the balloon loans, the servicer will not advance a default of the balloon payment due. However, the servicer will advance interest payments.

HOME EQUITY LOAN-BACKED SECURITIES

Home equity loan-backed securities are backed by home equity loans. A *home equity loan* (HEL) is a loan backed by residential property. Typically, the loan is a second lien on property that has already been pledged to secure a first lien. In some cases, the lien may be a third lien. In recent years, some loans have been first liens.

Home equity loans can be either closed end or open end. A closed-end HEL is structured the same way as a fully amortizing residential mortgage loan. That is, it has a fixed maturity and the payments are structured to fully amortize the loan by the maturity date. There are both fixed-rate and variable-rate closed-end HELs. Typically, variable-rate loans have a reference rate of 6-month LIBOR and have periodic caps and lifetime caps, just as with adjustable-rate mortgages. The cash flow of a pool of closed-end HELs is comprised of interest, regularly schedule principal repayments, and prepayments, just as with mortgage-backed securities. Thus, it is necessary to have a prepayment model and a default model to forecast cash flows. The prepayment speed is measured in terms of a conditional prepayment rate (CPR).

With an open-end HEL the homeowner is given a credit line and can write checks or use a credit card for up to the amount of the credit line. The amount of the credit line depends on the amount of the equity the borrower has in the property. There is a revolving period over which the homeowner can borrow funds against the line of credit. At the end of the term of the loan, the homeowner either pays off the amount borrowed in one payment or the outstanding balance is amortized.

Originators of HELs look at three key ratios when deciding to underwrite a loan — combined *loan-to-value ratio* (CLTV), *second-lien ratio*, and *payment-to-income ratio*. The CLTV looks at the ratio of all mortgage liens relative to the appraised value of the property. For example, suppose that an applicant seeking a $10,000 second mortgage lien via a HEL on property with an appraised value of $100,000 has a first mortgage-lien on that property of $80,000. Then the CLTV is 90% [($80,000 + $10,000)/$100,000]. The second lien ratio is found by dividing the amount of the second lien sought by the applicant by the combined mortgage liens. In our example, the second lien ratio is 11.11% [$10,000/($80,000 + $10,000)]. In calculating the payment-to-income ratio, the monthly mortgage payment includes all mortgage payments.

Borrowers are segmented into four general credit quality groups, A, B, C, and D. While there is no industrywide definition for classifying a borrower, the following definitions based on the borrower's credit history criteria appear to be what some originators use:

> A/A- *(excellent/good credit quality)*: (1) no more than two 30-day delinquencies in the past 12 months and (2) no prior bankruptcies
>
> B & C *(satisfactory/fair credit quality)*: (1) no more than four 30-day, two 60-day, and one 90-day delinquencies in the past 12 months and (2) no bankruptcies in the past 2 to 3 years
>
> D *(unsatisfactory/poor credit quality)*: (1) more than four 30-day, two 60-day, and 90-day delinquencies in the past 12 months and (2) no bankruptcies in the past 2 years

Bear Stearns reports the most common credit history criteria used for classifying the quality of borrowers employed by finance companies to be as follows:

> A *(good to excellent credit quality)*: (1) maximum of two 30-day delinquencies in the past 12 months and (2) no bankruptcies in the past 5 years
>
> B *(satisfactory credit quality)*: (1) maximum of three 30-day delinquencies in the past 12 months and (2) no bankruptcies in the past 3 years
>
> C *(fair/poor credit quality)*: (1) maximum of four 30-day and one 60-day delinquencies in the past 12 months and (2) no bankruptcies in the past two years

Cash Flow

The monthly cash flow for a home equity loan-backed security backed by closed-end HELs is the same as for mortgage-backed securities. That is, the cash flow consists of (1) net interest, (2) regularly scheduled principal payments, and (3) prepayments. The uncertainty about the cash flows arises from prepayments. We will discuss prepayment characteristics in Chapter 6.

Prospectus Prepayment Curve

Borrower characteristics and the seasoning process must be kept in mind when trying to assess prepayments for a particular deal. In the prospectus of an offering a base case prepayment assumption is made — the initial speed and the amount of time until the collateral is expected to be seasoned. Thus, the prepayment benchmark is issue specific. Investors are now using the concept of a *prospectus prepayment curve* or *PPC*. This is just a multiple of the base case prepayments assumed in the prospectus. For example, in the prospectus for the Contimortgage Home Equity Loan Trust 1996-1, the base case prepayment assumption for the fixed-rate mortgages in the pool is as follows (p. 3-37):

> ... a 100% Prepayment Assumption assumes conditional prepayment rates of 4% per annum of the then outstanding principal balance of the Home Equity Loans in the Fixed Rate Group in the first month of the life of the mortgage loans and an additional 1.455% (precisely 16/11%) per annum in each month thereafter until the twelfth month. Beginning in the twelfth month and in each month thereafter during the life of the mortgage loans, 100% Prepayment Assumption assumes a conditional prepayment rate of 20% per annum each month.

Therefore, if an investor analyzed the deal based on 200% PPC. this means doubling the CPRs cited in the excerpt and using 12 months for seasoning.

In the Champion Home Equity Loan Trust 1996-1, the base case prepayment assumption is specified in the prospectus as follows (S-28):

> The model used with respect to the Fixed Rate Certificates (the "Prepayment Ramp") assumes that the Home Equity Loans in Loan Group One prepay at a rate of 4% CPR in the first month after origination, and an additional 1.5% each month thereafter until the 14th month. Beginning in the 15th month and each month thereafter, the Prepayment Ramp assumes a prepayment rate of 25% CPR.

Thus, 100% PPC is based on the CPRs above assuming seasoning after 14 months.

Payment Structure

As with nonagency mortgage-backed securities discussed in the previous chapter, there are passthrough and paythrough home equity loan-backed structures. In the case of paythroughs, there are tranches with a schedule of principal payments. In the case of CMO structures, these tranches are called planned amortization tranches. In HEL structures, they are called *non-accelerating structures.*

Typically, home equity loan-backed securities are securitized by both closed-end fixed-rate and adjustable-rate (or variable-rate) HELs. The securities backed by the latter are called *HEL floaters* and most are backed by non-prime HELs. The reference rate of the underlying loans typically is 6-month LIBOR. The cash flow of these loans is affected by periodic and lifetime caps on the loan rate. To increase the attractiveness of home equity loan-backed securities to investors, the securities typically have been created in which the reference rate is 1-month LIBOR. Because of (1) the mismatch between the reference rate on the underlying loans and that of the HEL floater and (2) the periodic and lifetime caps of the underlying loans, there is a cap on the coupon rate for the HEL floater. Unlike a typical floater, which has a cap that is fixed throughout the security's life, the effective periodic and lifetime cap of a HEL floater is variable. The effective cap, referred to as the *available funds cap*, will depend on the amount of funds generated by the net coupon on the principal, less any fees.

Let's look at one issue, Advanta Mortgage Loan Trust 1995-2 issued in June 1995. At the offering, this issue had approximately $122 million closed-end HELs. There were 1,192 HELs, 727 fixed-rate loans and 465 variable-rate loans. There were five classes (A-1, A-2, A-3, A-4, and A-5) and a residual. The five classes are summarized below:

Class	Par amount ($)	Passthrough coupon rate (%)
A-1	9,229,000	7.30
A-2	30,330,000	6.60
A-3	16,455,000	6.85
A-4	9,081,000	floating rate
A-5	56,917,000	floating rate

As explained below, class A-5 had two sub-classes, A-5-I and A-5-II.

The collateral is divided into group I and group II. The 727 fixed-rate loans are included in group I and support Classes A-1, A-2, A-3, and A-4. The 465 variable-rate loans are in group II and support Classes A-5-I and A-5-II certificates. All classes receive monthly principal and interest (based on the passthrough coupon rate).

The initial investors in the A-5 floating-rate certificates were given a choice between two sub-classes that offered different floating rates. Sub-class A-5-I has a passthrough coupon rate equal to the lesser of (1) 12% and (2) 1-month LIBOR plus 32 basis points with a cap of 12%. Sub-class A-5-II has a passthrough coupon rate equal to the lesser of (1) the interest rate for sub-class A-5-I and (2) the group II available funds cap. The available funds cap, also called the net funds cap, is the maximum rate payable on the outstanding Class A-5 certificates principal balance based on the interest due on the variable-rate loans net of fees and minus 50 basis points.

The Class A-4 certificate also has a floating rate. The rate is 7.4% subject to the net funds cap for group I. This is the rate that is paid until the outstanding aggregate loan balances in the trust have declined to 10% or less. At that time, Class A-4 will accrue interest on a payment date that depends on the average net loan rate minus 50 basis points and the net funds cap rate for group I.

Credit Enhancement

All forms of credit enhancement described earlier in this chapter have been used for home equity loan-backed securities.

To illustrate the credit enhancement and structural characteristics, let's return to the Advanta Mortgage Loan Trust 1995-2. All of the classes (A-1 through A-5) received a rating of AAA by Standard & Poor's due to the credit enhancement. All the classes were credit enhanced through excess spread for both group I and group II collateral, and two bond insurance policies issued by MBIA that cover the amount of the certificates. The excess spread was the first layer of credit protection. For the group I loans, the excess spread is the difference between the weighted average loan rate for the fixed-rate loans and the passthrough coupon rate. For group II, the loans are variable-rate and the excess spread is the sum of (1) the difference between the floating rate on the loans (which is 6-month LIBOR) and the passthrough coupon rate (which is 1-month LIBOR) and (2) the weighted average margin on the loans. In determination of the excess spread, it is necessary to assume some prepayment speed. In stress testing the structure, Standard & Poor's used a 23% CPR.

MANUFACTURED HOUSING-BACKED SECURITIES

Manufactured housing-backed securities are backed by loans for manufactured homes. In contrast to site-built homes, manufactured homes are built at a factory and then transported to a manufactured home community or private land. These homes are more popularly referred to as mobile homes. The loan may be either a mortgage loan (for both the land and the mobile home) or a consumer retail installment loan.

Manufactured housing-backed securities are issued by Ginnie Mae and private entities. The former securities are guaranteed by the full faith and credit of the U.S. government. The manufactured home loans that are collateral for the securities issued and guaranteed by Ginnie Mae are loans guaranteed by the Federal Housing Administration (FHA) or Veterans Administration (VA).

Loans not backed by the FHA or VA are called conventional loans. Manufactured housing-backed securities that are backed by such loans are called conventional manufactured housing-backed securities. These securities are issued by private entities. The largest issuer is Green Tree Financial which has issued more than 70% of the manufactured housing-backed securities issued. Other issuers include Security Pacific Acceptance Corporation, Vanderbilt Mortgage and Finance, and Oakwood Mortgage Investors. The Resolution Trust Corporation was an issuer of these securities.

The typical loan for a manufactured home is 15 to 20 years. The loan repayment is structured to fully amortize the amount borrowed. Therefore, as with residential mortgage loans and HELs, the cash flow consists of net interest, regularly scheduled principal, and prepayments. Again, prepayment characteristics are described in Chapter 6.

As with residential mortgage loans and HELs, prepayments on manufactured housing-backed securities are measured in terms of CPR.

Payment Structure

The payment structure is the same as with nonagency mortgage-backed securities and home equity loan-backed securities. For example, consider the Green Tree

Manufactured Housing Contract Trust 1995-3 issue. There were four classes in this $502.1 million issue: A-1, M-1, B-1, and B-2. Class A-1 is the senior class, Classes M-1, B-1, and B-2 are the subordinated or junior classes. The priority of payments is as follows: first payments are made to Class A-1, then to Class M-1, then to Classes B-1, and then finally Class B-2.

Credit Enhancement

Credit enhancements are the same as in nonagency mortgage-backed securities and home equity loan-backed securities. In the Green Tree Manufactured Housing Contract Trust 1995-3 issue, there is a senior/subordinated structure and excess spread. The excess spread at the time of issuance was 4% and provided support for all four classes. There was an 18% subordination provided for Class A-1 by the three subordinated classes (M-1, B-1, and B-2). Class A-1 was rated AAA by Standard & Poor's. Class M-1 was supported by a 9% subordination provided by Class B-1 and Class B-2 in addition to the excess servicing spread and was rated AA-. Class B-1 had credit support from Class B-2 (4.5% subordination) and the excess servicing spread, and received a rating of BBB+. Class B-2 was rated BBB based on a guarantee by Green Tree of the timely payment of interest and principal, as well as the excess servicing spread.

CLASSIFICATION OF
NONAGENCY MORTGAGE PRODUCTS

We have described mortgage products that are classified as nonagency mortgage-backed securities and asset-backed securities (home equity loans and manufactured housing loans). There are mortgage products in which the underlying pool is a collection of different types of nonagency mortgage loans such that the security created could be classified as either a nonagency mortgage-backed security or an asset-backed security.

The Securities Data Corporation (SDC) has established criteria for classifying a mortgage product with mixed loans as either a nonagency mortgage-backed security or an asset-backed security. The purpose of the classification is *not* to aid in the analysis of these securities, but rather for constructing the so-called "league tables" for ranking investment banking firms by deal type. SDC's rules for classifying a deal as either a nonagency mortgage-backed security or an asset-backed security are as follows. If more than 50% of a deal consists of either manufactured housing loans, home equity loans, second mortgage loans, or home improvement loans, then the deal is classified as an asset-backed security. The percentage is based on the aggregate principal balance as of the cut-off date.

For deals in which more than 50% of the loans are first liens, SDC uses a *size test* to classify the deal. If more than 50% of the aggregate principal balance of the loans have a loan balance of more than $200,000, the deal is classified as a nonagency mortgage-backed security. A deal in which 50% of the loans are first liens but more than 50% of the aggregate principal balance of the loans is less than $200,000 is classified as an asset-backed security.

The key to the analysis of any mortgage-related product is an understanding of the characteristics of the underlying pool of loans, not the arbitrary classification of a deal.[2] The classification of a deal may become important to a portfolio manager in terms of any client-imposed restrictions on concentration limits in asset-backed securities and/or mortgage-backed securities.

---

[2] For an excellent discussion of how the arbitrary classification of deals affects the league tables, see "The League Tables — Not All Counts Were Created Equal," *PaineWebber Mortgage Strategist*, April 21, 1997, pp. 5-10.

Chapter 6

Prepayment Analysis

The projected cash flow for a mortgage-backed security depends on prepayments. We have discussed in Chapter 2 the market convention for describing prepayment behavior — the PSA prepayment benchmark. Recall that the PSA prepayment benchmark is not a forecast or projection of prepayments. Rather, it is an assumption about how prepayment behavior might be expected to occur over time — a ramp period of 29 months followed by a constant CPR for the remaining life of the mortgage pool. For credit-sensitive MBS products, defaults translate into prepayments. Consequently, default projection models are required to project prepayments for credit-sensitive MBS products. As with the PSA prepayment benchmark, the PSA standard default assumption model described in Chapter 4 is simply a market convention for describing the pattern of defaults. Finally, in Chapter 4, we discussed how a prospectus prepayment behavior is used in the case of home equity loans.

Astute portfolio managers need to go beyond these conventions to understand the factors that affect prepayment behavior for the underlying collateral of a mortgage-related product. In this chapter, we look at the evidence on prepayment behavior for mortgage loans underlying agency pools, mortgage loans underlying nonagency pools, home equity loans, and manufactured housing loans.

PREPAYMENTS ON MORTGAGE LOANS IN AGENCY POOLS

There has been extensive research on the factors that affect the prepayment behavior on loans included in agency passthrough securities. These factors include: (1) prevailing mortgage rate, (2) characteristics of the underlying mortgage pool, (3) seasonal factors, and (4) general economic activity. We discuss each below.

Prevailing Mortgage Rate

The current mortgage rate affects prepayments in three ways. First, the spread between the prevailing mortgage rate and the contract rate affects the incentive to refinance. Second, the path of mortgage rates since the loan was originated affects prepayments through a phenomenon referred to as *refinancing burnout*. Both the spread and path of mortgage rates affect prepayments that are the product of refinancing. The third way in which the prevailing mortgage rate affects prepayments is through its effect on the affordability of housing and housing turnover.

Spread Between Contract Rate and Prevailing Mortgage Rate

The single most important factor affecting prepayments because of refinancing is the current level of mortgage rates relative to the borrower's contract rate. The greater the difference between the two, the greater the incentive to refinance the mortgage loan. For refinancing to make sense, the interest savings must be greater than the costs associated with the process. These costs include legal expenses, origination fees, title insurance, and the value of the time associated with obtaining another mortgage loan. Some of these costs — such as title insurance and origination points — will vary proportionately with the amount to be financed. Other costs such as the application fee and legal expenses are typically fixed.

Historically, it has been observed that when mortgage rates fall to more than 200 basis points below the contract rate, prepayment rates increase. However, the creativity of mortgage originators in designing mortgage loans such that the refinancing costs are folded into the amount borrowed and the ability to obtain 100% financing has changed the view that mortgage rates must drop dramatically below the contract rate to make refinancing economic. Moreover, mortgage originators now do an effective job of advertising to make homeowners cognizant of the economic benefits of refinancing.

The present value of the benefits from refinancing depends on the initial level of the contract rate. Specifically, the present value of the benefits of a 200 basis point decline from an initial contract rate of 8% is greater than for a 200 basis point decline from an initial contract rate of 17%. Consequently, in modeling prepayment behavior one would expect that prepayments caused by refinancing might be more highly correlated with a percentage change in the rate rather than a spread.

Because of the lack of observations in a wide range of mortgage rate environments, it has not been possible to evaluate empirically whether a spread measured in basis points or in percentage terms better explains prepayment behavior. As a result, refinancing opportunities can be measured in a variety of ways. In the Goldman, Sachs prepayment model, for example, refinancing opportunities are measured by the ratio of the contract rate to the mortgage refinancing rate.[1] For a specific pool, the contract rate is the weighted average of the contract rates for the underlying mortgage loans. To reflect the lags in the refinancing process, the Goldman, Sachs prepayment model uses a weighted average of the past five month ratio of the contract rate to the mortgage refinancing rate.

Path of Mortgage Rates

The historical pattern of prepayments and economic theory suggest that it is not only the level of mortgage rates that affects prepayment behavior but also the path

---

[1] The Goldman, Sachs prepayment model is described in Scott F. Richard and Richard Roll, "Prepayments on Fixed-Rate Mortgage-Backed Securities," *Journal of Portfolio Management* (Spring 1989), pp. 73-74, and Scott F. Richard, "Relative Prepayment Rates on Thirty-Year FNMA, FHLMC and GNMA Fixed Rate Mortgage-Backed Securities," in Frank J. Fabozzi (ed.), *Advances and Innovations in the Bond and Mortgage Markets* (Chicago, IL: Probus Publishing, 1989), pp. 351-369.

that mortgage rates take to get to the current level. To illustrate why, suppose the underlying contract rate for a pool of mortgage loans is 11% and that three years after origination, the prevailing mortgage rate declines to 8%. Let's consider two possible paths of the mortgage rate in getting to the 8% level. In the first path, the mortgage rate declines to 8% at the end of the first year, then rises to 13% at the end of the second year, and then falls to 8% at the end of the third year. In the second path, the mortgage rate rises to 12% at the end of the first year, continues its rise to 13% at the end of the second year, and then falls to 8% at the end of the third year.

If the mortgage rate follows the first path, those who can benefit from refinancing will more than likely take advantage of this opportunity when the mortgage rate drops to 8% in the first year. When the mortgage rate drops again to 8% at the end of the third year, the likelihood is that prepayments because of refinancing will not surge; those who can benefit by taking advantage of the refinancing opportunity will have done so already when the mortgage rate declined for the first time. This is the prepayment behavior referred to as the refinancing burnout (or simply, burnout) phenomenon.

In contrast, the expected prepayment behavior when the mortgage rate follows the second path is quite different. Prepayment rates are expected to be low in the first two years. When the mortgage rate declines to 8% in the third year, refinancing activity and therefore prepayments are expected to surge. Consequently, the burnout phenomenon is related to the path of mortgage rates.

The difficulty in modeling prepayments has been to quantify path dependency. Some researchers have used the ratio of the remaining mortgage balance outstanding for the pool to the original mortgage balance. This ratio is called the *pool factor*. The argument is that the lower the pool factor, the greater prepayments have been historically and therefore the more likely it is that burnout will occur. One researcher who has tested various measures of path dependency reports that the pool factor is the best measure.[2] In contrast, the Goldman, Sachs prepayment model adjustment for burnout is a nonlinear function generated from the entire history of the ratio of the contract rate to the mortgage refinancing rate since the mortgage was issued.

Level of Mortgage Rates

Prepayments occur because of housing turnover and refinancing. Our focus so far has been on the factors that affect prepayments caused by refinancing. The level of mortgage rates affects housing turnover to the extent that a lower rate increases the affordability of homes. Such rate environments provide an opportune time to purchase a more expensive home (trade up) or to change location for other reasons.

---

[2] Charles N. Schorin, "Fixed-Rate MBS Prepayment Models," Chapter 10 in Frank J. Fabozzi (ed.), *Handbook of Mortgage-Backed Securities* (Chicago, IL: Probus Publishing, 1992).

Characteristics of the Underlying Mortgage Loans

The following characteristics of the underlying mortgage loans affect prepayments: (1) the contract rate, (2) whether the loans are FHA/VA-guaranteed or conventional, (3) the amount of seasoning, (4) the type of loan, for example, a 30-year level payment mortgage, 5-year balloon mortgage, etc., (5) the pool factor, (6) the geographical location of the underlying properties, and (7) presence of a prepayment penalty. We have already discussed how the contract rate affects prepayment behavior and how the pool factor has been used by some researchers as a measure to proxy for path dependency.

FHA/VA Mortgages versus Conventional Mortgages

The underlying mortgage loans for GNMA passthroughs are guaranteed by either the FHA or VA. FNMA and FHLMC passthroughs include conventional loans. There are four characteristics of FHA- and VA-guaranteed loans that cause their prepayment characteristics to differ from those of conventional loans.

First, FHA- and VA-guaranteed loans are assumable. Consequently, prepayments should be lower than for otherwise comparable conventional loans when the contract rate is less than the current mortgage rate. This is because purchasers will assume the seller's mortgage loan in order to acquire the below-market interest rate and, as a result, there will be no prepayment resulting from the sale of the property. Second, the amount of the mortgage loan is typically small, reducing the incentive to refinance as mortgage rates decline and thereby producing a rate of prepayment because of refinancing that is less than for conventional loans. Third, the income level of those who must obtain a mortgage loan guaranteed by the FHA or VA is typically less than that of borrowers with conventional loans. Their ability to take advantage of a refinancing opportunity is limited because they often do not have the funds to pay the costs associated with refinancing. While these three characteristics suggest that prepayments for these loans will be less than for conventional loans, the last characteristic also suggests faster prepayments. Historically, default rates are greater for FHA and VA-guaranteed loans compared to conventional loans. Defaults result in prepayments. However, faster prepayments because of default is swamped by the other characteristics that cause slower prepayments.

Empirical research suggests that for a given refinancing incentive, the prepayment rate is greater for FNMA/FHLMC passthroughs relative to GNMA passthroughs and that FNMA/FHLMC passthroughs burn out faster than GNMA passthroughs.[3]

Seasoning

Seasoning refers to the aging of the mortgage loans. Empirical evidence suggests that prepayment rates are low after the loan is originated and increase after the loan is somewhat seasoned. Then prepayment rates tend to level off, in which case

---

[3] Richard, "Relative Prepayment Rates on Thirty-Year FNMA, FHLMC and GNMA Fixed Rate Mortgage-Backed Securities," pp. 354 and 358.

the loans are referred to as fully seasoned. This is the underlying theory for the PSA prepayment benchmark.

Geographical Location of the Underlying Properties

The prepayment behavior described thus far is for generic pools. In some regions of the country the prepayment behavior tends to be faster than the average national prepayment rate, while other regions exhibit slower prepayment rates. This is caused by differences in local economies that affect housing turnover.[4]

Presence of a Prepayment Penalty

As explained in Chapter 2, there are mortgages (in both agency and nonagency passthroughs) that impose a prepayment penalty. The presence of a prepayment penalty is expected to reduce the economic incentive to refinance. Because prepayment penalty mortgages are relatively new, there is little historical evidence on their prepayment characteristics relative to regular mortgages (i.e., mortgages where there is no prepayment penalty).

There is some empirical evidence supporting slower prepayments for prepayment penalty mortgages. Exhibit 1 compares prepayment rates (CPRs) in August and September 1997 for Fannie Mae regular mortgage pools and Fannie Mae prepayment penalty pools. The prepayment rates are reported for 7%, 7.5%, and 8% coupon pools and by year of origination (1996 and 1997). For the 7% coupon pools, there is little incentive to refinance and therefore the difference in prepayment rates between regular and prepayment penalty pools is minor. Clearly, where the economic incentive to refinance is greatest, the 8% coupon pools, prepayment penalty pools show the most significant difference in prepayment rates.

Exhibit 1: Prepayment (CPRs) on Fannie Mae Regular and Prepayment Penalty Pools: August and September 1997

Coupon	Orig. Year	August			September		
		Regular	Penalty	Difference	Regular	Penalty	Difference
7.0%	1997	2.0	2.2	-0.2	2.0	1.8	0.2
	1996	5.9	2.9	3.0	5.9	6.0	-0.1
7.5%	1997	5.9	1.8	4.1	5.7	1.0	4.7
	1996	9.1	4.8	4.3	9.5	5.6	4.3
8.0%	1997	12.3	4.7	7.6	12.1	0.1	12.0
	1996	13.5	0.1	13.4	14.7	0.2	14.5

Source: Figure 5, *Global Relative Value*, Lehman Brothers, Fixed Income Research, October 27, 1997, MBS-4. *PERMISSION NEEDED*,

---

[4] Chuck Ramsey and J. Michael Henderson, "Investing in Specified Pools," Chapter 5 in *The Handbook of Mortgage-Backed Securities*.

Seasonal Factors

There is a well-documented seasonal pattern in prepayments. This pattern is related to activity in the primary housing market, with home buying increasing in the spring, and gradually reaching a peak in the late summer. Home buying declines in the fall and winter. Mirroring this activity are the prepayments that result from the turnover of housing as home buyers sell their existing homes and purchase new ones. Prepayments are low in the winter months and begin to rise in the spring, reaching a peak in the summer months. However, probably because of delays in passing through prepayments, the peak may not be observed until early fall.

General Economic Activity

Economic theory would suggest that general economic activity affects prepayment behavior through its effect on housing turnover. The link is as follows: a growing economy results in a rise in personal income and in opportunities for worker migration; this increases family mobility and as a result increases housing turnover. The opposite holds for a weak economy. Some researchers suggest that prepayments can be projected by identifying and forecasting the turnover rate of the single-family housing stock.[5]

Although some modelers of prepayment behavior may incorporate macroeconomic measures of economic activity such as gross disposable product, industrial production, or housing starts, the trend has been to ignore them or limit their use to specific applications. There are two reasons why macroeconomic measures have been ignored by some modelers. First, empirical tests suggest that the relationship between residuals of a prepayment forecasting model that does not include macroeconomic measures and various macroeconomic measures is either statistically insignificant or, if it is statistically significant, explanatory power is low.[6] Second, as explained later, prepayment models are based on a projection of a path for future mortgage rates. The inclusion of macroeconomic variables in a prepayment model would require the forecasting of the value of these variables over long time periods.

Macroeconomic variables, however, have been used by some researchers in prepayment models in two ways. One way is to capture the effect of housing turnover on prepayments by specifying a relationship between interest rates and housing turnover. This is the approach used in the Prudential Securities Model.[7] A second way is to incorporate macroeconomic variables and their forecasts in projecting short-term rather than long-term prepayments.

Housing turnover can be implied from PSA speeds. Exhibit 2 shows the average time to move implied by a PSA speed. So, for example, a 150 PSA assumption for a passthrough that is seasoned 24 months means that the average time to move for the homeowners in the mortgage pool is 10.7 years.

---

[5] See, for example, Joseph C. Hu, "An Alternative Prepayment Projection Based on Housing Activity," in *The Handbook of Mortgage-Backed Securities*.

[6] Richard and Roll, "Prepayments on Fixed-Rate Mortgage- Backed Securities," pp. 78-79.

[7] Lakbhir S. Hayre, Kenneth Lauterbach, and Cyrus Mohebbi, "Prepayment Models and Methodologies," in *Advances and Innovations in the Bond and Mortgage Markets*, p. 338.

Exhibit 2: Average Time (Years) to Move
Implied by a PSA Speed

Mortgage age (months)	PSA									
	75%	100%	125%	150%	175%	200%	225%	250%	275%	300%
0	22.9	17.4	14.1	11.8	10.3	9.1	8.1	7.4	6.8	6.3
6	22.5	17.0	13.6	11.4	9.8	8.6	7.7	7.0	6.4	5.8
12	22.2	16.6	13.3	11.1	9.5	8.3	7.4	6.6	6.0	5.5
24	21.8	16.2	12.9	10.7	9.1	7.9	7.0	6.2	5.6	5.1

Source: Karen Wault Wagner and Evan Firestone, "Homeowner Mobility and Mortgage Prepayment Forecasting," Chapter 11 in Frank J. Fabozzi, *Handbook of Mortgage-Backed Securities* (Chicago, IL: Probus Publishing, 1995).

Prepayment S Curve

While all the above factors (spread between the contract rate and the prevailing mortgage rate, the path of mortgage rates, the absolute level of the mortgage rate, seasoning, geographic concentration, seasonal factors, and general economic activity) affect the prepayment behavior on mortgage loans, the most dominating factor is by far the prevailing mortgage rate level. Specifically, it is the spread between the contract rate and the prevailing mortgage rate that provides the economic incentive for mortgagors to refinance. Unfortunately, this factor is also the least predictable and most volatile. Changes in housing turnover and general economic activity can cause prepayments to change by 20% to 40% gradually over a long period of time.

When mortgage rates move and current coupon mortgages all of a sudden become economically refinancable, i.e. the prepayment options become in the money, the prepayment rate can change fourfold to eightfold in a short period of time! Therefore, mortgage market participants focus a great deal of effort in the analysis of the relationship between mortgage rates and refinancing activity on generic mortgage loans. Once this is done on a macro level, the portfolio manager can then fine tune his or her prepayment projection based on the more detailed information on the loans such as geographic concentration, regional housing activity, embedded equity in the loan (loan-to-value ratio), seasoning, etc. Detailed collateral analyses will be illustrated in the next chapter.

No one can accurately predict future mortgage rate levels or the paths of mortgage rates consistently. But mortgage market participants have built prepayment models to predict prepayments given mortgage rate levels. Almost every Wall Street firm has built a proprietary econometric prepayment model based on empirical prepayment experience. These projections can be viewed on Bloomberg's DPE page (Dealer Prepayment Estimates). Bloomberg also has a function to aggregate all the dealers' reported estimates and calculates the median values. This function can be performed by typing in DMED (Dealers MEDian). For example, if one types in a current coupon passthrough (i.e., newly originated passthroughs) and performs the DMED function, one would get the following values:

Exhibit 3: Prepayment S Curve

Exhibit 3: Prepayment S Curve — %PSA vs Relative Coupon-Amount Out/In the Money (bps)

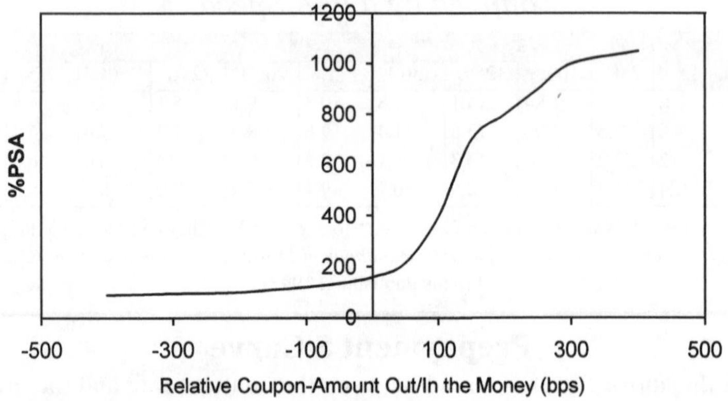

−300	−200	−100	−50	unchanged	+50	+100	+200	+300
1000	800	400	216	160	135	120	100	95

This means that the median Wall Street prepayment models' projection is that the current coupon passthrough would prepay at 160% PSA on average for the life of the loan if mortgage rates stay the same. If rates drop 50 basis points, the prepayment option becomes 50 basis points in the money and interest rate sensitive homeowners would refinance immediately to drive prepayment speeds up to 216% PSA. Note that not all prepayment options are exercised efficiently. If mortgage rates drop 200 basis points, which is more than enough to overcome any transaction costs of refinancing, more homeowners (even the less interest rate sensitive ones) would refinance and drive prepayment speeds up to 800% PSA. Once the refinancing option is in the money enough to overcome all transaction costs, the refinancing activity would start to level off because theoretically, all mortgagors would refinance except those who do not have sufficient equity or credit. If mortgage rates rise by 100 basis points, prepayments would slow down just a bit to 120% PSA because of the baseline prepayment activity due to housing turnover, divorces, relocations, etc.

The relationship between prepayment rates and mortgage rates (as a spread to the contract rate) holding everything else constant can be graphed. This is shown in Exhibit 3. From the exhibit, we can see that prepayments and mortgage rates are highly correlated but the relationship is not linear. In fact, the curve has an "S" shape and is generally known as the *prepayment S curve*. In other words, the prepayment S curve is a graphical depiction of prepayments as a function of the spread between the contract rate and the prevailing mortgage rate, holding other factors constant.

Passthroughs that are selling at a slight premium above par are often referred to as "cuspy collateral." This is because such collateral is on the "cusp" of the prepayment S curve where the economic incentive to refinance begins to become apparent.

PREPAYMENTS ON STANDARD MORTGAGE LOANS IN NONAGENCY POOLS[8]

Prepayment analysis typically has been limited to the value of the prepayment option as determined chiefly by the gap between the mortgage's coupon rate and the prevailing mortgage rate and, to a lesser extent, the impact of loan age or seasoning along with macroeconomic factors.

Analysts know that prepayment models ideally should discriminate between a homeowner's decision to refinance an existing mortgage — whether to obtain a lower rate or to obtain cash — and the decision to sell the property. Modeling these decisions accurately would require much more data, such as information on the homeowner's family composition, life style stage, and overall financial situation. Hence, the existing models with only the factors just noted are only proxies for the "real" model.

These model imperfections are not the result of any lack of creativity, but rather the limitations of the data released by Fannie Mae, Freddie Mac, and Ginnie Mae. The agencies release only aggregate information such as weighted average coupon/maturity (WAC/WAM) by quartile and geographic concentrations at the state level, average loan age, and average loan size. Moreover, prepayments are not reported by type.

Issuers of nonagency securities are much more forthcoming with data, generally releasing loan-level detail for the collateral backing their deals. These data generally are in a standard format such as the one developed by the Public Securities Association. This detail makes it possible to do much more complete prepayment analysis to answer the following kinds of questions:

- Is the prepayment function for loans taken out to purchase a house different from the function for loans that refinance a previous mortgage?
- What is the effect of homeowner's equity and changing property values on prepayments?
- Do alternate documentation or low/no-doc loans prepay differently from fully documented loans?

Traditional Agency/Nonagency Prepayment Comparisons

Several research reports have found that prepayments for nonagency securities tend to be faster than "comparable" agency securities. (The quotation marks are necessary because some analysts control only for the WAC and the WAM of the pools being compared.) Among the factors cited for the faster speeds are that:

---

[8] This section is adapted from Douglas L. Bendt, Chuck Ramsey, and Frank J. Fabozzi, "Prepayment Analysis for Non-Agency Mortgage-Backed Securities," Chapter 13 in Frank J. Fabozzi, Chuck Ramsey, Frank Ramirez, and Michael Marz (eds.), *The Handbook of Nonagency Mortgage-Backed Securities* (New Hope, PA: Frank J. Fabozzi Associates, 1997).

1. Greater variation in loan composition, such as greater WAC dispersion, can make WAC/WAM comparisons inadequate.
2. Larger loan sizes tend to prepay faster because the same size prepayment option in percentage terms is worth more in dollar terms.
3. More affluent borrowers tend to be more mobile.
4. California — traditionally a fast-prepaying state — is overrepresented in nonagency securities.

Other analysts correct for some of these factors. Adjusting for collateral diversity and geographic concentrations, Prudential finds prepayments speeds to average around 50% faster except during the depths of the last recession, when nonagency securities prepaid slower than agency securities.

Adjusted Agency/Nonagency Prepayment Comparisons

Often, prepayment rates for nonagency securities are cited as a multiple of expected prepayment rates on agency securities. Rather than compare nonagency and agency prepayment rates, it would be preferable to make such comparisons on a loan-level basis. This analysis would effectively remove the effects of WAC/WAM discrepancies and dispersions, allowing the effects of other factors to be seen more clearly.

With agency data, such comparisons are normally impossible. The data provided by Dow Jones/Telerate's Advance Factor Service, however, clearly show the effects of analyzing prepayments by pool coupon compared to analyzing prepayments using the actual mortgage rate. Using loan-level data, one study finds that the average "multiplier" for new-issue, lower coupons is about 2.5 — well above the range cited by analysts at the time — while multipliers for older, higher-rate collateral are about 1.5 — right in the middle of the range cited by other analysts at the time.

The higher multipliers for the lower coupons that have been measured were measuring the effects of the refinancing wave in 1992 and 1993. The barriers to refinancing have been lowered substantially with the increasing popularity of no-points mortgages. Thus, the value of the prepayment option for jumbo borrowers has increased in dollar terms relative to the value of the option for agency borrowers, given the same size of rate decrease.

Besides coupon and seasoning, there are three major influences on prepayment rates for nonagency securities. In order of importance, they are homeowner's equity, transaction type (purchase versus refinance), and level of documentation.

Homeowners' Equity

A homeowner's equity depends chiefly upon two major factors: (1) the initial down payment and (2) changes in home prices. Together, these factors determine the current LTV ratio. Amortization and partial prepayments are of lesser importance.

Homeowners with lower LTVs — greater equity — have more home financing choices. Most importantly, they could sell their houses to unlock the equity to use as a down payment on another house. Second, they could do a cash-out refinancing to unlock the equity even if they don't want to move or interest rates are not any lower. And finally, if interest rates are lower so that the prepayment option has value, there is no constraint on taking advantage of the lower interest rate.

A study by Bendt-Ramsey-Fabozzi found a clear pattern of faster speeds among mortgages with lower current LTVs where current market values are estimated by using indexes of home price changes.[9] This pattern helps explain California's reputation for being a fast-prepaying state throughout the 1980s. Housing prices exploded, allowing many homeowners to do equity-takeout refinancings and to trade up to bigger homes. Because housing prices having dropped in the early 1990s in most areas of California, prepayments have slowed dramatically.

Transaction Type

Mortgages taken out to purchase homes tend to be prepaid more slowly than mortgages taken out to refinance previous higher-rate mortgages. Refinance transactions in which the homeowner takes out cash tend to be more like purchase transactions. The Bendt-Ramsey-Fabozzi study finds this pattern especially clear for mortgages originated in the 1992-1993 and the 1986-1987 periods, when rates were low.

Homeowners refinancing an existing mortgage are different from homeowners who just purchased a house in two important ways. First, they have lived in their house for some amount of time. Therefore, they are more likely to have moved to a new stage in their life cycle and to require a different type of house. And second, the fact that they have refinanced their mortgage once already may make them more sensitive to future rate drops because they realize how easy the process can be. Mortgage brokers are more likely to be more aggressive with previous refinancers as well.

Level of Documentation

Nonagency mortgages that are fully documented are loans that would qualify for sale to the agencies, but for the fact that the loan amount is higher than the agencies' limits. (Loans may not qualify for sale to the agencies for other underwriting characteristics such as debt ratios as well, but these reasons are much less common.) Borrowers are required to submit forms verifying income and employment with W-2 forms, pay stubs, tax forms, and lenders verify the sources of the assets to be used for the down payment.

Loans that are deficient in at least one of these areas qualify under "alternative" or "low" documentation programs, usually at a slightly higher interest rate and a lower cap on the permissible LTV. In the extreme, no documentation may have been required as a trade-off for a higher rate and/or an even lower LTV.

---

[9] Bendt, Ramsey, and Fabozzi, "Prepayment Analysis of Nonagency Mortgage-Backed Securities."

The Bendt-Ramsey-Fabozzi study found that borrowers who qualified for full documentation programs in 1993 and 1994 have had higher prepayments. There are probably two reasons for this. First, the spectrum of lenders who will lend to such borrowers is wider; fewer lenders have a low or no-doc program than in the past because of higher default experience. Second, borrowers who qualified under a less-than-full-doc program are more likely to have fluctuations in their income — many are self-employed — that may limit their ability to refinance or trade up.

PREPAYMENTS ON HOME EQUITY LOANS

There are differences in the prepayment behavior for home equity loans and standard residential mortgage loans. In general it is expected that prepayments due to refinancings would be less important for HELs than for standard residential mortgage loans because typically the average loan size is less for HELs. In general it is thought that interest rates must fall considerably more for HELs than for traditional residential mortgage loans in order for a borrower to benefit from refinancing.

Wall Street firms involved in the underwriting and market making of home equity loan-backed securities have developed prepayment models for these loans. Several firms have found that the key difference between the prepayment behavior of HELs and traditional residential mortgages is the important role played by the credit characteristics of the borrower.

A study by Bear Stearns strongly suggests that borrower credit quality is the most important determinant of prepayments. These findings are consistent with those reported by other dealer firms.[10] The study looked at prepayments for four separate deals. The underlying HELs for each deal had a different level of borrower credit quality (with the credit quality of the loans being classified by the issuer). The four deals whose prepayments were analyzed were FICAL 90-1 (dominated by the highest credit quality borrowers, A++), GE Capital 91-1 (A– borrowers), Fleet Finance 90-1 (B/C borrowers), and Goldome Credit 90-1 (D borrowers). Prepayments were analyzed from the third quarter of 1991 to the third quarter of 1995, a period which encompassed the refinancing wave of 1992 and 1993. The main focus was on how borrower credit quality affected prepayments. The study found that prepayments for the Goldome Credit 90-1 deal (which was comprised of D borrowers) were completely uncorrelated to changes in interest rates. The deal with the highest credit quality borrowers, FICAL 90-1, exhibited prepayments similar to that of agency mortgage-backed securities in terms of their sensitivity to interest rates. The correlation between prepayments and interest rates for the deal with A– borrowers (Capital 91-1) was less than for FICAL 90-1 but greater than for the deal with B/C borrowers (Fleet Finance 90-1). Consequently, the sensitivity of refinancing to interest rates is reduced the lower the credit quality of the borrower.

---

[10] Dale Westhoff and Mark Feldman, "Prepayment Modeling and Valuation of Home Equity Loans Securities," Chapter 16 in *The Handbook of Nonagency Mortgage-Backed Securities*.

Exhibit 4: Bears Stearns' Findings for Prepayment Pattern on Home Equity Loans in a No-Change Interest Rate Scenario by Borrower Credit Quality

Borrower credit quality	Seasoning	CPR at Plateau
A	30 months	18% to 20% CPR
B	15 to 18 months	24% CPR
C	12 to 15 months	30% CPR

Source: Dale Westhoff and Mark Feldman, "Prepayment Modeling and Valuation of Home Equity Loans Securities," Chapter 16 in Frank J. Fabozzi, Chuck Ramsey, Frank Ramirez, and Michael Marz (eds.), *The Handbook of Nonagency Mortgage-Backed Securities* (New Hope, PA: Frank J. Fabozzi Associates, 1997).

Bear Stearns found that seasoning depends on the credit quality of the borrowers and the attributes of the loans. Some loans season in 10 months and some take as long as 30 months. The study by Bear Stearns found that the seasoning process consists of two phases. The first phase exhibits rapid seasoning and an eventual plateau in prepayments. In this phase, all other factors equal, lower credit quality loans tend to season faster and plateau at a higher level than loans of higher credit quality. Exhibit 4 reports the prepayment pattern in a no-change interest rate scenario by borrower credit quality.

Bear Stearns hypothesized that the reason for the more rapid seasoning and higher plateau for pools of lower credit quality borrowers is because those borrowers that make timely payments become eligible to move up in credit quality rating and can thereby take advantage of lower loan rates that may be available. Loan originators monitor such loans and solicit loan applications from such potential borrowers. Bear Stearns refers to this as the "credit cure" effect.

In the second phase there is a longer period of steadily declining prepayments. For lower credit quality loans, there is a significant slowdown in prepayments that lasts three to four years. Bear Stearns believes that this is due to the fact that borrowers who have improved their credit quality refinance in the first phase, which leaves in the remaining pool borrowers who are less able to refinance, as well as those who may exhibit a greater tendency to be delinquent. This phase is referred to as the "credit inertia" effect.

PREPAYMENTS ON MANUFACTURED HOUSING LOANS

Relative to the other mortgage-related products discussed in this chapter, prepayments on manufactured housing-backed securities tend to be more stable because they are not sensitive to refinancing. There are several reasons for this.[11]

First, the loan balances are typically small so that there is no significant dollar savings from refinancing. For example, consider the average 80% LTV 15-

[11] Thomas Zimmerman and Inna Koren, "Manufactured Housing Securities," Chapter 5 in Anand Bhattacharya and Frank J. Fabozzi (eds.), *Asset-Backed Securities* (New Hope, PA: Frank J. Fabozzi Associates, 1996).

year manufactured housing loan of $24,400 and average 80% LTV 15-year standard mortgage loan of $118,160.[12] The monthly loan payments and savings are shown in Exhibit 5. Notice that for a loan with a rate of 9%, refinancing at 7% (a 200 basis points lower rate) will only result in a monthly savings of $28.17 for the average manufacturing housing loan; in contrast, for a standard mortgage loan of $118,160 the monthly savings is $136.41.

Second, the rate of depreciation of mobile homes may be such that in the earlier years depreciation is greater than the amount of the loan paid off. This makes it difficult to refinance the loan. Finally, typically borrowers are of lower credit quality and therefore find it difficult to obtain funds to refinance.

A Morgan Stanley study by Abrahams, Esaki, and Restrick analyzed the factors driving refinancings and turnover in manufactured housing loans. The results are summarized in Exhibits 6 and 7. The Morgan Stanley study also finds that monthly defaults in many manufactured housing loan securitizations are about 0.1% to 0.2% of the original loan principal.[13]

PREPAYMENT MODELS

A prepayment model is a statistical model that is used to forecast prepayments. It begins by modeling the statistical relationships among the factors discussed in this chapter that are expected to affect prepayments.

Exhibit 5: Savings from Refinancing

Monthly Payment At:	Loan Size	
	$24,400	$118,160
9% Interest Rate	$247	$1,198
8% Interest Rate	$233	$1,129
7% Interest Rate	$219	$1,062
6% Interest Rate	$205	$997
Monthly Savings From Refinancing A 9% Interest Rate Loan to a:		
8% Interest Rate	$14.30	$69.26
7% Interest Rate	$28.17	$136.41
6% Interest Rate	$41.58	$201.36

Source: Exhibit 11 in Steven Abrahams, Howard Esaki, and Robert Restrick, "Manufactured Housing: Overview, Securitization, and Prepayments," Chapter 17 in Frank J. Fabozzi, Chuck Ramsey, Frank Ramirez, and Michael Marz (eds.), *The Handbook of Nonagency Mortgage-Backed Securities* (New Hope, PA: Frank J. Fabozzi Associates, 1997), p. 294.

---

[12] This example is from Steven Abrahams, Howard Esaki, and Robert Restrick, "Manufactured Housing: Overview, Securitization, and Prepayments," Chapter 17 in *The Handbook of Nonagency Mortgage-Backed Securities*.

[13] Abrahams, Esaki, and Restrick, "Manufactured Housing: Overview, Securitization, and Prepayments," p. 297.

Exhibit 6: Morgan Stanley Findings on the
Factors Driving Refinancings in Manufactured Housing Loans

Factor	Factor Levels	Proportional Prepayment Impact (% CPR)				
		Interest Rates Shift (bp from loan mortgage rate)				
		0	−50	−100	−200	−300
Refinancing	$18,000 balance (< avg size loan)	6	7	9	12	14
Incentive	$24,000 balance (avg size loan)	6	8	10	13	16
and Loan Size	$30,000 balance (> avg size loan)	6	9	12	14	17
Loan Age	< 24 Months	80% of average life speed				
	> 24 Months	105% of average life speed				
Seasonality	January, February	80% of average life speed				
	Other Months	105% of average life speed				
The	0.8 Million New Home Sales	Slower				
Economy	1.0 Million New Home Sales	Average				
	1.2 Million New Home Sales	Faster				
Lender	More	Raises prepayments				
Competition	Less	Lowers prepayment				

Source: Exhibit 10 in Steven Abrahams, Howard Esaki, and Robert Restrick, "Manufactured Housing: Overview, Securitization, and Prepayments," Chapter 17 in Frank J. Fabozzi, Chuck Ramsey, Frank Ramirez, and Michael Marz (eds.), *The Handbook of Nonagency Mortgage-Backed Securities* (New Hope, PA: Frank J. Fabozzi Associates, 1997), p. 294.

Exhibit 7: Morgan Stanley Findings on the
Factors Driving Turnovers in Manufactured Housing Loans

Factor	Factor Levels	Prepayment Impact
Loan Age	Month 1	3.7% CPR
	Months 2-23	Increases 0.1% CPR a month
	Months 24 and beyond	6.0% CPR
The Economy	0.8 Million New Home Sales	Slower
	1.0 Million New Home Sales	Average
	1.2 Million New Home Sales	Faster
Seasonality	January Low	80% of average annual speed
	July High	120% of average annual speed
Setting	On Borrower-Owned Land	Seasons over 36 Months
	In an MH Park	Seasons over 24 Months

Source: Exhibit 12 in Steven Abrahams, Howard Esaki, and Robert Restrick, "Manufactured Housing: Overview, Securitization, and Prepayments," Chapter 17 in Frank J. Fabozzi, Chuck Ramsey, Frank Ramirez, and Michael Marz (eds.), *The Handbook of Nonagency Mortgage-Backed Securities* (New Hope, PA: Frank J. Fabozzi Associates, 1997), p. 296.

In the case of standard mortgage loans in agency pools, one study suggests that the four factors discussed above explain about 95% of the variation in prepayment rates: refinancing incentives, burnout, seasoning, and seasonality.[14] These factors are then combined into one model. For example, in the Goldman,

[14] Richard, "Relative Prepayment Rates on Thirty-Year FNMA, FHLMC and GNMA Fixed Rate Mortgage-Backed Securities," pp. 359-360.

Sachs prepayment model the effects interact proportionally through the following multiplicative function, which is used to project prepayments:

monthly prepayment rate = (refinancing incentive) × (seasoning multiplier)
× (month multiplier) × (burnout multiplier)

where the various multipliers are adjustments for the effects we discussed earlier in this chapter.

For two of the effects, the only information that is needed is the amount of seasoning and the month. For the refinancing incentive and burnout, it is necessary to know the contract rate on the underlying pool and the refinancing mortgage rate. While the former is known and is unchanged over the life of the mortgage pool, the latter will change. The practice in prepayment modeling has been to generate a path of monthly mortgage rates as follows. First, a path for monthly short-term interest rates that is consistent with the prevailing term structure of interest rates is generated. Based on an assumed relationship between short-term interest rates and long-term interest rates, a path for monthly mortgage rates can be obtained. From these monthly mortgage rates, prepayment rates caused by refinancing incentives and burnout are projected. Consequently, the prepayment projection is contingent on the interest rate path projected.

The product of a prepayment forecast is not one prepayment rate but a set of prepayment rates for each month of the remaining term of a mortgage pool. The set of monthly prepayment rates, however, is not reported by Wall Street firms or vendors. Instead, a single prepayment rate is reported. One way to convert a set of monthly prepayment rates into a single prepayment rate is to calculate a simple average of the prepayment rates. The drawback to this approach is that it does not take into consideration the outstanding balance each month. An alternative approach is to use some type of weighted average, selecting the weights to reflect the amount of the monthly cash flow corresponding to a monthly prepayment rate. This is done by first computing the cash flow yield (discussed in Chapter 11) for a passthrough given its market price and the set of monthly prepayment rates. Then a single prepayment rate (CPR or PSA multiple) that gives the same cash flow yield is found.

Chapter 7

Collateral Analysis of Derivative Mortgage Products

This chapter provides a common sense approach for addressing general collateral issues, regardless of the tranche type the investor is considering. We discuss the two broad types of underlying collateral used in the construction of derivative mortgage products (collateralized mortgage obligations and mortgage strips): agency passthroughs and whole loan mortgages. Whole loan collateral involves the additional dimension of analyzing mortgage credit.

AGENCY COLLATERAL

The portfolio manager contemplating investing in a derivative mortgage product is indirectly lending money to homeowners. As a lender, the portfolio manager will want to have as much information as possible about the borrowers, the properties, and the loan terms granted to the homeowner. Agency CMOs and PO mortgage strips effectively minimize credit risk, because the agency guarantees the principal and interest in the event of homeowner default. Collateral analysis of these deals thus emphasizes primarily the loan terms, and secondarily the properties.

When the yield curve steepens, a wider variety of mortgage products become available and more attractive to homeowners. In the rate environment of the early 1990s, there was greater issuance of 15-year and balloon products, loans that were increasingly used as collateral in CMO deals. As the yield curve flattened in 1994, issuance shifted back to 30-year products.

Exhibit 1 details the changing composition of collateral for agency CMOs since 1990. The diversity of collateral makes its careful analysis all the more important. Agency CMO investors should concentrate on the impact of the *gross weighted average coupons* and the *weighted average maturities*, as well as the dispersions of these statistics, as they have a significant effect on prepayment speeds. Geographic location of properties is a factor as well

Gross Weighted Average Coupon

The initial step in the analysis of any derivative mortgage product involves looking at the gross weighted average coupon (GWAC) of the deal. Exhibit 2 shows an example of an existing FHLMC 10%, 30-year collateral CMO deal. This deal has a GWAC of 10.74% compared to that of 10.60% on generic FHLMC 10%s of similar WAM.

Exhibit 1: Agency CMO Collateral Market Share

	1990	1991	1992	1993	1994	1995	1996	1997	1998*
30-Year Conventionals	83%	67%	58%	58%	68%	63%	61%	80%	84%
30-Year GNMAs	13	19	14	11	13	26	21	16	12
20-Year Conventionals	0	0	0	2	1	0	0	0	0
15-Year Conventionals	4	14	26	27	17	10	10	4	4
Balloons	0	0	2	2	1	1	9	1	0

* January through April 1998

Source: Bloomberg Financial Markets.

Exhibit 2: Collateral Gross WAC: Impact on Prepayment Speeds

	FHLMC Series 202	Generic FHLMC 10s
Coupon	10.00%	10.00%
GWAC	10.74%	10.60%
	Prepayments in CPR as of January 1995	
1 month speed	19.2	16.3
3 month speed	21.2	17.6
6 month speed	20.6	19.8
12 month speed	30.8	30.1

Source: Bloomberg Financial Markets.

Portfolio managers should realize that it is the GWAC that determines prepayments, not the net weighted average coupon (NWAC or net coupon) of the collateral. Exhibit 2 shows that, as expected, the FHLMC 10% CMO experienced faster prepayment speeds relative to the generic collateral when measured over several different periods. This, of course, would be good for purchasers of the discount bonds, but bad for the premium bondholders.

The difference in GWACs between same net coupon deals will have varying impacts on prepayments depending on overall mortgage rates. This impact can be either large or small according to the area of the prepayment curve where the GWAC lies. Exhibit 3 shows the prepayment "S" curve for FNMA collateral. This curve displays the January 1995 prepayments across a range of net coupons.

When 30-year mortgage rates were around 8% in early 1994, the 14 basis point difference in GWACs from the example in Exhibit 2 between 10.74% and 10.60% was fairly insignificant. This collateral was highly refinanceable, and the 12-month prepayment difference between this deal and generic collateral was therefore fairly insignificant. However, by the end of 1994, mortgage rates rose to around 9.5%, which made FNMA and FHLMC 10% collateral much less refinanceable given the transaction costs associated with the process. The same 14 basis point difference in GWACs between 10.74% and 10.6% became more significant as indicated by the difference in the recent 3-month prepayment speeds of this deal and generic collateral as reported in Exhibit 2 (21.2% CPR versus 17.6% CPR).

Exhibit 3: FNMA Prepayments (January 1995)

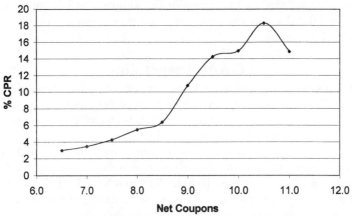

Source: Federal National Mortgage Association

Exhibit 4: Collateral Gross WAC: Impact on Prepayment Speeds

	FHLMC Series 1058	Generic FHLMC 8.5s
Coupon	8.50%	8.50%
GWAC	9.35%	9.25%
	Prepayments in CPR as of January 1995	
1 month speed	10.9	9.4
3 month speed	10.8	9.8
6 month speed	14.2	11.6
12 month speed	34.5	28.7

Source: Bloomberg Financial Markets.

If this same 14 basis point difference existed on the other end of the coupon range, the difference in prepayments would have been more significant in early 1994. Take another example as shown in Exhibit 4. FHLMC Series 1058 is an existing FHLMC 8.5% deal with a GWAC of 9.35% and a WAM of 24-9 as of January 1995 versus generic FHLMC 8.5% collateral of similar WAM with a GWAC of 9.25%. When rates were lower and the yield curve was steep in early 1994, a slight difference in the GWAC could cause these loans to be refinanced by rolling down the curve either into 15-year, 7-year or 5-year balloons, or adjustable-rate mortgages. Exhibit 4 shows quite a difference in the 12-month prepayment speeds of the deal versus generic collateral (34.5% CPR versus 28.7% CPR). As mortgage rates rose to around 9.5% by the end of 1994, both the 9.25% and 9.35% loans became non-economically refinanceable and there was very little difference in the recent prepayment speeds as reported in the exhibit.

The greatest impact on bond valuations will occur when portfolio managers are considering derivative mortgage products backed by mortgages that lie on the steepest part of the prepayment S curve. These "cuspy" coupons can move into or out of their prepayment options with relatively small movements in mortgage rates. As illustrated by the examples in Exhibits 2 and 4, the overall mortgage rates and the shape of the yield curve are very important in the analysis of the GWACs of the collateral.

GWAC Dispersion

Because the prepayment curve is not linear, the degree of dispersion of the GWAC will have a significant impact on the actual prepayment experience of a derivative mortgage product. The best way to illustrate this is to look at an extreme example using the prepayment S curve shown in Exhibit 3.

Consider two CMOs, each with a net coupon of 8.5% and GWAC of 9.0%. The first bond has collateral consisting entirely of loans with a GWAC of 9.0%. The second bond is collateralized by 50% in 8.5% GWAC loans and 50% in 9.5% GWAC loans. If the prepayment curve were linear, one would expect prepayments on these two issues to be the same, and there would be very little need to know how widely dispersed the coupons were.

Because the prepayment S curve is positively convex around that coupon, however, linear interpolation between the 8.0%s and 9.0%s indicates that the weighted average prepayment experience on the barbelled position will be greater than that on the bullet CMO. Therefore, one would expect the barbelled bond to prepay at a faster rate than the bullet bond, despite identical average GWACs.

This estimation problem exists for coupons on the higher part of the prepayment S curve as well. Consider another example using Exhibit 3, where one FNMA 10.5% CMO is backed solely by 11% GWAC loans, and another deal is evenly collateralized by 10.5%s and 11.5%s. In this situation, the prepayment rate for the bullet CMO will be greater than that for the barbelled issue because the prepayment S curve is negatively convex around that coupon.

These two examples point out the need to look at GWAC dispersion, especially in the case of derivative mortgage products backed by cuspy collateral. Moreover, portfolio managers must actively monitor their holdings of derivative mortgage products because interest rate changes will shift the prepayment S curve. Conditions when GWAC dispersion may not seem important can change quickly in volatile interest rate environments. Also, over time high GWAC loans will pay off first, which will result in a downward drift on the GWAC.

Weighted Average Maturity

The weighted average maturity (WAM) affects prepayments in two ways. First, nonrefinanceable mortgages exhibit slow prepayments in the first few years, because most homeowners are unlikely to move again in the first couple of years after taking out the mortgage. After three to five years of seasoning, such mortgages begin to prepay at a faster rate. Therefore, newly originated loans, i.e., longer WAM pools, tend to prepay more slowly than more seasoned paper with the same GWAC.

Exhibit 5: Collateral WAM: Impact on Prepayment Speeds

	Trust 136 IO/PO	Trust 25 IO/PO
GWAC	10.58%	10.81%
WAM	294	173
	Prepayments in CPR as of January 1995	
3 month speed	17.8	11.3
6 month speed	22.5	15.7
12 month speed	31.2	22.1

Source: Bloomberg Financial Markets.

The WAM will affect the prepayment experience on premium refinance-able coupons in an opposite way because of "burnout." Burnout refers to the fact that those homeowners who have had the chance to refinance and have not (for whatever reason) are less likely to refinance the next time the opportunity arises. Seasoned collateral that experienced the 1987, early 1992, and late 1992 prepayment waves is now less sensitive to interest rate movements. Therefore, longer WAM premium loans tend to prepay faster than more seasoned paper.

Burnout has the greatest impact on securities that have the most prepayment sensitivity. Exhibit 5 compares a long WAM and a short WAM security, both FNMA Trust IO/PO Strips. Prepayments on the shorter WAM IO are significantly lower than those on the long WAM IO, partially reflecting the effects of burnout.

Caution should be exercised when making blanket assumptions about the effect of burnout. The degree to which burnout affects levels of prepayments depends to a great degree on the absolute decline in mortgage rates, the shape of the yield curve, and the accessibility of information on refinancing opportunities.

WAM Dispersion

In much the same way that GWAC dispersion affects prepayments, WAM dispersion can affect the potential yield of a tranche, especially for premium and discount securities. All things equal, the longer the WAM, the higher the potential yield on a premium security, and the lower the potential yield on a discount security.

Widely dispersed WAM collateral can exhibit unexpected shortenings or lengthenings in periods of fast prepayments in contrast to a bullet WAM deal, where the collateral can be expected to roll down the curve corresponding to the passage of time. In the case of premium collateral, the WAM will shorten by more than the passage of time. This is a result of the longer-maturity loans prepaying faster than the shorter-maturity loans that have experienced some burnout.

New deals using discount collateral can actually experience a slight extension of their WAM. This occurs when the new loans in the collateral are not prepaying and the slightly aged loans (i.e., over two years) begin prepaying at a faster rate. Again, the effect of this will depend on how widely dispersed the maturities are, as well as how seasoned the entire collateral is.

Exhibit 6: Geographic Concentration of Collateral (January 1995)

	FN Trust 43 FN 9.5%	FN Trust 26 FN 9.5%
GWAC	10.26%	10.33%
WAM	267	256
Prepayments in CPR as of January 1995		
3 month speed	11.9	24.2
6 month speed	14.0	21.9
12 month speed	26.9	30.3
Life speed	22.3	27.1
Four Largest Geographical Concentrations (%)		
Massachusetts	44.4	—
California	—	16.3
New Jersey	28.5	13.7
New York	—	11.7
Connecticut	8.9	—
Rhode Island	8.1	—
Texas	—	10.6

Source: Bloomberg/CMO Passport

Portfolio managers can protect themselves by paying close attention to the GWAC and WAM and their dispersion before buying a secondary issue. Many commercially available mortgage computer systems allow portfolio managers to access this information. In the primary market, where CMOs are priced for forward settlement with TBA collateral, investors can specify GWAC and WAM ranges and establish formulas to adjust the final prices if the actual collateral falls outside of these ranges.

Geography

Geographic location of the underlying loans has a significant impact on prepayments. Regional economies have characteristics that impact the housing market in those areas. The strength of local real estate markets and regional economies determine the extent to which housing activity (turnovers, upgrades, equity take-out refinancings) contributes to prepayments across different geographic sectors.

In the late 1980s, for example, the Northeast was in recession and, real estate prices followed a general downward decline. The California economy, however, was fairly robust, and housing turnover was high. As a result, loans in the Northeast had slower prepayment speeds versus the national average, while loans in California had much faster speeds.

Exhibit 6 shows deal information for FNMA Trust 43 versus FNMA Trust 26 that illustrates this phenomenon. The slower speeds on Trust 43 versus Trust 26 can be explained by the differences in the geographical concentration of the collateral. As the exhibit shows, Trust 43 is backed predominantly by Northeast collateral, while Trust 26 has a large exposure to California.

Portfolio managers investing in mortgage products, particularly derivative mortgage products, should also be aware that geographic concentration of collateral will change over time. Collateral that is dispersed evenly between slow prepaying regions and fast prepaying regions will become skewed toward the slower regions as the faster pools are paid off. Also, particular regions themselves change from being slow to fast and vice versa; geographic conditions are dynamic.

For example, the Northeast, which historically prepaid slowly, is now speeding up as that region's economy recovers. California, on the other hand, which was among the fastest prepaying regions, has slowed down in response to the economic downturn in that state from 1991 to 1996. However, the California housing market seems to be heating up again in 1997 and 1998.

Portfolio managers should also be aware of regional property values and their effects on collateral characteristics. Defaults tend to be high where real estate markets are severely depressed. Because agency mortgage-backed securities are guaranteed as to principal, any defaults that occur on the underlying collateral are of course reflected as prepayments. Also, during times of falling interest rates, higher anticipated levels of refinancings may be offset by lack of equity in areas where housing prices have fallen dramatically. Similarly, equity takeout motivated refinancings may be unexpectedly high in areas where home prices have soared.

These circumstances must be taken into consideration when analyzing collateral because of the potential impact on prepayment speeds. What may be favorable prepayment conditions for a derivative mortgage product today may be discouraging tomorrow. Constant monitoring of local economic strength as well as the geographic diversity of the collateral over time is necessary for relative value assessment and management of derivative mortgage products.

WHOLE LOAN COLLATERAL

In the nonagency mortgage area the typical derivative mortgage product created is the CMO backed by whole loan collateral. Analysis of the collateral requires analyzing the additional element of credit risk, which, if managed correctly, can provide the opportunity for superior returns. A methodology for analyzing whole loan CMOs will allow the portfolio manager to identify securities that can offer value to the overall portfolio.

The largest issuers of whole loan CMO deals have been Pru-Home, Residential Funding Corporation (RFC), and GE Mortgate. Many types of loans are used as collateral for whole loan CMOs, including 30-year and 15-year mortgages, ARMs, TPMs, balloons, and RELOs.

The first step in analyzing whole loan CMOs is to make use of the credit ratings assigned to the various classes by the major credit agencies. These ratings provide a first cut at assessing whether the security in question offers value relative to similar bonds with the same rating.

In assigning these ratings, the agencies calculate potential losses in a variety of scenarios. These losses are calculated by multiplying the rate at which the mortgages are foreclosed by the dollar amount of the losses suffered on those loans.

In general terms, in order to receive a triple-A rating, a security must be able to withstand losses on collateral comparable to what would occur in an economic depression, while a double-A rating would require protection from a severe recession. Each rating agency has its own methodology for determining these standards, and within a given rating, there can be significant variability in collateral and credit support, which can have an important impact on value.

The analysis of whole loan CMOs should be undertaken according to a bottom-up approach. The portfolio manager should begin with a thorough analysis of the underlying collateral, which can be viewed as the raw material that goes into the finished product, the CMO. This should be followed by analysis of any internal credit enhancements built into the structure of the deal. These enhancements redistribute default risk on the collateral from one class to another. Next, the portfolio manager should evaluate any external, or third party, credit enhancements that are used to provide additional credit support to the overall deal.

Finally, the portfolio manager should look at any cash flow tranching that might be built into the CMO. This last step is the same as that used to analyze agency CMOs that will be discussed in the next chapter. In the case of whole loan CMOs, this is the least important consideration. An attractive CMO structure can be rendered irrelevant given poor collateral and inadequate credit support.

Whole loan CMO analysis must begin at the collateral level. There are many different components to be scrutinized.

Loan-to-Value Ratio

The weighted average loan-to-value (LTV) ratio is a highly reliable predictor of future mortgage defaults. Exhibit 7 shows the relationship between LTVs and default rates. LTVs over 80 exhibit markedly higher default rates. The portfolio manager should also pay close attention to second lien mortgages and the dispersion of LTVs among the loans.

For example, consider a deal backed by loans all with a weighted average LTV of 75. Compare this with a deal constituted of 50% 65 LTV loans and 50% 85 LTV loans, which also has a weighted average LTV of 75. The second deal has a much higher default exposure than the first deal because the loans are not cross-collateralized. The solid equity on the 65 LTV loans cannot make up for any losses that might occur on the 85 LTV loans. Clearly, a portfolio manager would prefer the first deal, all else equal.

In general, the lower the weighted average LTV, the better, but portfolio managers should pay close attention to the percent of loans with LTVs over 80. Additionally, investors should look for private mortgage insurance (PMI) on over 80 LTV loans.

Exhibit 7: Historical Default Rates by LTV

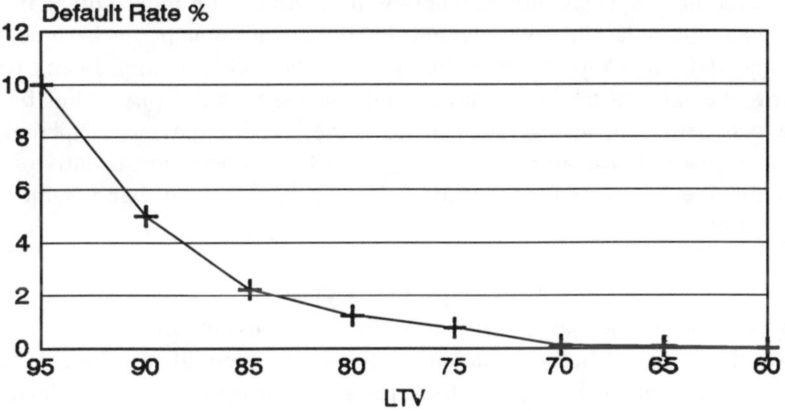

Source: Moody's Investors Service

On more seasoned securities changes in LTV can alter the overall credit quality of the collateral. Therefore, the investor should focus on current LTV whenever possible, as opposed to original LTV due to changes in housing values and second mortgage liens. This is especially true in a period of declining home prices, which can often wipe out any equity homeowners have built up and increase the likelihood of defaults. Current LTV information is available on a few specialized databases such as Mortgage Risk Assessment Corporation.

Delinquencies

For obvious reasons, delinquencies are highly correlated with defaults. Portfolio managers should pay close attention to delinquency rates, especially delinquencies over 90 days, as these often end in foreclosure.

Underwriting Standards

Portfolio managers should look for a high proportion of loans underwritten with a full set of supporting documents. Generally, deals backed by a significant percentage of loans with only partial or limited documentation reflect a lower quality of underwriting standards, which may reflect lower overall loan quality.

Loan Purpose

A high proportion of cash-out refinancings increases the default risk of a security. Portfolio managers should look for a deal backed primarily by purchase loans or refinance loans where all the funds are used for financing the home.

Seasoning

The amount of time for which the loans have been outstanding may have an important impact on default exposure. This is particularly true in areas that have experienced significant home price appreciation or depreciation. In areas of appreciated home prices, homeowners will have built up more equity in their homes and will be less likely to default. In contrast, if home prices have declined over time, defaults would be more likely, given the lack of equity. In an extreme scenario, the value of the home may actually be less than the outstanding balance of the loan. Seasoning also gives evidence of the degree of payment experience of the homeowners. For example, a homeowner who has been consistently on time with mortgage payments for ten years is less likely to default than a homeowner with no such track record.

Property Type

The type of properties backing the deal affects not just the likelihood of default but also the ability to liquidate the properties in the event of foreclosure. Therefore, portfolio managers should look for a high proportion of single-family homes, which default less often and are relatively easy to sell compared to condominiums and planned unit developments (PUDs).

Occupancy

Loans on nonowner-occupied property default at a much higher rate than homes where the borrower actually lives on the property. Therefore, a portfolio manager should discount securities of deals that have a high proportion of either investment property or vacation or second homes.

Geography

The geographic distribution of the collateral is important for security valuation. First, the overall distribution of whole loan collateral is somewhat different from that for agency collateral. For example, a much larger percentage of whole loan collateral is originated in California. Whole loan collateral consists primarily of jumbo loans which are excluded from agency securitization. Because of the higher home prices in California, more jumbo loans are originated there.

Thus, it is important to recognize the extent to which rising or falling home prices in a particular region affect possible default experience, especially in more seasoned collateral. Portfolio managers should also look for collateral from areas, including California, that have a high degree of economic diversification. This reduces exposure to economic downturns in one particular industry, similar to the recession that hit the oil industry in the Southwest during the 1980s.

Credit Enhancements

Once the collateral has been thoroughly analyzed, the portfolio manager should then take a close look at any internal or external forms of credit enhancement built into the structure of the deal. For a deal with generic collateral, the rating agencies have determined a minimum level of enhancement that is required to obtain each successive rating.

Internal credit enhancements are most often in the form of senior/subordi-nated structures, where the subordinated class provides protection to the senior class in the event of losses on the underlying collateral. In this case, the subordinated class will absorb all losses to the degree possible before the senior class is touched.

A relatively recent development in this area is referred to as a *super senior structure*, which creates two AAA bonds, one senior and one super senior; the senior bond acts as support for the super senior bond. Other forms of internal credit enhancement include cash reserve funds and excess servicing accounts, which provide a cash buffer to absorb initial

External credit enhancements come in the form of third party guarantees that provide for protection against losses up to a specified level. The most com-mon forms of external enhancements are letters of credit, pool insurance, and cor-porate guarantees.

In general, for the same level of credit support, a portfolio manager should prefer internal to external credit support. A deal with external support is subject to the credit risk of the third party guarantor. Should the third party be downgraded, the bonds in the deal could be subject to downgrade themselves. This can become a serious matter, as more issuers are placed on watch for possi-ble downgrade.

CONCLUSION

A systematic methodology will help investors analyze the collateral of an agency or nonagency derivative mortgage product. Analysis of all aspects of the collateral in a particular deal should precede evaluation of the structure itself.

Chapter 8

Structure Analysis for Derivative Mortgage Products

Investors must recognize that not all derivative mortgage products are created equal. Each deal is backed by different collateral. Moreover, each has its own structure. These two facts have several implications for portfolio managers.

First, managers in derivative mortgage products must develop their own assumptions regarding valuation inputs. Managers should have expectations about collateral prepayments, interest rates, rate volatilities, and prepayment volatilities.

Second, tranche descriptions should be taken to indicate only the generic cash flow characteristics of each security. Similarly named bonds from separate deals will react differently to market movements because of differences in their structures. Therefore, managers should understand the entire structure, not just the tranche they are buying.

Finally, managers should evaluate derivative mortgage products using variable prepayment assumptions. It is important to look at the deal as a whole as well as at each individual tranche to examine the cash flow variabilities. Managers must be able to identify interactions among different tranches and shifts in pay-down priority under variable prepayments.

This chapter is structured around examples that demonstrate the latter two points. While all three must be considered together, forecasting prepayments or interest rates is not addressed here.[1] The goal of the illustrations is to help portfolio managers better understand the dynamics of the structures of derivative mortgage products and to avoid unexpected changes in their holdings of these securities.

VARIABLE PREPAYMENT EFFECTS: IO/PO EXAMPLE

One of the fundamental assumptions a portfolio manager must make in purchasing a derivative mortgage product involves determining the prepayment speed at which to run the analysis. Many tranches are highly sensitive to even small changes in prepayments, so this assumption can be critical in ascertaining the value of a particular tranche.

---

[1] The factors considered in forecasting prepayments are discussed in Chapter 6.

Exhibit 1: Analysis of an IO/PO Trust

	Vector 1	Vector 2	500 PSA
IO Yield	8.16%	9.67%	9.45%
PO Yield	4.50%	4.35%	4.36%

Vector 1:	Vector 2:
700 × 6 Months	300 × 6 Months
300 × 6 Months	700 × 6 Months
500 Thereafter	500 Thereafter

Market convention dictates running a bond at a single static speed for life, but given that prepayment speeds vary over time for both economic and demographic reasons, using only one speed for life is unrealistic. Portfolio managers must incorporate variable prepayment assumptions into their analysis. The choice of prepayment vectors can have a significant impact on bond performance versus a comparable static speed.

This point is demonstrated in Exhibit 1 using the least complicated derivative mortgage structure, a straight IO/PO strip. The structure in this example is backed by generic FNMA 10%s. The bond is run assuming three different prepayment vectors. The first vector assumes that the collateral prepays at 700 PSA for the first six months, 300 PSA for the next six months, and 500 PSA thereafter. The second vector assumes 300 PSA for the first six months, 700 PSA for the next six months, and 500 PSA thereafter. The third vector assumes a constant prepayment speed of 500 PSA for life. These vectors represent realistic seasonal patterns of prepayments that vary according to whether the security was purchased in front of the fast summer months or the slow winter months.

Note that all three of the vectors result in a long-term prepayment speed of approximately 500 PSA. Because of this, one might expect minimal overall impact on the bond's cash flow yield[2] under each scenario. In fact, this is not the case. The yield on the IO class is highest under the second vector and lowest under the first vector, with the third vector falling in between the two.

The IO, which benefits from slower prepayments, clearly performs better when speeds are slower initially and then accelerate. The opposite is true for the PO class, which benefits from front-loaded prepayment vectors. This example shows that portfolio managers should use prepayment vectors carefully, and that they should be conscious of the effects of changes in these vectors on a bond's performance.

SHIFTING PAYDOWN PRIORITY: JUMP Z EXAMPLE

Exhibit 2 shows the structure of an old FHLMC deal. This deal serves as a good example for two reasons. It shows the importance of looking at the deal under

---

[2] The cash flow yield and its limitations as a measure of potential return are explained in Chapter 11. Throughout this chapter when we refer to "yield" we mean "cash flow yield."

variable prepayments and also demonstrates that a bond does not always react as might be expected given the tranche description.

This deal has eight different groups of bonds. There are two PAC sequences (I and II) with PAC IOs stripped off them, one TAC sequence, one support bond, one Z accrual bond, and one IOette.[3] The exhibit shows how the principal payments are allocated to the different tranches over time, given a static prepayment pricing speed of 155 PSA.

Further analysis shows that the accrual bond is a jump Z bond with a strike of 157 PSA.[4] A jump Z bond behaves like a normal Z bond as long as speeds remain below the strike speed. It has no cash flows until all other bonds in the structure have paid down. However, even one month of prepayments at 2 PSA in excess of the pricing speed will cause the accrual bond to "jump" and stay in front of most other bonds in priority of receiving principal until principal is paid off entirely.

Exhibit 3 shows the impact on the entire deal of varying the prepayments by 2 PSA for only one month. This clearly shows the value of looking at deals using variable prepayment expectations and not relying on static pricing speeds. This is especially true for those investing in the TAC and PAC II bonds in this deal who may be concerned with extension risk.

As illustrated in Exhibits 2 and 3, shifting principal payments will have an impact on many tranches of the deal. Exhibit 4 shows how these shifts will affect the average life on the PAC I and PAC II sequential pays. Two prepayment scenarios are shown: (1) a combination of only one month of 157 PSA, and 155 thereafter, and (2) the static pricing speed of 155 PSA. Notice that for the Type I PACs, the average life is unaffected across the scenarios because the prepayments fall within the preset PAC band.

Exhibit 2: FHLMC at Pricing Speed of 155 PSA

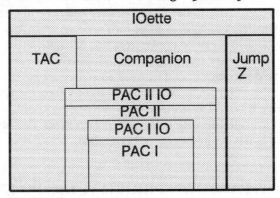

---

[3] An IOette is an IO tranche with a *nominal* (not notional) principal. Prior to a change in the REMIC provisions notional IOs could not be created in a CMO structure. Consequently, to comply with the REMIC requirements that specified every tranche must have some principal, IOettes were created.

[4] For more description of a jump Z, see Chapter 4.

Exhibit 3: FHLMC at 155 PSA with Jump Z
Jumped at 157 for 1 Month

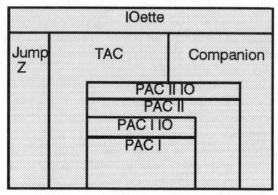

Exhibit 4: Average Life for FHLMC: PAC Is versus PAC IIs

	Jump/155	155
Type I PAC (95 - 310)	9.13	9.13
Type II PAC (135 - 295)	4.65	4.32

Source: CMO Passport

The average life changes, however, for the Type II PACs. Unlike the Type I PACs, whose paydown schedule is independent of the behavior of the jump Z bond, the Type II PACs will be impacted. When their amortization schedules were calculated, it was assumed that the accrual bond was last in principal priority. The Type II PACs would be paid off sooner, while the Z bond accrued. When the Z bond jumps to the front of the principal payment priority, however, it no longer accrues. The principal goes to the Z bondholders and is no longer available to the PAC II bonds, which lengthen in average life.

Two conclusions can be drawn from this example. First, variable prepayment analysis is critically important. Second, portfolio managers cannot rely solely on tranche descriptions to understand what they are buying. In other words, not all PACs or Z accrual bonds are the same. In this case, the PAC IIs have average life volatility at only 2 PSA faster than the pricing speed, while the jump Z exhibits a short average life with front-loaded cash flows. Clearly, the belief that similarly named bonds are homogeneous is a fallacy.

SHIFTING PAYDOWN PRIORITY: TAC PO EXAMPLE

Exhibit 5 shows another deal. This structure is backed by FNMA 9.5% POs; the pricing speed at issuance was 500 PSA. Like the first example, this one also illustrates the importance of creating a vector of variable prepayment speeds to analyze specific bonds.

Exhibit 5: FNMA 9.5% PO Deal

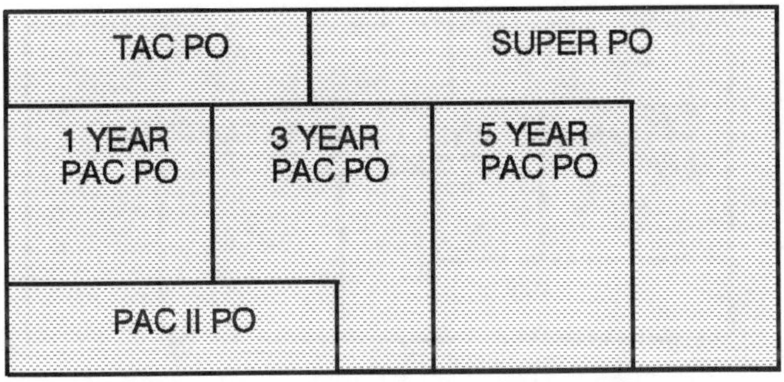

Exhibit 6: TAC PO Yield and Average Life Profile

PSA	750	500	375	275	Vector 1
WAL	0.62	1.00	3.93	8.09	4.23
Yield	22.40	13.90	3.44	1.62	3.61

Vector 1 = 700 × 2 Months; 900 × 4 Months; 500 × 6 Months; 350 thereafter

Source: CMO Passport

Exhibit 6 isolates the TAC PO in the deal. From the PO description, the portfolio manager would assume that higher prepayments would benefit the holder of this bond. Indeed, looking at the four static speeds, the bond exhibits the expected PO characteristics. At higher speeds, the average life decreases, and the yield increases. At lower speeds, the opposite occurs.

Vector 1, however, reiterates the importance of not relying on the generic categorization of bonds as indicative of future performance. At higher speeds, one would expect the average life of this bond to shorten, and the yield to rise. Yet temporarily fast prepayment speeds for one year do not necessarily benefit the 1-year average life TAC PO. Instead, if prepayments subsequently decline, the bond extends and the yield falls.

In this case, the structure is such that the paydown priority of the under-lying tranches shifts in a fashion similar to the jump Z example. Exhibit 7 shows how at speeds greater than 500 PSA, the TAC PO maintains its amortization schedule, and all excess prepayments go toward the paydown of the super PO. Therefore, the TAC PO does not receive the benefit of any fast prepayments until the super PO has expired. To compound the problem, when the super PO is paid off there are no longer any support bonds left to maintain the TAC schedule, and the bond extends dramatically with any slowdown of prepayment speeds.

The most important point to take from this example is not that a template with a fixed set of vectors for various coupons will suffice. Rather, portfolio man-agers need to analyze the changing performance of any deal in a wide range of environments.

Exhibit 7: FNMA 9.5% PO at PSA Greater Than 500 PSA

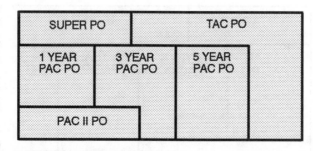

Empirical evidence shows us that actual prepayment experience is rarely static. Even for the most interest rate insensitive bonds, fluctuations in prepayment speeds will occur due to seasonality. Therefore, common sense dictates that derivative mortgage products be evaluated under conditions that reflect the portfolio manager's views on interest rates and prepayments.

Appropriate prepayment vectors will depend upon the collateral and should be altered according to changing market conditions. If, in fact, the investor is anticipating very fast prepayment speeds that extend well beyond the expiration of the super PO, the TAC PO could look very attractive.

LIMITATIONS OF PAC PROTECTION: PAC IO EXAMPLE

This example compares two bonds from a CMO deal that, on the surface, have similar characteristics. Both bonds are PAC IOs with similar collateral. Both are backed by FNMA 8%s with a gross weighted average coupon (GWAC) of 8.6%, and both have 6-year average lives within the PAC bands. In addition, the PAC bands on both bonds are similar.

All else equal, a portfolio manager would prefer the bond with the slightly wider PAC band, which gives more call protection. Yet analysis of both bonds under variable prepayment assumptions shows how much one bond can differ from the other, especially at speeds outside the PAC bands.

Exhibits 8 and 9 show a yield and average life matrix for these two PAC IOs. Inside the PAC bands, the bonds would have the same yield. Outside the PAC bands, the yields change. At 300 PSA the first bond declines by 262 basis points and shortens by 0.85 years, while the second bond declines by 577 basis points and shortens by one year. At 500 PSA, which can be viewed as a worst case scenario, the first bond declines by over 1,600 basis points and shortens by 2.7 years, while the second bond declines by over 3,200 basis points and shortens by three years. This divergence in performance is a function of the structure of each deal.

Exhibit 8: Yield and Average Life Matrix for FNMA 8% PAC IO — #1

PAC Band (100 - 230)	100 PSA - 230 PSA	300 PSA	500 PSA	600 x 6 Months 200 Thereafter	600 x 12 Months 200 Thereafter
Yield	10.001	7.378	-6.235	10.003	10.343
WAL	5.996	5.147	3.259	5.997	6.196

Source: CMO Passport

Exhibit 9: Yield and Average Life Matrix for FNMA 8% PAC IO — #2

PAC Band (115 - 240)	115 PSA - 240 PSA	300 PSA	500 PSA	600 x 6 Months 200 Thereafter	600 x 12 Months 200 Thereafter
Yield	10.000	4.229	-22.308	10.005	8.187
WAL	5.878	4.868	2.885	5.879	5.531

Source: CMO Passport

Analyzing the bonds under variable prepayment scenarios shows the exaggeration of this effect and the intrinsic strength of the PAC bands. Under a scenario of 600 PSA for six months and 200 PSA thereafter, both bonds perform identically. However, stretching the fast prepayments out to 12 months and then slowing them back down indicates that the first bond gains in yield by 34 basis points and extends by two months. The second bond falls in yield by 181 basis points and shortens by three months.

CONCLUSION

It should be clear how varied structures can be, and how important it is for portfolio managers to analyze bonds individually as well as within the context of the entire deal. New CMO structures will continue to be developed in the future. Portfolio managers with a flexible, yet disciplined, approach to analyzing these structures, will be able to identify value in the market. Most commercially available mortgage analysis systems allow portfolio managers to perform the type of evaluation discussed in this chapter.

Chapter 9

Leveraging MBS Portfolios: Repos, Dollar Rolls, and Mortgage Swaps

There are investment strategies in which a portfolio manager borrows funds to purchase mortgage-backed securities. The expectation of the portfolio manager is that the return earned by investing in the securities purchased with the borrowed funds will exceed the borrowing cost. When securities are to be purchased with the borrowed funds, the most common practice is to use the securities as collateral for the loan. In this chapter, we will look at the common types of collateralized loan involving mortgage-backed securities — repurchase agreements and dollar rolls. We also describe an instrument for synthetically leveraging a position — mortgage swaps.

REPURCHASE AGREEMENT

A *repurchase agreement* is the sale of a security with a commitment by the seller to buy the same security back from the purchaser at a specified price at a designated future date. The price at which the seller must subsequently repurchase the security for is called the *repurchase price* and the date that the security must be repurchased is called the *repurchase date*. Basically, a repurchase agreement is a collateralized loan, where the collateral is the security sold and subsequently repurchased. The agreement is best explained with an illustration.

Suppose a dealer has purchased $10 million of a particular MBS. The dealer can use the repurchase agreement or "repo" market to obtain financing. In the repo market the dealer can use the $10 million of the security as collateral for a loan. The term of the loan and the interest rate that the dealer agrees to pay are specified. The interest rate is called the *repo rate*. When the term of the loan is one day, it is called an *overnight repo*; a loan for more than one day is called a *term repo*. The transaction is referred to as a repurchase agreement because it calls for the sale of the security and its repurchase at a future date. Both the sale price and the repurchase price are specified in the agreement. The difference between the repurchase price and the sale price is the dollar interest cost of the loan.

Back to the dealer who needs to finance $10 million of an MBS that it purchased and plans to hold overnight. Suppose that a customer of the dealer has excess funds of $10 million. The dealer would agree to deliver ("sell") $10 million of the security to the customer for an amount determined by the repo rate and buy ("repurchase") the same MBS from the customer for $10 million the next day. Suppose that the overnight repo rate is 6.5%. Then, as will be explained below, the dealer would agree to deliver the MBS for $9,998,195 and repurchase the same security for $10 million the next day. The $1,805 difference between the "sale" price of $9,998,195 and the repurchase price of $10 million is the dollar interest on the financing.

The following formula is used to calculate the dollar interest on a repo transaction:

$$\text{Dollar interest} = (\text{Dollar principal}) \times (\text{Repo rate}) \times \text{Repo term}/360$$

Notice that the interest is computed on a 360-day basis. In our example, at a repo rate of 6.5% and a repo term of one day (overnight), the dollar interest is $1,805 as shown below:

$$\$9,998,195 \times 0.065 \times 1/360 = \$1,805$$

While the example illustrates financing a dealer's long position in the repo market, dealers can also use the market to cover a short position. For example, suppose a dealer sold $10 million of an MBS two weeks ago and must now cover the position — that is, deliver the securities. The dealer can do a *reverse repo* (agree to buy the securities and sell them back). Of course, the dealer eventually would have to buy the security in the market in order to cover its short position. In this case, the dealer is actually making a collateralized loan to its customer. The customer is then using the funds obtained from the collateralized loan to create leverage.

There is a good deal of Wall Street jargon describing repo transactions. To understand it, remember that one party is lending money and accepting a security as collateral for the loan; the other party is borrowing money and providing collateral to borrow. When someone lends securities in order to receive cash (i.e., borrow money), that party is said to be "reversing out" securities. A party that lends money with the security as collateral is said to be "reversing in" securities. The expressions "to repo securities" and "to do repo" are also used. The former means that someone is going to finance securities using the security as collateral; the latter means that the party is going to invest in a repo. Finally, the expressions "selling collateral" and "buying collateral" are used to describe a party financing a security with a repo on the one hand, and lending on the basis of collateral, on the other.

Most participants in the United States use the Public Securities Association (PSA) Master Repurchase Agreement. In the agreement, Paragraph 1 refers to one party as the "Seller" and the other party as the "Buyer." The Seller is the party delivering the security or equivalently borrowing funds. The "Buyer" is the party lending funds. The agreement covers all repurchase transactions where a party is the lender of funds and the other party is the borrower of funds.

Credit Risks

Despite the fact that there may be high-quality collateral underlying a repo transaction, both parties to the transaction are exposed to credit risk. Repos should be
carefully structured to reduce credit risk exposure. The amount lent should be less
than the market value of the security used as collateral, thereby providing the
lender with some cushion should the market value of the security decline. The
amount by which the market value of the security used as collateral exceeds the
value of the loan is called *repo margin* or simply margin. Margin is also referred
to as the "haircut." Repo margin is generally between 1% and 3%. For borrowers
of lower credit worthiness and/or when less liquid securities are used as collateral, the repo margin can be 10% or more.

   Another practice to limit credit risk is to mark the collateral to market on a
regular basis. (Marking a position to market means recording the value of a position at its market value.) When market value changes by a certain percentage, the
repo position is adjusted accordingly. The decline in market value below a specified
amount will result in a *margin deficit*. Paragraph 4(a) of The PSA Master Repurchase Agreement gives the "Seller" the option to cure the margin deficit by either
providing additional cash to the "Buyer" or by transferring "additional Securities
reasonably acceptable to Buyer." Suppose instead that the market value rises above
the amount required for margin. This results in a *margin excess*. In such instances,
Paragraph 4(b) grants the "Buyer" the option to give the "Seller" cash equal to the
amount of the margin excess or to transfer purchased securities to the "Seller."

   Since the PSA Master Repurchase Agreement covers all transactions
where a party is on one side of the transaction, the discussion of margin maintenance in Paragraph 4 is in terms of "the aggregate Market Value of all Purchased
Securities in which a particular party hereto is acting as Buyer" and "the aggregate
Buyer's Margin Account for all such Transactions." Thus, maintenance margin is
not looked at from an individual transaction or security perspective. However,
Paragraph 4(e) permits the "Buyer" and "Seller" to agree to override this provision
so as to apply the margin maintenance requirement to a single transaction.

   The price to be used to mark positions to market is defined in Paragraph
2(h) — definition of "Market Value." The price is one "obtained from a generally
recognized source agreed to by the parties or the most recent closing bid quotation from such a source." For complex securities that do not trade frequently,
there is difficulty in obtaining a price at which to mark a position to market.

   One concern in structuring a repo is delivery of the collateral to the lender.
The most obvious procedure is for the borrower to deliver the collateral to the
lender or to the cash lender's clearing agent. In such instances, the collateral is said
to be "delivered out." At the end of the repo term, the lender returns the collateral to
the borrower in exchange for the principal and interest payment. This procedure
may be too expensive though, particularly for short-term repos, because of costs
associated with delivering the collateral. The cost of delivery would be factored into
the transaction by a lower repo rate that the borrower would be willing to pay. The

risk of the lender not taking possession of the collateral is that the borrower may sell the security or use the same security as collateral for a repo with another party.

As an alternative to delivering out the collateral, the lender may agree to allow the borrower to hold the security in a segregated customer account. Of course, the lender still faces the risk that the borrower may use the collateral fraudulently by offering it as collateral for another repo transaction. If the borrower of the cash does not deliver out the collateral, but instead holds it, then the transaction is called a *hold-in-custody repo* (HIC repo). Despite the credit risk associated with a HIC repo, it is used in some transactions when the collateral is difficult to deliver (such as in whole loans) or the transaction amount is small and the lender of funds is comfortable with the reputation of the borrower of the cash.

Another method is for the borrower to deliver the collateral to the lender's custodial account at the borrower's clearing bank. The custodian then has possession of the collateral that it holds on behalf of the lender. This practice reduces the cost of delivery because it is merely a transfer within the borrower's clearing bank. If, for example, a dealer enters into an overnight repo with Customer A, the next day the collateral is transferred back to the dealer. The dealer can then enter into a repo with Customer B for, say, five days without having to redeliver the collateral. The clearing bank simply establishes a custodian account for Customer B and holds the collateral in that account. This specialized type of repo arrangement is called a *tri-party repo*. In fact, for some regulated institutions, for example, federal credit unions, this is the only type of repo arrangement permitted.

Determinants of the Repo Rate

There is not one repo rate. The rate varies from transaction to transaction depending on a variety of factors: quality of collateral, term of the repo, delivery requirement, and availability of collateral.

The higher the credit quality and liquidity of the collateral, the lower the repo rate. The effect of the term of the repo on the rate depends on the shape of the yield curve. If delivery of the collateral to the lender is required, the repo rate will be lower. If the collateral can be deposited with the bank of the borrower, a higher repo rate is paid.

The more difficult it is to obtain the collateral, the lower the repo rate. To understand why this is so, remember that the borrower (or equivalently the seller of the collateral) has a security that lenders of cash want, for whatever reason. Such collateral is referred to as *hot* or *special collateral*. (Collateral that does not have this characteristic is referred to as *general collateral*.) The party that needs the hot collateral will be willing to lend funds at a lower repo rate in order to obtain the collateral.

Hot (Special) Collateral and Arbitrage

A portfolio manager can use collateralized borrowing to create a leveraged position. In certain circumstances a borrower of funds via a repo transaction (or dollar roll discussed below) can generate an arbitrage opportunity. This occurs when it is possible to borrow funds at a lower rate than the rate that can be earned by reinvesting those funds.

Such opportunities arise when a portfolio includes particular securities that are hot or special and the portfolio manager can reinvest at a rate higher than the repo rate. For example, suppose that a portfolio manager has hot collateral in an MBS portfolio, that lenders of funds are willing to take as collateral for 30 days charging a repo rate of 4.5%. Suppose further that the portfolio manager can invest the funds in a 30-day Treasury bill (the maturity date being the same as the term of the repo) and earn 5%. Assuming that the repo is properly structured so that there is no credit risk, then the portfolio manager has locked in a spread of 50 basis points for 30 days. This is a pure arbitrage. The portfolio manager faces no risk. Of course, the portfolio manager is exposed to the risk that the security may decline in value, but this risk would exist as long as the portfolio manager intended to hold that security in the portfolio anyway.

"Risk" Arbitrage

The term arbitrage in its purest sense means that there is no risk in a strategy but that the strategy offers the opportunity to earn a positive return without investing any funds. The illustration that we just gave is an example of an arbitrage.

Unfortunately, some market participants use the term arbitrage in a more cavalier way. Even if there is risk in a strategy, so long as that risk is perceived to be small — small being a quantity defined by the user of the term — the term arbitrage is used. Some market participants will qualify the term by using the adjective "risk" — that is, risk arbitrage. In such a context, arbitrage with no risk is then referred to as "riskless arbitrage."

Let's look at a so-called risk arbitrage that has been used by some portfolio managers. Suppose that a portfolio manager buys an agency adjustable-rate passthrough security with a coupon rate that resets monthly based on the following coupon formula:

1-month LIBOR + 80 basis points   with a cap of 9%.

Suppose further that the portfolio manager can use these securities in a repo transaction in which: (1) a repo margin of 5% is required, (2) the term of the repo is one month, and (3) the repo rate is 1-month LIBOR plus 10 basis points. Also assume that the portfolio manager wishes to invest $1 million of his own funds in these securities. The portfolio manager can purchase $20 million in par value of these securities since only $1 million of equity is required. The amount borrowed would be $19 million. The leverage is 20-to-1. Thus, the portfolio manager realizes a spread of 70 basis points on the $19 million borrowed since LIBOR plus 80 basis points is earned in interest each month (coupon rate) and LIBOR plus 10 basis point is paid each month (repo rate).

This strategy is sometimes referred to as an "arbitrage." However, it has two risks. First, the price of the security may decline because the market may require a spread greater than 80 basis points over LIBOR. Thus, there is price risk if the security must be sold prior to maturity. Second, there is the risk that the cost of funds may exceed the cap. For example, if 1-month LIBOR is 9.9% in some month, the coupon rate on the security would be capped at 9%. However, the cost of funds would be 10% (1-month LIBOR plus 10 basis points), the borrowing cost not being capped. Thus, the dollar return and percent return for the month would be:

9% coupon on $20 million par value	$1,800,000
10% borrowing cost on $19 million	$1,900,000
Dollar return for month	−$100,000
Return on equity for month	−10%

The risk that the financing cost will exceed the coupon rate due to a restriction on the coupon rate is called *cap risk*.

DOLLAR ROLLS

In the MBS market, a special type of collateralized loan has developed because of the characteristics of these securities and the need of dealers to borrow these securities to cover short positions. This arrangement is called a *dollar roll* because the dealer is said to "roll in" securities borrowed and "roll out" securities when returning the securities to the portfolio manager.

As with a repo agreement, it is a collateralized loan that calls for the sale and repurchase of a security. Unlike a repo agreement, the dealer who borrows the securities need not return the identical security. That is, the dealer need only return a "substantially identical security." This means that the security returned by the dealer that borrows the security must match the coupon rate and security type (i.e., issuer and mortgage collateral). This provides flexibility to the dealer. In exchange for this flexibility, the dealer provides 100% financing. That is, there is no over collateralization or margin required. Moreover, the financing cost may be cheaper than in a repo because of this flexibility. Finally, unlike in a repo, the dealer keeps the coupon and any principal paid during the period of the loan.

Determination of the Financing Cost

Determination of the financing cost is not as simple as in a repo. The key elements in determining the financing cost assuming that the dealer is borrowing securities/lending cash are:

1. the sale price and the repurchase price
2. the amount of the coupon payment
3. the amount of the principal payments due to scheduled principal payments

4. the projected prepayments of the security sold (i.e., rolled in to the dealer)
5. the attributes of the substantially identical security that is returned (i.e., rolled out by the dealer)
6. the amount of under- or over-delivery permitted

Let's look at these elements. In a repo agreement, the repurchase price is greater than the sale price, the difference representing interest and is called the *drop*. In the case of a dollar roll, the repurchase price need not be greater than the sale price. In fact, in a positively sloped yield curve environment (i.e., long-term rates exceed short-term rates), the repurchase price will be less than the purchase price. The reason for this is the second element, the coupon payment. The dealer keeps the coupon payment.

The third and fourth elements involve principal repayments. The principal payments include scheduled principal and prepayments. As with the coupon payments, the dealer retains the principal payments during the period of the agreement. A gain will be realized by the dealer on any principal repayments if the security is purchased by the dealer at a discount and a loss if purchased at a premium. Because of prepayments, the principal that will be paid is unknown and, as will be seen, represents a risk in the determination of the financing cost.

The fifth element is another risk since the effective financing cost will depend on the attributes of the substantially identical security that the dealer will roll out (i.e., the security it will return to the lender of the securities) at the end of the agreement. Finally, as explained in Chapter 3, there are delivery tolerances. For example, PSA delivery standards permit under- or over-delivery of up to 1%. In a dollar roll, the portfolio manager and the dealer have the option to under or over-deliver: the portfolio manager when delivering the securities at the outset of the transaction and the dealer when returning the securities at the repurchase date.

To illustrate how the financing cost for a dollar roll is calculated, suppose that a portfolio manager enters into an agreement with a dealer in which it agrees to sell $10 million par value (i.e., unpaid aggregate balance) of Ginnie Mae 8s at 101⁷⁄₃₂ and repurchase substantially identical securities a month later at 101 (the repurchase price). The drop is therefore ⁷⁄₃₂. While under- or over-delivery is permitted, we will assume that $10 million par value will be delivered to the dealer by the portfolio manager and the same amount of par value will be returned to the portfolio manager by the dealer. Since the sale price is 101⁷⁄₃₂, the portfolio manager will receive in cash $10,121,875 (101.21875 × $10 million). At the repurchase date, the portfolio manager can repurchase substantially identical securities for 101 or $10,100,000. Therefore, the portfolio manager can sell the securities for $10,121,875 and buy them back for $10,100,000. The difference — which is the drop — is $21,875.

To offset this, the portfolio manager forfeits the coupon interest during the period of the agreement to the dealer. Since the coupon rate is 8%, the coupon interest forfeited is $66,666 (8% × $10 million/12). The dealer is also entitled to any principal repayments, both regularly scheduled and prepayments. Since the dealer purchases the securities from the portfolio manager at $101⁷/₃₂, any principal repayments will result in a loss of $1⁷/₃₂ per $100 of par value of principal repaid. From the portfolio manager's perspective, this is a benefit and effectively reduces the financing cost. While the regularly scheduled amount can be determined, prepayments must be projected based on some PSA speed. In our illustration, for simplicity let's assume that the regularly scheduled principal payment for the month is $6,500 and the prepayment is projected to be $20,000 based on some PSA speed. Since $1⁷/₃₂ is lost per $100 par value repaid, the dealer loses $79 due to the regularly scheduled principal payment (1⁷/₃₂ × $6,500/100) and $244 from prepayments (1⁷/₃₂ × $20,000/100).

The monthly financing cost is then:

Lost coupon interest		$66,666
Offsets		22,198
Drop (gain from repurchase)	21,875	
Principal repayment premium gained	323	
Due to regularly schedule principal	79	
Due to prepayments	244	
Total financing cost		$44,468
Monthly financing cost[1]		0.00439
Annual financing cost (monthly rate × 12)		5.27%

The financing cost as calculated, 5.27%, must be compared with alternative financing opportunities. For example, funds can be borrowed via a repo agreement using the same Ginnie Mae collateral. In comparing financing costs, it is important that the dollar amount of the cost be compared to the amount borrowed. For example, in our illustration we annualized the cost by multiplying the monthly rate by 12. The convention in other financing markets may be different for annualizing. Moreover, it is not proper to compare financing costs of other alternatives without giving recognition to the risks associated with a dollar roll.

Before discussing these risks, it is important to note that there is a factor that can reduce the financing cost. When a dollar roll is entered into, the agreement calls for delivery of the securities by the portfolio manager to the dealer at some specified future date. The sale price and repurchase price are established prior to the actual delivery. Since the agreement allows the portfolio manager to under-deliver by as much as 1%, the manager will do so if the market price of the securities has increased prior to the delivery date. Similarly, if the market price has fallen, the manager will over-deliver.

Because of the unusual nature of the dollar roll transaction as a collateralized borrowing vehicle, it is only possible to estimate the financing cost. From our illustration, it can be seen that when the transaction prices are above par value, then the speed of prepayments affects the financing cost. The maximum financing cost

---

[1] This cost is found by dividing the total financing cost of $44,468 by the proceeds received of $10,121,875.

can be determined by assuming no prepayments. In this case, the total financing cost would be $244 greater or $44,712. This increases the annual financing cost from 5.27% to 5.29%, or 2 basis points. In practice, a portfolio manager can perform sensitivity analysis to determine the effect of prepayments on the financing cost.

MORTGAGE SWAPS

While a dollar roll is an effective way of making a leveraged investment in a pool of mortgages, an alternative strategy is through a mortgage swap. A *mortgage swap* is an asset-based swap between two counterparties based on the cash flows and performance of a pool of mortgages. It is a synthetic leveraged position on mortgages. It is economically equivalent to borrowing funds at LIBOR (± a spread) and investing in a pool of mortgages.

As with other generic swaps, it has two legs: the mortgage leg and the funding leg. The mortgage leg replicates the cash flows of a pool of mortgages, including the monthly coupon payments, monthly regular principal amortization, monthly irregular principal prepayments, monthly gain (discounts) or loss (premiums) on paydown, and the price appreciation or depreciation on the remaining balance at the end of the holding period. The funding leg replicates the cost of carrying the investment, usually at LIBOR. The notional balance of the mortgage swap (both the mortgage leg and the funding leg) amortizes down simultaneously with actual prepayments on the specific pool of reference mortgages.

Mortgage Swap Structure

A typical mortgage swap has the following structure and terms:

Notional amount:	$100 million
Term:	3 years
Reference asset:	GNMA 8%, pool#*xxxxx*
Initial price:	103% of notional face
Reference pool WAC:	8.5%
Reference pool WAM:	330 months
Projected prepayment rate:	12% CPR, 1.06% SMM
Initial 1-month LIBOR:	5.50%
Receive:	Fixed coupon of 8% (30/360) on current balances of reference pool
Pay:	LIBOR flat (actual/360) on current value (current balance × initial price) of reference pool
Receive:	Principal paydown × discount if initial price is below par

Pay:	Principal paydown × premium if initial price is above par
Payment frequency:	Monthly
Expiration:	Cash settlement on difference between initial and market price on remaining balance

As the terms indicate, the portfolio manager will receive the full economics (coupon income, actual prepayment experience, gain or loss on paydown, and price appreciation or depreciation at the end of holding period) of owning $100 million of GNMA 8% pool#*xxxxx*, and will incur the variable cost of funding at LIBOR.

This transaction can be replicated by "dollar rolling" GNMA 8% on a monthly basis, except that the funding cost on the dollar roll is unknown from month to month. With a mortgage swap, the portfolio manager is locked into a funding rate for the rest of the term, although unwinding the swap may be more costly than unwinding a dollar roll.

Exhibit 1 shows the projected cash flows for this hypothetical mortgage swap.

Exhibit 1: Cash Flows of the Hypothetical Mortgage Swap

Structure:

Principal	100	WAC	8.500%	Coupon	8.00%	1-month LIBOR	5.50%
WAM	330	CPR	12.00%	SMM	1.060%	PSA	200%
MBS Price ⟹ 103.00		Ending Price ⟹ 101		MY	7.349%	BEY	7.463%

Term	Principal Payment	Net Interest	Prepayment	MBS Balance	Principal Settlement	LIBOR Flat	Swaps Cash Flow
1	0.0764	0.6667	1.0588	98.8648	–0.03406	0.4786	0.1540
2	0.0761	0.6591	1.0468	97.7419	–0.03369	0.4732	0.1522
3	0.0759	0.6516	1.0349	96.6311	–0.03332	0.4678	0.1505
4	0.0756	0.6442	1.0231	95.5324	–0.03296	0.4625	0.1487
5	0.0753	0.6369	1.0115	94.4456	–0.03260	0.4573	0.1470
6	0.0750	0.6296	1.0000	93.3706	–0.03225	0.4521	0.1453
7	0.0748	0.6225	0.9886	92.3072	–0.03190	0.4469	0.1437
8	0.0745	0.6154	0.9773	91.2554	–0.03155	0.4418	0.1420
9	0.0742	0.6084	0.9662	90.2149	–0.03121	0.4368	0.1404
10	0.0740	0.6014	0.9552	89.1858	–0.03087	0.4318	0.1388
11	0.0737	0.5946	0.9443	88.1679	–0.03054	0.4269	0.1372
12	0.0734	0.5878	0.9335	87.1609	–0.03021	0.4220	0.1356
13	0.0732	0.5811	0.9228	86.1650	–0.02988	0.4172	0.1340
14	0.0729	0.5744	0.9123	85.1798	–0.02956	0.4124	0.1325
15	0.0727	0.5679	0.9018	84.2053	–0.02923	0.4077	0.1309
16	0.0724	0.5614	0.8915	83.2414	–0.02892	0.4030	0.1294
17	0.0721	0.5549	0.8813	82.2880	–0.02860	0.3984	0.1279
18	0.0719	0.5486	0.8712	81.3449	–0.02829	0.3939	0.1264
19	0.0716	0.5423	0.8612	80.4121	–0.02798	0.3893	0.1250
20	0.0714	0.5361	0.8513	79.4894	–0.02768	0.3849	0.1235
21	0.0711	0.5299	0.8415	78.5768	–0.02738	0.3805	0.1221
22	0.0709	0.5238	0.8319	77.6741	–0.02708	0.3761	0.1207
23	0.0706	0.5178	0.8223	76.7812	–0.02679	0.3718	0.1193
24	0.0703	0.5119	0.8128	75.8980	–0.02650	0.3675	0.1179
25	0.0701	0.5060	0.8035	75.0244	–0.02621	0.3633	0.1165
26	0.0698	0.5002	0.7942	74.1603	–0.02592	0.3591	0.1151
27	0.0696	0.4944	0.7851	73.3056	–0.02564	0.3550	0.1138
28	0.0693	0.4887	0.7760	72.4603	–0.02536	0.3509	0.1125
29	0.0691	0.4831	0.7671	71.6241	–0.02509	0.3468	0.1112
30	0.0688	0.4775	0.7582	70.7970	–0.02481	0.3428	0.1099
31	0.0686	0.4720	0.7495	69.9790	–0.02454	0.3389	0.1086
32	0.0684	0.4665	0.7408	69.1699	–0.02427	0.3349	0.1073
33	0.0681	0.4611	0.7322	68.3695	–0.02401	0.3311	0.1060
34	0.0679	0.4558	0.7237	67.5779	–0.02375	0.3272	0.1048
35	0.0676	0.4505	0.7154	66.7949	–0.02349	0.3235	0.1036
36	0.0674	0.4453	0.7071	66.0205	–1.34364	0.3197	–1.2181

Chapter 10

Measuring the Interest Rate Risk of a Mortgage-Backed Security

A portfolio of mortgage-backed securities is exposed to interest rate risk. More specifically, a portfolio of mortgage-backed securities is exposed to both level risk and yield curve risk. *Level risk* refers to shifts in the interest rate level (normally parallel shifts of the yield curve) while *yield curve risk* refers to changes in the shape or slope of the curve (yield curve twists). It is essential for a portfolio manager to be able to quantify the exposure to changes in interest rates in order to control that risk. In this chapter we will discuss the measures used for quantifying the level and yield curve risk of an individual security and a portfolio.

MEASURING LEVEL RISK

The two measures of level risk used by managers are duration and convexity. Duration is a first approximation as to how the value of an individual security or the value of a portfolio when interest rates change. Convexity measures the change in the value of a security or portfolio that is not explained by duration.

Duration

The most obvious way to measure a bond's price sensitivity as a percentage of its current price to changes in interest rates is to change rates by a small number of basis points and calculate how its price will change. To do this, we introduce the following notation. Let

V_0 = initial value or price of the security
Δy = change in the yield of the security (in decimal)
V_- = the estimated value of the security if the yield is decreased by Δy
V_+ = the estimated value of the security if the yield is increased by Δy

There are two key points to keep in mind in the foregoing discussion. First, the change in yield referred to above is the same change in yield for all maturities. This assumption is commonly referred to as a *parallel yield curve shift assumption*. Thus, the foregoing discussion about the price sensitivity of a security to interest rate changes is limited to parallel shifts in the yield curve. Later in this chapter we will address the case where the yield curve shifts in a nonparallel manner.

Second, the notation refers to the estimated value of the security. This value is obtained from a valuation model. Consequently, *the resulting measure of the price sensitivity of a security to interest rates changes is only as good as the valuation model employed to obtain the estimated value of the security.*

Now let's focus on the measure of interest. We are interested in the percentage change in the price of a security when interest rates change. The percentage change in price per basis point change is found by dividing the percentage price change by the number of basis points (times 100). That is:

$$\frac{V_- - V_0}{V_0(\Delta y)100}$$

Similarly, the percentage change in price per basis point change for an increase in yield (Δy times 100) is:

$$\frac{V_0 - V_+}{V_0(\Delta y)100}$$

The percentage price change for an increase and decrease in interest rates is not the same. Consequently, the average percentage price change per basis point change in yield is calculated. This is done as follows:

$$\frac{1}{2}\left[\frac{V_- - V_0}{V_0(\Delta y)100} + \frac{V_0 - V_+}{V_0(\Delta y)100}\right]$$

or equivalently,

$$\frac{V_- - V_+}{2V_0(\Delta y)100}$$

The approximate percentage price change for a 100 basis point change in yield is found by multiplying the previous formula by 100. The name popularly used to refer to the approximate percentage price change is *duration*. Thus,

$$\text{Duration} = \frac{V_- - V_+}{2V_0(\Delta y)} \tag{1}$$

To illustrate this formula, consider the following option-free bond: a 9% 20-year bond trading to yield 6%. The initial price or value (V_0) is 134.6722. Suppose the yield is changed by 20 basis points. If the yield is decreased to 5.8%, the value of this bond (V_-) would be 137.5888. If the yield is increased to 6.2%, the value of this bond (V_+) would be 131.8439. Thus,

$$\begin{aligned}
\Delta y &= 0.002 \\
V_0 &= 134.6722 \\
V_- &= 137.5888 \\
V_+ &= 131.8439
\end{aligned}$$

Substituting these values into the duration formula,

$$\text{Duration} = \frac{137.5888 - 131.8439}{2(134.6722)(0.002)} = 10.66$$

*The duration of a security can be interpreted as the approximate percent-
age change in price for a 100 basis point parallel shift in the yield curve.* Thus a
bond with a duration of 4.8 will change by approximately 4.8% for a 100 basis
point parallel shift in the yield curve. For a 50 basis point parallel shift in the
yield curve, the bond's price will change by approximately 2.4%; for a 25 basis
point parallel shift in the yield curve, 1.2%, etc.

A manager who anticipates a decline in interest rates may decide to
extend (i.e., increase) the portfolio's duration. Suppose that the manager increases
the present portfolio duration of 4 to 6. This means that for a 100 basis point
change in interest rates, the portfolio will change by about 2% more than if the
portfolio duration was left unchanged.

Duration is related to percentage price change. However, for two bonds
with the same duration, the dollar price change will not be the same if their prices
are different. For example, consider two bonds, W and X. Suppose that both
bonds have a duration of 5, but that W is trading at par while X is trading at 90. A
100 basis point change for both bonds will change the price by approximately 5%.
This means a price change of $5 (5% times $100) for W and a price change of
$4.5 (5% times $90) for X.

The dollar price volatility of a bond can be measured by multiplying
modified duration by the full dollar price and the number of basis points (in decimal form). That is:

Dollar price change
= Modified duration × Dollar price × Yield change (in decimal)

The dollar price volatility for a 100 basis point change in yield is:

Dollar price change = Modified duration × Dollar price × 0.01

or equivalently,

Dollar price change = Modified duration × Dollar price/100

The dollar price change calculated using the above formula is called *dollar duration*. In some contexts, dollar duration refers to the price change for a 100
basis point change in yield. The dollar duration for any number of basis points
can be computed by scaling the dollar price change accordingly. For example, for
a 50 basis point change in yields, the dollar price change or dollar duration is:

Dollar price change = Modified duration × Dollar price/200

Modified Duration Versus Effective Duration

A popular form of duration that is used by practitioners is *modified duration*.
Modified duration is the approximate percentage change in a bond's price for a
100 basis point parallel shift in the yield curve *assuming that the bond's cash flow*

does not change when the yield curve shifts. What this means is that in calculating the values of V_- and V_+ in equation (1), the same cash flow used to calculate V_0 is used. Therefore, the change in the bond's price when the yield curve is shifted by a small number of basis points is due solely to discounting at the new yield level.

The assumption that the cash flow will not change when the yield curve shifts in a parallel fashion makes sense for option-free bonds such as noncallable Treasury securities. This is because the payments made by the U.S. Department of the Treasury to holders of its obligations do not change when the yield curve changes. However, the same cannot be said for mortgage-backed securities. For these securities, a change in yield will alter the expected cash flow because it will change expected prepayments.

The price/yield relationship for a mortgage passthrough security is shown in Exhibit 1. As yields in the market decline, the likelihood that yields will decline further so that the mortgagor will benefit from refinancing increases. The exact yield level at which investors begin to view the issue likely to be refinanced may not be known, but we do know that there is some level. In Exhibit 1, at yield levels below y^*, the price/yield relationship for the mortgage passthrough security departs from the price/yield relationship for the option-free bond. Suppose, for example, the market yield is such that an option-free bond would be selling for 110. However, since the passthrough is callable at par, investors would not pay 110. If they did and the passthrough is called, investors would receive 100 for a security they purchased for 110. Notice that for a range of yields below y^* in Exhibit 1, there is price compression — that is, there is limited price appreciation as yields decline. The portion of the passthrough price/yield relationship below y^* is said to be *negatively convex*.

Negative convexity means that the price appreciation will be less than the price depreciation for a large change in yield of a given number of basis points. An option- free bond is said to exhibit *positive convexity*; that is, the price appreciation will be greater than the price depreciation for a large change in yield. The price changes resulting from bonds exhibiting positive convexity and negative convexity are summarized below:

Change in interest rates	Absolute value of percentage price change for:	
	Positive convexity	Negative convexity
−100 basis points	X%	less than Y%
+100 basis points	less than X%	Y%

The valuation model that we describe in the next chapter takes into account how parallel shifts in the yield curve will affect the cash flow. Thus, when V_- and V_+ are the values produced from the valuation model, the resulting duration takes into account both the discounting at different interest rates and how the cash flow can change. When duration is calculated in this manner, it is referred to as *effective duration* or *option-adjusted duration*.

Exhibit 1: Price/Yield Relationship for an Option-Free Bond and a Mortgage Passthrough Security

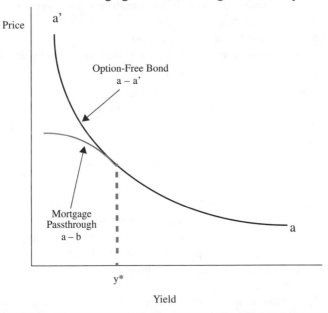

The difference between modified duration and effective duration for mortgage-backed securities can be quite dramatic. For example, for certain collateralized mortgage obligation tranches, the modified duration could be 7 and the effective duration 20! (We'll give one example of this later.) Thus, using modified duration as a measure of the price sensitivity of a mortgage-backed security to a parallel shift in the yield curve would be misleading. The more appropriate measure for a mortgage-backed security is effective duration.

The values used in the duration formula are those obtained from a valuation model. In the Monte Carlo simulation model for valuation described in the next chapter, the short-term rates are shifted up and down on each interest rate path and the security revalued.

Macaulay Duration It is worth comparing the modified duration formula presented above to that commonly found in the literature. It is common in the literature to find the following formula for modified duration:[1]

$$\frac{1}{(1 + \text{yield}/k)}\left[\frac{1\text{PVCF}_1 + 2\text{PVCF}_2 + 3\text{PVCF}_3 + ... + n\text{PVCF}_n}{k \times \text{Price}}\right] \quad (2)$$

where

---

[1] More specifically, this is the formula for modified duration for a bond on a coupon anniversary date.

k = number of periods, or payments, per year (e.g, $k = 2$ for semiannual pay bonds and $k = 12$ for monthly pay bonds)

n = number of periods until maturity (i.e., number of years to maturity times k)

yield   = yield to maturity of the bond

$PVCF_t$ = present value of the cash flow in period t discounted at the yield to maturity

The expression in the brackets of the modified duration formula given by equation (2) is a measure formulated in 1938 by Frederick Macaulay.[2] This measure is popularly referred to as *Macaulay duration*. Thus, modified duration is commonly expressed as:

$$\text{Modified duration} = \frac{\text{Macaulay duration}}{(1 + \text{yield}/k)}$$

The general formulation for duration as given by equation (1) provides a short-cut procedure for determining a bond's modified duration. Because it is easier to calculate the modified duration using the short-cut procedure, most vendors of analytical software will use equation (1) rather than equation (2) to reduce computation time. But, once again, it must be emphasized that modified duration is a flawed measure of a mortgage-backed security's price sensitivity to interest rate changes for a bond with an embedded option.

Market-Based Approaches to Duration Estimation

For mortgage-backed securities, two completely different approaches than modified and effective duration are used by some managers — empirical duration and coupon curve duration. The two approaches are based on observed market prices.

Empirical Duration Empirical duration, sometimes referred to as *implied duration*, is the sensitivity of a mortgage-backed security as estimated empirically from historical changes in prices and yields.[3] Regression analysis is used to estimate the relationship. More specifically, the relationship estimated is the percentage change in the price of the MBS of interest to the change in the general level of Treasury yields.

To obtain the empirical duration, Paul DeRossa, Laurie Goodman, and Mike Zazzarino suggest the following relationship be estimated using multiple regression analysis:[4]

---

[2] Frederick Macaulay, *Some Theoretical Problems Suggested by the Movement of Interest Rates, Bond Yields, and Stock Prices in the U.S. Since 1856* (New York: National Bureau of Economic Research, 1938).

[3] The first attempt to calculate empirical duration was by Scott M. Pinkus and Marie A. Chandoha, "The Relative Price Volatility of Mortgage Securities," *Journal of Portfolio Management* (Summer 1986), pp. 9-22.

[4] Paul DeRossa, Laurie Goodman, and Mike Zazzarino, "Duration Estimates on Mortgage-Backed Securities," *Journal of Portfolio Management* (Winter 1993), pp. 32-37.

Percentage change in price $= c + b_1 (\Delta y) + b_2 (P - 100) (\Delta y)$
$$+ b_3 [(P - 100)^2 (\Delta y) \text{ if } P > 100, \text{ otherwise } 0] + \text{error term}$$

where

P =   price (with par equal to 100)
Δy =   change in yield

and c, b_1, b_2, and b_3 are the parameters to be estimated. The inclusion of the second and third terms in the relationship is to allow for the price sensitivity to vary depending on the price level of the mortgages.

The expectation is that the parameter c would be equal to zero when the relationship is estimated. The expected sign of b_1 is negative. That is, there is an inverse relationship between yield changes and price changes. Finally, the terms b_2 and b_3 are expected to have a positive sign.

DeRossa, Goodman, and Zazzarino estimated the relationship using daily data for a 5-year period (11/19/86 to 11/18/91) for Ginnie Mae and Fannie Mae 8s, 9s, 10s, and 11s. The Treasury yield used was the 10-year Treasury, although they indicate that nearly identical results were realized if they used the 7-year Treasury. In all of their estimated regressions, all of the parameters had the expected sign.

Given the estimated relationship, the empirical duration for different coupons at different price levels can be found by dividing the estimated relationship by the change in yield. That is:

$$\text{Duration} = \frac{\text{Percentage change in price}}{\Delta y}$$

$$= c + b_1 + b_2(P - 100) + b_3[(P - 100)^2 \text{ if } P > 100, \text{ otherwise } 0]$$

For an MBS trading at par, P is 100, and the empirical duration is therefore b_1.

There are three advantages to the empirical duration approach.[5] First, the duration estimate does not rely on any theoretical formulas or analytical assumptions. Second, the estimation of the required parameters are easy to compute using regression analysis. Finally, the only inputs that are needed are a reliable price series and Treasury yield series.

There are disadvantages.[6] First, a reliable price series for the data may not be available. For example, there may be no price series available for a thinly traded mortgage derivative security or the prices may be matrix priced or model priced rather than actual transaction prices. Second, an empirical relationship does not impose a structure for the options embedded in an MBS and this can dis-

---

[5] See Bennett W. Golub, "Towards a New Approach to Measuring Mortgage Duration," Chapter 32 in Frank J. Fabozzi (ed.), *The Handbook of Mortgage-Backed Securities* (Chicago: Probus Publishing, 1995), p. 672.
[6] Golub, "Towards a New Approach to Measuring Mortgage Duration."

tort the empirical duration. Third, the price history may lag current market conditions. This may occur after a sharp and sustained shock to interest rates has been realized. Finally, the volatility of the spread to Treasury yields can distort how the price of an MBS reacts to yield changes.

Coupon Curve Duration The coupon curve duration is a second approach that uses market prices to estimate the duration of an MBS. It is an easier approach to duration estimation than empirical duration. The approach, first suggested by Douglas Breeden,[7] starts with the coupon curve of prices for similar MBS. By rolling up and down the coupon curve of prices, the duration can be obtained. Because of the way it is estimated, this approach to duration estimation was referred to by Breeden as the "roll-up, roll-down approach." The prices obtained from rolling up and rolling down the coupon curve of prices are substituted into the approximation formula for duration given by equation (1).

To illustrate this approach, let's use the coupon curve of prices for Ginnie Maes in June 1994. A portion of the coupon curve of prices for that month was as follows:

Coupon	Price
6%	85.19
7%	92.06
8%	98.38
9%	103.34
10%	107.28
11%	111.19

Suppose that the coupon curve duration for the 8s is sought. If the yield declines by 100 basis points, the assumption is that the price of the 8s will increase to the price of the 9s. Thus, the price will increase from 98.38 to 103.34. Similarly, if the yield increases by 100 basis points, the assumption is that the price of the 8s will decline to the price of the 7s (92.06). Using the duration formula given by equation (1), the corresponding values are:

$$V_0 = 98.38$$
$$V_- = 103.34$$
$$V_+ = 92.06$$
$$\Delta y = 0.01$$

The estimated duration based on the coupon curve is then:

$$\text{Duration} = \frac{103.34 - 92.06}{2(98.38)(0.01)} = 5.73$$

---

[7] Douglas Breeden, "Risk, Return, and Hedging of Fixed-Rate Mortgages," *Journal of Fixed Income* (September 1991), pp. 85-107.

Breeden of Smith Breeden Associates tested the coupon curve durations and found them to be relatively accurate.[8] Bennett Golub of BlackRock Financial Management reports a similar finding.[9]

While the advantages of the coupon curve duration are the simplicity of its calculation and the fact that current prices embody market expectations. The approach is limited to generic MBS and difficult to use for mortgage derivatives.

Duration of a Floating-Rate MBS

Our discussion of duration thus far has focused on fixed-rate mortgage-backed securities. There are floating-rate mortgage-backed products. These include adjustable-rate passthrough securities and floating-rate CMOs.

For a floating-rate security, or floater, the coupon rate is reset periodically based on a formula. In general the formula is as follows:

Reference rate + Spread

The spread is fixed over the floater's life. A floater will have a cap (i.e., a maximum coupon rate).

The change in the price of a fixed-rate security when market rates change is due to the fact that the security's coupon rate differs from the prevailing market rate. By contrast, for a floater, the coupon rate is reset periodically, reducing a floater's price sensitivity to changes in rates. A floater's price will change depending on three factors:

1. time remaining to the next coupon reset date
2. whether or no the cap is reached
3. whether the spread that the market wants changes

The longer the time to the next coupon reset date, the greater a floater's potential price fluctuation. Conversely, the less time to the next coupon reset date, the smaller the floater's potential price fluctuation. For a CMO floater whose coupon resets monthly, assuming the other two factors remain constant, the price will change by a minimal amount when rates change. That is, for such a floater, the duration is close to zero.

With respect to the cap, once the coupon rate as specified by the coupon reset formula rises above the cap, the floater then offers a below market coupon rate, and its price will decline. Turning to the spread, at the initial offering of a floater, the spread is market determined so that the security will trade near par. If after the initial offering the market requires a higher spread, the floater's price will decline to reflect the higher spread. For example, consider a CMO floater whose coupon reset formula is 1-month LIBOR plus a spread of 40 basis points. If market rates change such that investors want a spread of 50 basis points rather

---

[8] Breeden, "Risk, Return, and Hedging of Fixed-Rate Mortgages."
[9] Golub, "Towards a New Approach to Measuring Mortgage Duration," p. 673.

than 40 basis points, this floater would be offering a coupon rate that is 10 basis points below the market. As a result, the floater's price will decline.

Two measures have been developed to estimate the sensitivity of a floater to each component of the coupon reset formula. Specifically, *index duration* is a measure of the price sensitivity of a floater to changes in the reference rate (i.e., index) holding the spread constant. *Spread duration* measures a floater's price sensitivity to a change in the spread assuming that the reference rate is unchanged.

Duration of an Inverse Floater

As explained in Chapter 4, an inverse floater is a security whose coupon rate changes inversely with the change in the reference rate. It is created by splitting a fixed-rate security into a floater and an inverse floater.

The duration of an inverse floater will be a multiple of the duration of the collateral from which it is created. To see this, suppose that a 30-year fixed-rate CMO tranche with a market value of $100 million is split into a floater and an inverse floater with a market value of $80 million and $20, respectively. Assume also that the duration for the tranche from which the floater/inverse floater combination is created is 8. For a 100 basis point change in interest rates, the tranche's value will change by approximately 8% or $8 million (8% times $100 million). This means that by splitting the tranche's value, the combined change in value for a 100 basis change in rates for the floater and inverse floater must be $8 million. If the duration of the floater is small as just explained, this means that the entire $8 million change in value must come from the inverse floater. For this to occur, the duration of the inverse floater must be 40. That is, a duration of 40 will mean a 40% change in value of the inverse floater for a 100 basis point change in interest rates and a change in value of $8 million (40% times $20 million).

Notice from our illustration that the duration of the inverse floater is greater than the number of years to maturity of the collateral used to created the CMO itself. For example, the underlying mortgage pool may be 360 months (30 years). Portfolio managers who interpret duration in terms of years (i.e., Macaulay duration) are confused that a security can have a duration greater than the collateral from which it is created.

In general, assuming that the duration of the floater is close to zero, it can be shown that the duration of an inverse floater is:[10]

Duration of inverse floater

$$= (1 + L)(\text{Duration of collateral}) \times \frac{\text{Collateral price}}{\text{Inverse price}}$$

where L is the leverage of inverse floater.

---

[10] William Leach, "A Portfolio Manager's Perspective of Inverses and Inverse IOs," in Frank J. Fabozzi (ed.), *CMO Portfolio Management* (Summit, NJ: Frank J. Fabozzi Associates, 1994), p. 159.

Portfolio Duration

A portfolio's (effective) duration can be obtained by calculating the weighted average of the duration of the securities in the portfolio. The weight is the proportion of the portfolio that a security comprises. Mathematically, a portfolio's duration can be calculated as follows:

$$W_1 D_1 + W_2 D_2 + W_3 D_3 + ... + W_K D_K$$

where

W_i = market value of security i/market value of the portfolio
D_i = effective duration of security i
K = number of securities in the portfolio

To illustrate this calculation, consider the following three-security MBS portfolio:

Security	Par amount owned	Market value
1	$4 million	$4,000,000
2	5 million	4,231,375
3	1 million	1,378,586

The market value for this MBS portfolio is $9,609,961. The market price per $100 value and the duration of each bond are given below:

Security	Price	Yield to Maturity (%)	Duration
1	100.0000	10	3.86
2	84.6275	10	8.05
3	137.8590	10	9.17

In this illustration, K is equal to 3 and

$$W_1 = 4,000,000/9,609,961 = 0.416 \quad D_1 = 3.861$$

$$W_2 = 4,231,375/9,609,961 = 0.440 \quad D_2 = 8.047$$

$$W_3 = 1,378,586/9,609,961 = 0.144 \quad D_3 = 9.168$$

The portfolio's duration is

$$0.416 (3.86) + 0.440 (8.05) + 0.144 (9.17) = 6.47$$

A portfolio duration of 6.47 means that for a 100 basis change in the yield for *all* three securities, the market value of the portfolio will change by approximately 6.47%. But keep in mind, the yield on all three bonds must change by 100 basis points for the duration measure to be meaningful. This is a critical assumption and its importance cannot be overemphasized. We shall return to this point later in this chapter when we discuss yield curve risk measures.

Similarly, the dollar duration of a portfolio can be obtained by calculating the weighted average of the dollar duration of the bonds in the portfolio.

Portfolio Duration When There is a Borrowing In the previous chapter we discussed the use of various vehicles that a manager can use to create leverage by borrowing funds. When funds are borrowed, the portfolio's value is equal to:[11]

Portfolio's value = Market value of the assets – Value of the liabilities

The portfolio's duration is then found as follows. First, compute the dollar duration of the assets and the liabilities for a 50 basis point rise in rates. Second, calculate the following ratio:

$$\frac{\text{Change in value of assets} - \text{Change in value of liabilities}}{\text{Market value of the assets} - \text{Value of the liabilities}} \times 200$$

The duration of the liabilities is the sensitivity of the liabilities to a change in rates. Suppose that the borrowing is short-term, say one month. Then the duration of the liabilities will be close to zero based on the same arguments given above as to why the duration of a floater with a one month reset will be close to zero. Thus, the change in the value of the liabilities for a 50 basis point change in rates will be close to zero.

Consider a manager with $10 million to invest. Suppose the manager decides to invest in one mortgage-backed security with a duration of 4. The duration of the portfolio is then 4. Suppose instead that the manager borrows an additional $40 million in a reverse repo transaction and buys $50 million of the same mortgage-backed security with a duration of 4. The manager uses the $50 million of the security purchased as collateral for the reverse repo borrowing and assume the term of the repo agreement is 30 days. Suppose interest rates rise by 50 basis points. The change in the value of the assets is determined as follows. A 50 basis point increase will decrease the value of the $50 million of the asset by $1 million $(0.5 \times 4\% \times \$50$ million$)$. As noted above, the change in the value of the liabilities is approximately zero. Therefore, the duration of the portfolio is

$$\frac{\$1 \text{ million} - 0}{\$50 \text{ million} - \$40 \text{ million}} \times 200 = 20$$

The duration for the portfolio is 20. Notice that the duration of the portfolio is five times the duration of the asset whose duration is 4.

Convexity Measure

The duration measure indicates that regardless of whether the yield curve is shifted up or down, the approximate percentage price change is the same. However, this does not agree with the properties of a bond's price volatility. Specifically, while for small changes in yield the percentage price change will be the

---

[11] In the case of a mutual fund, the portfolio's duration is the duration of the net asset value.

same for an increase or decrease in yield, for large changes in yield this is not true. This suggests that duration is only a good approximation of the percentage price change for a small change in yield.

To see this, consider a 9% 20-year bond selling to yield 6% with a duration of 10.66. If yields increase instantaneously by 10 basis points (from 6% to 6.1%), then using duration the approximate percentage price change would be −1.066% (−10.66% divided by 10, remembering that duration is the percentage price change for a 100 basis point change in yield). The actual percentage price change is −1.07%. Similarly, if the yield decreases instantaneously by 10 basis points (from 6.00% to 5.90%), then the percentage price change would be +1.066%. The actual percentage price change would be +1.07%. This example illustrates that for small changes in yield, duration does an excellent job of approximating the percentage price change

Instead of a small change in yield, let's assume that yields increase by 200 basis points, from 6% to 8%. The approximate percentage price change is −21.32% (−10.66% times 2). The actual percentage price change is only −18.40%. Moreover, if the yield decreases by 200 basis points from 6% to 4%, the approximate percentage price change based on duration would be +21.32%, compared to an actual percentage price change of +25.04%. Thus, the approximation is not as good for a 200 basis point change in yield.

Duration is in fact a first approximation for a small parallel shift in the yield curve. The approximation can be improved by using a second approximation. This approximation is referred to as "convexity." The use of this term in the industry is unfortunate since the term convexity is also used to describe the shape or curvature of the price/yield relationship. The *convexity measure* of a security can be used to approximate the change in price that is not explained by duration.

The convexity measure of any security can be approximated using the following formula:

$$\text{Convexity measure} = \frac{V_+ + V_- - 2V_0}{2V_0(\Delta y)^2} \tag{3}$$

where the notation is the same as used earlier for duration [equation (1)].

For our hypothetical 9% 20-year bond selling to yield 6%, we know that for a 20-basis-point-change in yield

$$\Delta y = 0.002$$
$$V_0 = 134.6722$$
$$V_- = 137.5888$$
$$V_+ = 131.8439$$

Substituting these values into the convexity measure formula,

$$\text{Convexity measure} = \frac{137.5888 + 131.8439 - 2(134.6722)}{2(134.6722)(0.002)^2} = 81.96$$

Given the convexity measure, the approximate percentage price change adjustment due to the security's convexity (i.e., the percentage price change not explained by duration) is:

Convexity measure $\times (\Delta y)^2$

For example, for the 9% coupon bond maturing in 20 years, the convexity adjustment to the percentage price change if the yield increases from 6% to 8% is

$$81.96 \times (0.02)^2 = 0.0328 = 3.28\%$$

If the yield decreases from 6% to 4%, the convexity adjustment to the approximate percentage price change would also be 3.28%.

The approximate percentage price change based on duration and the convexity adjustment is found by simply adding the two estimates. So, for example, if yields change from 6% to 8%, the estimated percentage price change would be:

Estimated change approximated by duration	=	−21.32%
Estimated adjustment for convexity	=	+3.28%
Total estimated percentage price change	=	−18.04%

The actual percentage price change is −18.40%.

For a decrease of 200 basis points, from 6% to 4%, the approximate percentage price change would be as follows:

Estimated change approximated by duration	=	+21.32%
Estimated adjustment for convexity	=	+3.28%
Total estimated percentage price change	=	+24.60%

The actual percentage price change is +25.04%. Thus, duration with the convexity adjustment does a good job of estimating the sensitivity of a security's price change to large changes in yield.

Notice also that when the convexity measure is positive, we have the situation described earlier that the gain is greater than the loss for a given large change in yield. We can see this in the example above. However, if the convexity measure is negative, we have the situation where the loss will be greater than the gain. For example, suppose that a mortgage-backed security has an effective duration of 4 and a convexity measure of −30. This means that the approximate percentage price change for a 200 basis point change is 8%. The convexity adjustment for a 200 basis point change in yields is then

$$-30 \times (0.02)^2 = -0.012 = -1.2\%$$

Therefore, the approximate percentage price change after adjusting for convexity is:

Estimated change approximated by duration = −8.0%
Estimated adjustment for convexity   = −1.2%
Total estimated percentage price change   = −9.2%

For a decrease of 200 basis points, the approximate percentage price change would be as follows:

Estimated change approximated by duration = +8.0%
Estimated adjustment for convexity   = −1.2%
Total estimated percentage price change   = +6.8%

Notice that the loss is greater than the gain — a property called negative convexity that we discussed earlier.

Modified Convexity and Effective Convexity

The prices used in equation (3) to calculate convexity can be obtained by either assuming that when the yield curve shifts in a parallel way the expected cash flow does not change or it does change. In the former case, the resulting convexity is referred to as modified convexity. Actually, in the industry, convexity is not qualified by the adjective "modified." Thus, in practice the term convexity typically means the cash flow is assumed not to change when yields change. *Effective convexity*, in contrast, assumes that the cash flow does change when yields change. This is the same distinction made for duration.

As with duration, for mortgage-backed securities there can be quite a difference between the calculated modified convexity and effective convexity. In fact, for all option-free bonds, either convexity measure will have a positive value. For mortgage-backed securities, the calculated effective convexity can be negative when the calculated modified convexity gives a positive value.

YIELD CURVE RISK

The duration and convexity measures are measures of level risk. That is, if all Treasury rates shifted up or down by the same number of basis points, these measures do a good job of approximating the exposure of a portfolio to a rate change. However, yield curves do not change in a parallel fashion. Consequently, two MBS portfolios with the same duration can perform quite differently when the yield curve shifts in a nonparallel fashion. In fact, two MBS can have the same duration and Portfolio 1 can have a greater convexity than Portfolio 2, but the former portfolio can underperform the latter under certain types of shift in the yield curve despite its better convexity.

Several approaches have been suggested for measuring the exposure to a shift in the yield curve. A basic approach used is to shift the yield in some nonparallel fashion and assess the impact on the value of the security or the value of a portfolio.[12] However, the most popular approach to measuring yield curve risk is to change the yield for a particular maturity of the yield curve and determine the sensitivity of a security or portfolio to this change holding all other yields constant. The sensitivity of the change in value to a particular change in yield is called *rate duration*. There is a rate duration for every point on the yield curve. Consequently, there is not one rate duration, but a profile of rate durations representing each maturity on the yield curve. The total change in value if all rates change by the same number of basis points is simply the duration of a security or portfolio to a change in the level of rates. That is, it is the measure of level risk for a parallel shift in the yield curve discussed in the previous section.

This approach was first suggested by Donald Chambers and Willard Carleton in 1988 who called it "duration vectors."[13] Robert Reitano suggested a similar approach in a series of papers and called the durations "partial durations."[14] The most popular version of this approach is that developed by Thomas Ho in 1992.[15]

Ho's approach focuses on 11 key maturities of the spot rate curve. The rate durations are called *key rate durations*. The specific maturities on the spot rate curve for which a key rate duration is measured are 3 months, 1 year, 2 years, 3 years, 5 years, 7 years, 10 years, 15 years, 20 years, 25 years, and 30 years. Changes in rates between any two key rates are calculated using a linear interpolation.

The impact of any type of yield curve shift can be quantified using key rate durations. A level shift can be quantified by changing all key rates by the same number of basis points and determining based on the corresponding key rate durations the affect on the value of a portfolio. The impact of a steepening of the yield curve can be found by (1) decreasing the key rates at the short end of the yield curve and determining the change in the portfolio value using the corresponding key rate durations, and (2) increasing the key rates at the long end of the yield curve and determining the change in the portfolio value using the corresponding key rate durations.

The key rate durations can be computed for an individual security or for a portfolio. At the security level, Ho computed the key rate durations for a Ginnie Mae 30-year 10% passthrough and a PO and IO created from Ginnie Mae passthroughs. Exhibit 2 shows the key rate duration profile for the passthroughs and Exhibit 3 shows the key rate duration profiles for the PO and IO. At the time of Ho's analysis, the Ginnie Mae passthrough was a new issue.

---

[12] For two examples of this approach, see Thomas E. Klaffky, YY. Ma, and Ardavan Nozari, "Managing Yield Curve Exposure: Introducing Reshaping Durations," *Journal of Fixed Income* (December 1992), pp. 5-15, and Michael P. Schumacher, Daniel C. Dektar, and Frank J. Fabozzi, "Yield Curve Risk of CMO Bonds," *CMO Portfolio Management.*

[13] Donald Chambers and Willard Carleton, "A Generalized Approach to Duration," *Research in Finance* 7(1988).

[14] See, for example, Robert R. Reitano, "Non-Parallel Yield Curve Shifts and Durational Leverage," *Journal of Portfolio Management* (Summer 1990), pp. 62-67, and "A Multivariate Approach to Duration Analysis," *ARCH* 2(1989).

[15] Thomas S.Y. Ho, "Key Rate Durations: Measures of Interest Rate Risks," *Journal of Fixed Income* (September 1992), pp. 29-44.

Exhibit 2: Key Rate Duration Profile for a 30-Year Ginnie Mae Passthrough

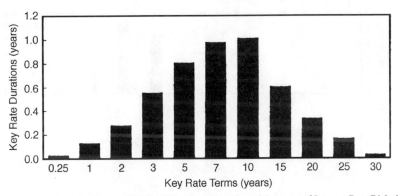

Source: Exhibit 12 in Thomas S.Y. Ho, "Key Rate Durations: Measures of Interest Rate Risks," *Journal of Fixed Income* (September 1992), p. 38.
This copyrighted material is reprinted with permission from Institutional Investor, Inc.
Journal of Fixed Income, 488 Madison Avenue, New York, NY 10022.

From Exhibit 2 it can be seen that the new issue passthrough exhibits a bell-shaped curve with the peak of the curve between 5 and 15 years. Adding up the key rate durations from 5 to 15 years (i.e., the 5-year, 7-year, 10-year, and 15-year key rate durations) indicates that of the total interest rate exposure, about 70% is within this maturity range. That is, the effective duration alone masks the fact that the interest rate exposure for this passthrough is due to yield changes in the 5-year to 15-year maturity range.

Let's look at the PO. A PO will have a high positive duration. From the key rate duration profile for the PO shown in Exhibit 3 it can be seen that the key rate durations are negative up to year 7. Thereafter, the key rate durations are positive and have a high value. While the total risk exposure (i.e., effective duration) may be positive, there is exposure to yield curve risk. For example, the key rate durations suggest that if the long end of the yield curve is unchanged, but the short end of the yield curve (up to year 7) decreases, the PO's value will decline despite an effective duration that is positive.

IOs have a high negative duration. However, from the key rate duration profile in Exhibit 3 it can be seen that the key rate durations are positive up to year 10 and then takes on high negative values. As with the PO, this security is highly suspectable to how the yield curve changes.

From the key rate duration of each security in the portfolio, a key rate duration for the portfolio can be computed. A profile of the portfolio's key rate durations then shows the exposure of the portfolio to a change in the shape of the yield curve.

Exhibit 3: Key Rate Duration Profiles for a PO and an IO for Current Coupon Ginnie Mae

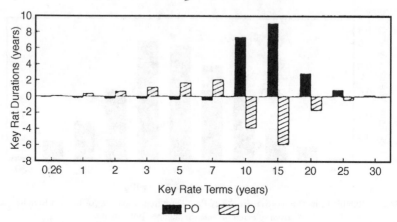

Source: Exhibit 13 in Thomas S.Y. Ho, "Key Rate Durations: Measures of Interest Rate Risks," *Journal of Fixed Income* (September 1992), p. 38.
This copyrighted material is reprinted with permission from Institutional Investor, Inc.
Journal of Fixed Income, 488 Madison Avenue, New York, NY 10022.

Chapter 11

OAS Analysis Using Monte Carlo Simulation

In this chapter we show how to value mortgage-backed securities. We begin by reviewing the conventional framework — static cash flow yield analysis — and its limitations. Then we discuss a more advanced technology, the option-adjusted spread analysis. The static cash flow yield methodology is the simplest of the two valuation technologies to apply, although it may offer little insight into the relative value of a mortgage-backed security. The option-adjusted spread technology while far superior in valuation is based on assumptions that must be recognized by the manager and the sensitivity of the security's value to changes in those assumptions must be tested.

STATIC CASH FLOW YIELD ANALYSIS

The yield on any financial instrument is the interest rate that makes the present value of the expected cash flow equal to its market price plus accrued interest. For mortgage-backed securities, the yield calculated is called a *cash flow yield*. The problem in calculating the cash flow yield of a mortgage-backed security is that because of prepayments the cash flow is unknown. Consequently, to determine a cash flow yield some assumption about the prepayment rate must be made.

The cash flow for a mortgage-backed security is typically monthly. The convention is to compare the yield on a mortgage-backed security to that of a Treasury coupon security by calculating the MBS's *bond-equivalent yield*. The bond-equivalent yield for a Treasury coupon security is found by doubling the semiannual yield. However, it is incorrect to do this for a mortgage-backed security because the investor has the opportunity to generate greater interest by reinvesting the more frequent cash flows. The market practice is to calculate a yield so as to make it comparable to the yield to maturity on a bond-equivalent yield basis. The formula for annualizing the monthly cash flow yield for a mortgage-backed security is as follows:

$$\text{Bond-equivalent yield} = 2[(1 + i_M)^6 - 1]$$

where i_M is the monthly interest rate that will equate the present value of the projected monthly cash flow equal to the market price (plus accrued interest) of the mortgage-backed security.

All yield measures suffer from problems that limit their use in assessing a security's potential return. The yield to maturity has two major shortcomings as a measure of a bond's potential return. To realize the stated yield to maturity, the investor must: (1) reinvest the coupon payments at a rate equal to the yield to maturity, and (2) hold the bond to the maturity date. The reinvestment of the coupon payments is critical and for long-term bonds can be as much as 80% of the bond's return. The risk of having to reinvest the interest payments at less than the computed yield is called *reinvestment risk*. The risk associated with having to sell the security prior to the maturity date is called *interest rate risk* and in Chapter 9 we discussed how to quantify that risk.

These shortcomings are equally applicable to the cash flow yield measure: (1) the projected cash flows are assumed to be reinvested at the cash flow yield, and (2) the mortgage-backed security is assumed to be held until the final payout based on some prepayment assumption. The importance of reinvestment risk, the risk that the cash flow will have to be reinvested at a rate lower than the cash flow yield, is particularly important for many mortgage-backed securities, because payments are monthly and both interest and principal must be reinvested. Moreover, an additional assumption is that the projected cash flow is actually realized. If the prepayment experience is different from the prepayment rate assumed, the cash flow yield will not be realized.

Given the computed cash flow yield and the average life for a mortgage-backed security based on some prepayment assumption, the next step is to compare the yield to the yield for a comparable Treasury security. "Comparable" is typically defined as a Treasury security with the same maturity as the average life of the mortgage-backed security. The difference between the cash flow yield and the yield on a comparable Treasury security is called a *nominal spread.*

Unfortunately, it is the nominal spread that some managers will use as a measure of relative value. However, this spread masks the fact that a portion of the nominal spread is compensation for accepting prepayment risk. For example, CMO support tranches were offered at large nominal spreads. However, the spread embodied the substantial prepayment risk associated with support tranches. The manager who bought solely on the basis of nominal spread — dubbed a "yield hog" — failed to determine whether that nominal spread offered potential compensation given the substantial prepayment risk faced by the holder of a support tranche.

Instead of nominal spread, managers need a measure that indicates the potential compensation after adjusting for prepayment risk. This measure is called the *option- adjusted spread* (OAS). We will now explain how this measure is computed.

VALUATION USING MONTE CARLO SIMULATION

In fixed income valuation modeling, there are two methodologies commonly used to value securities with embedded options — the binomial model and the Monte Carlo model. The latter model involves simulating a sufficiently large number of potential interest rate paths in order to assess the value of a security along these different paths. This model is the most flexible of the two valuation methodologies for valuing interest rate sensitive instruments where the history of interest rates is important. Mortgage-backed securities are commonly valued using this model. As explained below, a byproduct of a valuation model is the OAS.

The binomial model is used to value callable agency debentures and corporate bonds.[1] This valuation model accommodates securities in which the decision to exercise a call option is not dependent on how interest rates evolved over time. That is, the decision of an issuer to call a bond will depend on the level of the rate at which the issue can be refunded relative to the issue's coupon rate, and not the path interest rates took to get to that rate. In contrast, there are fixed income securities and derivative instruments for which the periodic cash flows are interest rate path-dependent. This means that the cash flow received in one period is determined not only by the current interest rate level, but also by the path that interest rates took to get to the current level.

In the case of passthrough securities, prepayments are interest rate path-dependent because this month's prepayment rate depends on whether there have been prior opportunities to refinance since the underlying mortgages were originated — the phenomenon we referred to earlier in this book as prepayment burnout. Moreover, in the case of adjustable-rate mortgage passthroughs (ARMs), prepayments are not only path-dependent but the periodic coupon rate depends on the history of the reference rate upon which the coupon rate is determined. This is because ARMs have periodic caps and floors as well as a lifetime cap and floor. For example, an ARM whose coupon rate resets annually could have the following restriction on the coupon rate: (1) the rate cannot change by more than 200 basis points each year and (2) the rate cannot be more than 500 basis points from the initial coupon rate.

Pools of passthroughs are used as collateral for the creation of CMOs. Consequently, there are typically two sources of path dependency in a CMO tranche's cash flows. First, the collateral prepayments are path-dependent as discussed above. Second, the cash flow to be received in the current month by a CMO tranche depends on the outstanding balances of the other tranches in the deal. Thus, we need the history of prepayments to calculate these balances.

Conceptually, the valuation of passthroughs using the Monte Carlo model is simple. In practice, however, it is very complex. The simulation involves generating a set of cash flows based on simulated future mortgage refinancing rates, which in turn imply simulated prepayment rates.

Valuation modeling for CMOs is similar to valuation modeling for passthroughs, although the difficulties are amplified because the issuer has sliced and diced both the prepayment risk and the interest rate risk into tranches. The sensitivity of the passthroughs comprising the collateral to these two risks is not

---

[1] For an explanation of this valuation model, see Chapter 6 and 7 in Frank J. Fabozzi, *Valuation of Fixed Income Securities and Derivatives: Third Edition* (New Hope, PA: Frank J. Fabozzi Associates, 1998).

transmitted equally to every tranche. Some of the tranches wind up more sensitive to prepayment risk and interest rate risk than the collateral, while some of them are much less sensitive.

The objective is to figure out how the value of the collateral gets transmitted to the CMO tranches. More specifically, the objective is to find out where the value goes and where the risk goes so that one can identify the tranches with low risk and high value: the tranches a manager wants to consider for purchase. The good news is that this combination usually exists in every deal. The bad news is that in every deal there are usually tranches with low value and high risk, that managers want to avoid purchasing.

Simulating Interest Rate Paths and Cash Flows

The typical model that Wall Street firms and commercial vendors use to generate these random interest rate paths takes as input today's term structure of interest rates and a volatility assumption. The term structure of interest rates is the theoretical spot rate (or zero coupon) curve implied by today's Treasury securities. The volatility assumption determines the dispersion of future interest rates in the simulation. The simulations should be calibrated so that the average simulated price of a zero-coupon Treasury bond equals today's actual price.

Some models use the on-the-run Treasury issues in the calibration process. Other dealers, such as Lehman Brothers, use off-the-run Treasury issues. The argument for using off-the-run Treasury issues is that the price/yield of on-the-run Treasury issues will use not reflect their true economic value because the market price reflects their value for financing purposes (i.e., an issue may be on special in the repo market).

Each model has its own model of the evolution of future interest rates and its own volatility assumptions. Typically, there are no significant differences in the interest rate models of dealer firms and vendors, although their volatility assumptions can be significantly different.

The random paths of interest rates should be generated from an arbitrage-free model of the future term structure of interest rates. By arbitrage-free it is meant that the model replicates today's term structure of interest rates, an input of the model, and that for all future dates there is no possible arbitrage within the model.

The simulation works by generating many scenarios of future interest rate paths. In each month of the scenario (i.e., path), a monthly interest rate and a mortgage refinancing rate are generated. The monthly interest rates are used to discount the projected cash flows in the scenario. The mortgage refinancing rate is needed to determine the cash flows because it represents the opportunity cost the mortgagor is facing at that time.

If the refinancing rates are high relative to the mortgagor's original coupon rate (i.e., the rate on the mortgagor's loan), the mortgagor will have less incentive to refinance, or even a positive disincentive (i.e., the homeowner will avoid moving in order to avoid refinancing). If the refinancing rate is low relative to the mortgagor's original coupon rate, the mortgagor has an incentive to refinance.

Prepayments are projected by feeding the refinancing rate and loan characteristics into a prepayment model. Given the projected prepayments, the cash flows along an interest rate path can be determined.

To make this more concrete, consider a newly issued mortgage passthrough security with a maturity of 360 months. Exhibit 1 shows N simulated interest rate path scenarios. Each scenario consists of a path of 360 simulated 1-month future interest rates. Just how many paths should be generated is explained later. Exhibit 2 shows the paths of simulated mortgage refinancing rates corresponding to the scenarios shown in Exhibit 1. Assuming these mortgage refinancing rates, the cash flows for each scenario path are shown in Exhibit 3.

Exhibit 1: Simulated Paths of 1-Month Future Interest Rates

	Interest Rate Path Number						
Month	1	2	3	...	n	...	N
1	$f_1(1)$	$f_1(2)$	$f_1(3)$	...	$f_1(n)$	...	$f_1(N)$
2	$f_2(1)$	$f_2(2)$	$f_2(3)$	...	$f_2(n)$	...	$f_2(N)$
3	$f_3(1)$	$f_3(2)$	$f_3(3)$	...	$f_3(n)$	...	$f_3(N)$
...	...	...	...	...	...	...	...
t	$f_t(1)$	$f_t(2)$	$f_t(3)$	...	$f_t(n)$	...	$f_t(N)$
...	...	...	...	...	...	...	...
358	$f_{358}(1)$	$f_{358}(2)$	$f_{358}(3)$	...	$f_{358}(n)$	...	$f_{358}(N)$
359	$f_{359}(1)$	$f_{359}(2)$	$f_{359}(3)$	...	$f_{359}(n)$	...	$f_{359}(N)$
360	$f_{360}(1)$	$f_{360}(2)$	$f_{360}(3)$	...	$f_{360}(n)$	...	$f_{360}(N)$

Notation:

$f_t(n)$ = 1-month future interest rate for month t on path n

N = total number of interest rate paths

Exhibit 2: Simulated Paths of Mortgage Refinancing Rates

	Interest Rate Path Number						
Month	1	2	3	...	n	...	N
1	$r_1(1)$	$r_1(2)$	$r_1(3)$	...	$r_1(n)$	...	$r_1(N)$
2	$r_2(1)$	$r_2(2)$	$r_2(3)$	...	$r_2(n)$	...	$r_2(N)$
3	$r_3(1)$	$r_3(2)$	$r_3(3)$	...	$r_3(n)$	...	$r_3(N)$
...	...	...	...	...	...	...	...
t	$r_t(1)$	$r_t(2)$	$r_t(3)$	...	$r_t(n)$	...	$r_t(N)$
...	...	...	...	...	...	...	...
358	$r_{358}(1)$	$r_{358}(2)$	$r_{358}(3)$	...	$r_{358}(n)$	...	$r_{358}(N)$
359	$r_{359}(1)$	$r_{359}(2)$	$r_{359}(3)$	...	$r_{359}(n)$	...	$r_{359}(N)$
360	$r_{360}(1)$	$r_{360}(2)$	$r_{360}(3)$	...	$r_{360}(n)$	...	$r_{360}(N)$

Notation:

$r_t(n)$ = mortgage refinancing rate for month t on path n

N = total number of interest rate paths

Exhibit 3: Simulated Cash Flows on Each of the Interest Rate Paths

Month	Interest Rate Path Number						
	1	2	3	...	n	...	N
1	$C_1(1)$	$C_1(2)$	$C_1(3)$	...	$C_1(n)$	...	$C_1(N)$
2	$C_2(1)$	$C_2(2)$	$C_2(3)$	...	$C_2(n)$	...	$C_2(N)$
3	$C_3(1)$	$C_3(2)$	$C_3(3)$	...	$C_3(n)$	...	$C_3(N)$
...	...	...	...	...	...	...	...
t	$C_t(1)$	$C_t(2)$	$C_t(3)$	...	$C_t(n)$	...	$C_t(N)$
...	...	...	...	...	...	...	...
358	$C_{358}(1)$	$C_{358}(2)$	$C_{358}(3)$	...	$C_{358}(n)$	...	$C_{358}(N)$
359	$C_{359}(1)$	$C_{359}(2)$	$C_{359}(3)$	...	$C_{359}(n)$	...	$C_{359}(N)$
360	$C_{360}(1)$	$C_{360}(2)$	$C_{360}(3)$	...	$C_{360}(n)$	...	$C_{360}(N)$

Notation:
$C_t(n)$ = cash flow for month t on path n
N = total number of interest rate paths

Calculating the Present Value for a Scenario Interest Rate Path

Given the cash flows on an interest rate path, the path's present value can be calculated. The discount rate for determining the present value is the simulated spot rate for each month on the interest rate path plus an appropriate spread. The spot rate on a path can be determined from the simulated future monthly rates. The relationship that holds between the simulated spot rate for month T on path n and the simulated future 1-month rates is:

$$z_T(n) = \{[1 + f_1(n)][1 + f_2(n)]...[1 + f_T(n)]\}^{1/T} - 1$$

where

$z_T(n)$ = simulated spot rate for month T on path n
$f_j(n)$ = simulated future 1-month rate for month j on path n

Consequently, the interest rate path for the simulated future 1-month rates can be converted to the interest rate path for the simulated monthly spot rates as shown in Exhibit 4. Therefore, the present value of the cash flows for month T on interest rate path n discounted at the simulated spot rate for month T plus some spread is:

$$PV[C_T(n)] = \frac{C_T(n)}{[1 + z_T(n) + K]^T}$$

where

$PV[C_T(n)]$ = present value of cash flows for month T on path n
$C_T(n)$ = cash flow for month T on path n

Exhibit 4: Simulated Paths of Monthly Spot Rates

Month	Interest Rate Path Number						
	1	2	3	...	n	...	N
1	$z_1(1)$	$z_1(2)$	$z_1(3)$	...	$z_1(n)$	...	$z_1(N)$
2	$z_2(1)$	$z_2(2)$	$z_2(3)$	...	$z_2(n)$	...	$z_2(N)$
3	$z_3(1)$	$z_3(2)$	$z_3(3)$	...	$z_3(n)$	...	$z_3(N)$
...	...	...	...	...	...	...	...
t	$z_t(1)$	$z_t(2)$	$z_t(3)$	...	$z_t(n)$	...	$z_t(N)$
...	...	...	...	...	...	...	...
358	$z_{358}(1)$	$z_{358}(2)$	$z_{358}(3)$	...	$z_{358}(n)$	...	$z_{358}(N)$
359	$z_{359}(1)$	$z_{359}(2)$	$z_{359}(3)$	...	$z_{359}(n)$	...	$z_{359}(N)$
360	$z_{360}(1)$	$z_{360}(2)$	$z_{360}(3)$	...	$z_{360}(n)$	...	$z_{360}(N)$

Notation:

$z_t(n)$ = spot rate for month t on path n

N   = total number of interest rate paths

$z_T(n)$ = spot rate for month T on path n

K = spread

The present value for path n is the sum of the present value of the cash flows for each month on path n. That is,

$$PV[\text{Path}(n)] = PV[C_1(n)] + PV[C_2(n)] + ... + PV[C_{360}(n)]$$

where $PV[\text{Path}(n)]$ is the present value of interest rate path n.

Determining the Theoretical Value

The present value of a given interest rate path can be thought of as the theoretical value of a passthrough if that path was actually realized. The theoretical value of the passthrough can be determined by calculating the average of the theoretical values of all the interest rate paths. That is, the theoretical value is equal to

$$\text{Theoretical value} = \frac{PV[\text{Path}(1)] + PV[\text{Path}(2)] + ... + PV[\text{Path}(N)]}{N}$$

where N is the number of interest rate paths.

This procedure for valuing a passthrough is also followed for a CMO tranche or a mortgage strip. The cash flow for each month on each interest rate path is found according to the principal repayment and interest distribution rules of the deal. In order to do this for a CMO, a structuring model is needed.

Distribution of Path Present Values

The Monte Carlo model is a commonly used management science tool in business. It is employed when the outcome of a business decision depends on the outcome of several random variables. The product of the simulation is the average value and the probability distribution of the possible outcomes.

Unfortunately, the use of Monte Carlo simulation to value fixed income securities has been limited to just the reporting of the average value, which is referred to as the theoretical value of the security. This means that all of the information about the distribution of the path present values is ignored. Yet, this information is quite valuable.

For example, consider a well protected PAC bond. The distribution of the present value for the paths should be concentrated around the theoretical value. That is, the standard deviation should be small. In contrast, for a support tranche, the distribution of the present value for the paths could be wide, or equivalently, the standard deviation could be large.

Therefore, before using the theoretical value for a mortgage-backed security generated from the Monte Carlo model, information about the distribution of the path present values should be obtained.

Option-Adjusted Spread

In the Monte Carlo model, the OAS is the spread K that when added to all the spot rates on all interest rate paths will make the average present value of the paths equal to the observed market price (plus accrued interest). Mathematically, OAS is the spread that will satisfy the following condition:

$$\text{Market price} = \frac{\text{PV}[\text{Path}(1)] + \text{PV}[\text{Path}(2)] + \dots + \text{PV}[\text{Path}(N)]}{N}$$

where N is the number of interest rate paths.

The procedure for determining the OAS is straightforward, although time consuming. The next question, then, is how to interpret the OAS. Basically, the OAS is used to reconcile value with market price. On the left-hand side of the previous equation is the market's statement: the price of a mortgage-backed security. The average present value over all the paths on the right-hand side of the equation is the model's output, which we refer to as value.

What a portfolio manager seeks to do is to buy securities where value is greater than price. By using a valuation model such as the Monte Carlo model, a portfolio manager could estimate the value of a security, which at this point would be sufficient in determining whether to buy a security. That is, the portfolio manager can say that this bond is 1 point cheap or 2 points cheap, and so on. The model does not stop here. Instead, it converts the divergence between price and value into some type of yield spread measure since, as most market participants find it more convenient to think about yield spread than price differences.

The OAS was developed as a measure of the yield spread that can be used to convert dollar differences between value and price. But what is it a "spread" over? In describing the model above, we can see that the OAS is measuring the average spread over the Treasury spot rate curve, not the Treasury yield curve. It is an average spread since the OAS is found by averaging over the interest rate paths for the possible Treasury spot rate curves

The measure is superior to the nominal spread which gives no recognition to the prepayment risk. The OAS is "option adjusted" because the cash flows on the interest rate paths are adjusted for the option of the borrowers to prepay.

Effective Duration and Convexity

In Chapter 9 we explained how to determine the effective duration and effective convexity for any security. These measures can be calculated using the Monte Carlo model as follows. First the bond's OAS is found using the current term structure of interest rates. Next, the initial short-term rate used to generate the interest rate paths in Exhibit 1 is increased by a small number of basis points and new paths of interest rates are generated. Given the new paths, the security is revalued holding the OAS constant. Similarly, the initial short-term rate used to generate the interest rate paths in Exhibit 1 is decreased by a small number of basis points and the security is then revalued holding the OAS constant. The two calculated values are then used in the formula for effective duration and convexity given in Chapter 9.

Simulated Average Life

The average life of a mortgage-backed security is the weighted average time to receipt of principal payments (scheduled payments and projected prepayments). The average life reported in a Monte Carlo model is the average of the average lives along the interest rate paths. That is, for each interest rate path, there is an average life. The average of these average lives is the average life reported by the model.

Additional information is conveyed by the distribution of the average life. The greater the range and standard deviation of the average life, the more uncertainty there is about the bond's average life.

OAS Convergence

Since the OAS employs the Monte Carlo simulation methodology, it is essentially a statistical sampling approach. The underlying assumption is that the sample of 300 or so simulated interest rate paths statistically represents all the possible outcomes of rates movement with the forward curve being the mean and the market implied volatility being the distribution. The confidence level of this assumption obviously depends on the sample size, i.e. the number of interest rate paths simulated. Consequently, the larger number of paths provides more reliable or more statistically significant OAS prices.

Theoretically, one would prefer to run a million paths to obtain accurate OAS pricing. However, in the real world, some times bonds have to trade in a relatively short period of time and a million path OAS simulation may not be feasible or timely depending on the computer speed. The number of paths required to obtain statistically reliable OAS pricing depends on the type of bond. A relatively simple security or well structured tranches such as passthroughs and PAC tranches may only require 200 to 300 paths to approach price convergence. More leveraged and prepayment sensitive tranches such as IOs, POs, and inverse floaters may need up to 2,000 to 3,000 paths to approach price convergence.

Exhibit 5: Constant OAS Prices with a Different Number of Paths

Security Type	Number of Paths						OAS (bp)
	100	300	500	1,000	2,000	3,000	
10-year Treasury	103.50	103.50	103.50	103.50	103.50	103.50	0
FNMA 7% Passthrough	101.05	101.15	101.00	101.06	101.08	100.99	58
FNR 97-78 PR, Interm. PAC	100.39	100.50	100.58	100.56	100.53	100.57	46
FNR 93-8 HA, PAC IO	5,296.00	5,315.00	5,297.00	5,305.00	5,300.00	5,302.00	295
FNR 94-108 S, Inv IO	36.00	36.08	36.12	36.06	36.02	35.97	900
FNMA Strip 240 PO	72.23	72.04	72.24	72.03	72.12	72.12	80

Values obtained using *Derivative Solutions Fixed Income System.*

The following examples illustrate this concept. We can calculate the fair market prices of various types of bonds using market implied OASs. We will perform this exercise on a 10-year Treasury, a FNMA passthrough, an intermediate PAC bond, a PAC IO, a strip PO, and an inverse IO. We will repeat the OAS calculations using different numbers of simulated paths but constant OAS. One would expect to get a different price from each run because of the randomness of the simulation process but the "noise" would decrease as the sample size increases. Exhibit 5 shows the results.

Since there is no embedded option in the 10-year Treasury, a 100-path Monte Carlo simulation would generate the same OAS price as a 3,000-path simulation. Each run generates a different price but the variation (noise) is relatively small on the passthrough and the intermediate PAC. The price fluctuation is noticeably large on the increasingly complex (more interest rate leveraged or prepayment sensitive) securities. Since these securities have different prices, it is easier to normalize them for comparison. Here, we assume the 3,000-path price to be the convergent price and we express the other prices as a percentage of the 3,000-path convergent price. The result is summarized in Exhibit 6.

Note that the inverse IO, because of its leveraged sensitivity to both rates and prepayments, has the most randomness in pricing relative to the convergent price. IOs and POs are also prepayment sensitive and also have significant randomness. The generic passthrough and PAC bond can get within 0.1% of the convergent price with only 1,000 paths. The PAC IO, even though it is interest rate leveraged and prepayment sensitive, can also get within 0.1% of the convergent price with 1,000 paths because of the call protection from the PAC band. The PO needs a minimum of 2,000 paths to get within 0.1% of the convergent price while the inverse needs more than 2,000 paths.

Assumptions in OAS Analysis

As described previously, the Monte Carlo simulation/OAS methodology relies on many assumptions. If the assumptions are not accurate, the resulting pricing is probably not accurate either. Therefore, it is important to test the sensitivity of the OAS pricing result on the input assumptions. Exhibit 7 highlights the sensitivity to the common OAS input parameters.

Exhibit 6: OAS Price Convergence

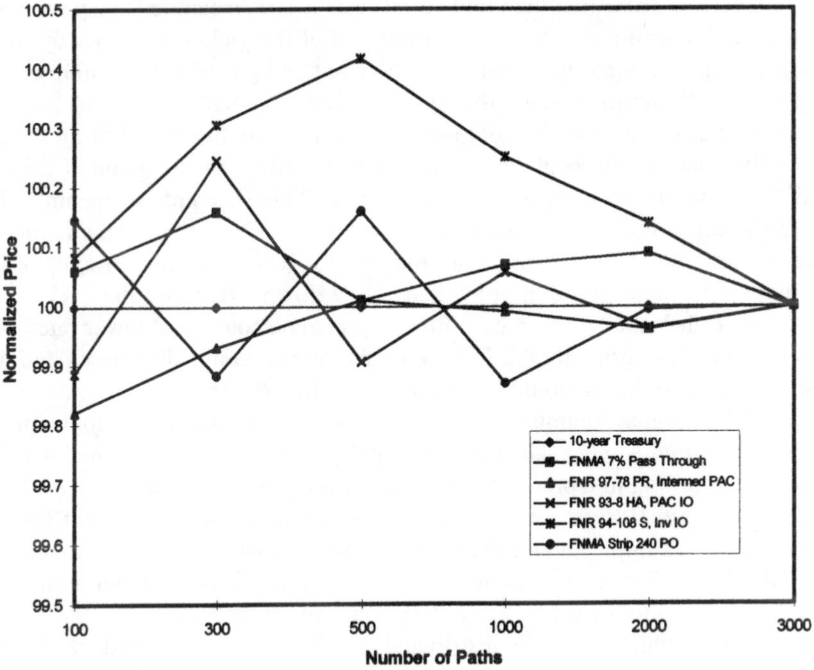

Values obtained using *Derivative Solutions Fixed Income System*.

Exhibit 7: OAS Assumption Sensitivity

Security Type	Assumption				
	Duration	Convexity	Rotate	Prepay	Vega
10-year Treasury	7.08	0.63	−2.60	0	0
FNMA 7% Passthrough	3.95	−1.30	0.16	−0.08	−0.30
FNR 97-78 PR, Interm. PAC	3.25	−1.20	1.10	−0.20	−0.15
FNR 93-8 HA, PAC IO	−15.50	−6.40	10.10	−3.00	−0.28
FNR 94-108 S, Inv IO	37.35	−2.60	17.90	−1.80	−0.74
FNMA Strip 240 PO	13.77	10.70	−8.20	2.30	0.30

Values obtained using *Derivative Solutions Fixed Income System*.

Effective duration is the price sensitivity of a fixed income instrument to changes in interest rates (typically defined as a 100 basis point parallel shift in the yield curve). For instance, the 10-year Treasury has a duration of 7.08, which implies that it has a price sensitivity of roughly 7.08% per 100 basis point movement in rates. The price movement is actually different from that because of the convexity. The 10-year Treasury having positive convexity would go up in price by more than 7.08% if rates go down by 100 basis points and would go down in price by less than 7.08% if rates go up by 100 basis points. Most mortgage-backed securities are short prepayment options and therefore have negative convexity.

Both the duration and convexity numbers assume parallel shifts in the yield curve. We know that the yield curve does rotate, meaning it may steepen or tighten. A steepening means that the front end of the yield curve goes up by less than the long end of the yield curve, or the front end goes down by more than the long end. A flattening means the reverse. The "Rotate" number in Exhibit 7 describes that sensitivity. The rotation of the curve is defined as shifting the front end of the curve down by 50 basis points while shifting the long end of the curve up 50 basis points, pivoting at the 5-year, i.e. a 100 basis points steepening. Holding OAS constant, the inverse IO price would go up by 17.9%. This is intuitive because under such an environment, the inverse IO earns a higher coupon from the inverse formula, while prepayments slow down extending the average life. The extra front loaded coupon cash flows are also discounted at lower rates. A PO would go down in price by 8.2% since prepayments would slow down and those pushed-back cash flows would be discounted at higher rates.

The "Prepay" number in Exhibit 7 describes the sensitivity to the prepayment assumption. Along each simulated path, prepayments are assumed to behave perfectly according to a prepayment model. If the prepayment model is shifted up or down by say, 10%, it will affect the OAS pricing on prepayment sensitive tranches. For example, if the prepayment model misestimates prepayments by 10%, the PAC IO price would be off by 3% under a constant OAS assumption. The PO price would be off by 2.3% in the opposite direction.

How tightly or widely distributed the simulated paths are depends on the volatility assumption. Most mortgage-backed securities are short prepayment options and the value of the options depends on volatility. The volatility assumption in the OAS model is also critical. The "Vega" number in Exhibit 7 describes the sensitivity to volatility. An increase of one percentage point in the volatility term structure would lower the price of the inverse IO by 0.74%, holding OAS constant. The inverse IO has an embedded short volatility position. The same increase in volatility would increase the PO price by 0.3%. This is because a PO is not short an option. Instead, a PO has an embedded long volatility position and therefore benefits if volatility increases.

VALUING ARMS

As described in Chapter 2, the basic structure and attributes of an adjustable-rate mortgage security (ARM) are the teaser rate, teaser period, index, margin, reset frequency, periodic cap, and lifetime cap. For example, a 5.5% 1-year CMT + 2.25% ARM with 2/12 caps means the security has a 5.5% net coupon for the first year. It will reset the second year coupon to the then 1-year CMT index rate plus 2.25% on the anniversary date subject to the 2% periodic cap and 12% lifetime cap constraints. Due to all these features, an ARM has other embedded options such as periodic caps and lifetime caps in addition to the normal prepayment option on a mortgage. The value of an ARM is also interest rate path dependent and it has to be valued using a Monte Carlo simulation/OAS framework.

To illustrate how this framework is used to value ARMs, consider the two almost identical ARMs shown in Exhibit 8. One ARM has tight periodic and life caps and the other has higher caps. The market would obviously trade the high cap ARM at a higher price because of the better periodic and life caps. The question is how much higher; how much are the caps worth?

One simple way to approach it is to calculate the yield or effective margin. The convention in the ARM market is to trade ARMs based on effective margin or BEEM (bond equivalent effective margin). This method uses the current index level to project the future coupon resets based on the periodic and life cap constraints. The future cash flows would then be discounted to obtain a bond equivalent yield and the excess yield above the current index level is the BEEM. Due to the tight periodic cap of 1% on the low cap ARM, the projected coupon on the next reset may not be fully indexed, therefore generating less coupon cash flows than the high cap ARM. The BEEM calculation would factor that in and price the low cap ARM at a lower price.

For example, if we were to price both ARM securities at 1.5% BEEM, the price of the low cap ARM would be 99.17 and the price of the high cap ARM would be 99.72. However, this methodology assumes the current CMT index to be static, and ignores the optionality of the periodic and life caps due to the volatility of the CMT index, the changes in the shape of the yield curve, and the interest rate paths. In fact, the OASs obtained from a 300-path Monte Carlo simulation using those equal BEEM prices are 118 basis points versus 134 basis points on the low cap ARM and high cap ARM, respectively.

To price both ARM securities at an equal OAS (134 basis points), the price of the low cap ARM has to be lowered to 98.72, a point lower than that of the high cap ARM. In addition, the effective duration of the low cap ARM is 2.15 compared to the 1.28 duration of the high cap ARM. The results are summarized in Exhibit 9.

Exhibit 8: Two Hypothetical ARMs

	Low Cap	High Cap
Teaser Rate	5.5%	5.5%
Index	1yearCMT	1yearCMT
Net Margin	2.25%	2.25%
Gross Margin	3.0%	3.0%
Age	2 months	2 months
WAM	30 years	30 years
Reset Frequency	Annual	Annual
Periodic Cap	1%	2%
Life Cap	11%	12%
Next Reset	10 months	10 months
Stated Delay	45 days	45 days
Look Back	45 days	45 days

Exhibit 9: Summary of Analysis of Two Hypothetical ARMs

	High Cap	Low Cap Based on Price Equal to	
		BEEM of High Cap	OAS of High Cap
Price (% of Par)	99.72	99.17	98.72
BEEM (bps)	150	150	164
OAS (bps)	134	118	134
Average Life (years)	3.1	3.6	3.6
Effective Duration	1.28	2.16	2.15
Effective Convexity	−0.59	−0.69	−0.67

Values obtained using *Derivative Solutions Fixed Income System.*

Chapter 12

Component Analysis of Complex Derivative Mortgage Products

Derivatives are commonly defined as instruments whose values are derived from other underlying assets. For example, a call option on a bond gives the holder the right, but not the obligation, to buy the underlying bond at a preset strike price regardless of the then market price. Thus, a call option derives its value from the underlying bond. Of course, there are other contractual terms in the agreement such as time to expiration, exercise style (European, American, or Bermudan), delivery variance, and market condition (such as volatility) that would fine tune the pricing of the option contract.

CMO derivatives are not different. A CMO is collateralized by mortgages and derives its value from the cash flows of the underlying mortgages. In most cases, the underlying mortgages/collateral are in the form of mortgage passthroughs, but the collateral can be another CMO tranche or a portfolio of various CMO securities. The individual values of the specific tranches within a CMO depend on the specific CMO structure.

The focus of this chapter is the analysis of the underlying components from which a CMO derivative derives its value. Once these components are identified, the portfolio manager can better understand the pricing of a CMO derivative, the sensitivity of price due to a change in the level of interest rates (i.e., duration and convexity) and the yield curve, how to assess relative value, and how to hedge individual positions. At the end of this chapter we demonstrate how to hedge out the undesirable components embedded in specific CMO derivatives.

Technically, all CMO tranches are derivatives since they derive their values from the underlying collateral subject to the CMO structures. However, the investment industry and the CMO marketplace apply the term "derivatives" generally to CMO tranches that are not plain vanilla structures like sequentials or PACs. CMO derivatives generally imply interest-only strips (IOs), principal-only strips (POs), inverse floaters, inverse IOs, two-tiered index bonds (TTIBs), or any other complex structures. Using these structures as specific examples, we will illustrate component analysis of CMO derivatives.

CMO AS A NEAR-ZERO-SUM GAME

CMO structuring is a near-zero-sum exercise regardless of the structure of the CMO. It is a zero-sum exercise with respect to principal, interest, maturity, aver-

189

age life, and risks. Whether the CMO is a sequential structure or a PAC/support structure, whether it is stripped into IOs and POs, whether it has floaters, and inverse floaters, the total principal amount (excluding notional principal on the IOs) of all the tranches must be equal to the principal amount of the collateral. The net weighted average coupon of all the tranches (discounts, premiums, floaters, and inverses) must be equal to the coupon of the collateral. The final maturity of the last tranche of the deal is equal to that of the collateral. The combined average lives of all the tranches must be equal to the average life of the collateral. The total prepayment risks of all the tranches must be equal to that of the collateral.

However, CMO structuring may not be a zero-sum exercise in terms of price and, consequently, dollar duration and dollar convexity. The sum of the prices of all the tranches is equal to the price of the collateral plus issuance fees and reasonable arbitrage profit margin. Consequently, the total dollar duration and dollar convexity of all the tranches is equal to those of the collateral only before fees and profits. However, it should still give the manager an approximation on the price and characteristics of the CMO. This principle forms the basis for both the structural component analysis and derivative component analysis of CMO derivatives.

IO and PO Strips

IOs and POs are typically created from separating the interest cash flows from the principal cash flows of a fixed-rate mortgage. For example, the principal and interest cash flows from $100 million of a 7% mortgage can be separated into a PO and an IO. The PO has a principal amount of $100 million and the IO has a notional amount of $100 million, as illustrated in Exhibit 1.

POs are known to managers to behave like zero-coupon bonds, i.e., discount price, long duration, and positive convexity. If the 7% mortgage has a market price of $95, duration of 6, convexity of −1, and the PO has a price of $60, duration of 15 and a convexity of +3, then the zero-sum principle implies that the IO should have a price of around $35 ($95 − $60), a duration of −9.4 [($95 × 6 − $60 × 15)/$35], and a convexity of −7.9 [($95 × (−1) − $60 × 3)/$35]. The extremely negative duration and convexity of an IO become apparent and rational and make economic sense if the manager views the IO as two components: a long position on the 7% fixed-rate mortgage and a short position on the PO.

Exhibit 1: Creation of an IO/PO Strip

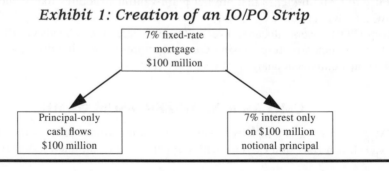

Exhibit 2: Fair Price, Duration, and Convexity of Synthetic POs and IOs

Synthetic Coupon	Price	Duration	Convexity
Collateral 7%	$95	6.0	−1.0
PO	60	15.0	3.0
IO	35	−9.4	−7.9
1%	65	13.1	2.2
2%	70	11.5	1.4
3%	75	10.1	0.8
4%	80	8.9	0.3
5%	85	7.8	−0.2
6%	90	6.9	−0.6
7%	95	6.0	−1.0
8%	100	5.2	−1.3
9%	105	4.5	−1.7
10%	110	3.9	−1.9
11%	115	3.3	−2.2
12%	120	2.8	−2.4
13%	125	2.3	−2.6
14%	130	1.8	−2.8
15%	135	1.4	−3.0

IOs and POs are the extreme examples of strips. Synthetic discounts and premiums can be created by uneven or partial stripping of the same collateral. From the same $100 million 7% fixed-rate mortgage, one can create a $50 million 5% tranche and a $50 million 9% tranche. This is because the weighted average coupon of the two tranches always add up to 7%, which is the coupon of the underlying collateral. The same logic applies in the creation of any synthetic coupon desired. Every coupon can be replicated by an appropriate combination of IO and PO. A synthetic 9% coupon has two components: seven parts of PO and nine parts of IO. A synthetic 5% coupon has two components: seven parts of PO and five parts of IO. The duration and convexity can also be deducted from the zero-sum-game principle.

Exhibit 2 shows the fair price, duration and convexity of each integer synthetic coupon from 0% to 15%. Note that the one-to-one IO/PO combination is the same as collateral and therefore has the same price, duration, and convexity as the 7% collateral. Extremely high coupons such as 90% or 900% are generally referred to as *IO-ettes*. They are mostly IOs with a tiny bit of principal.

Inverse Floaters

Inverse floaters are CMO tranches with coupons that float inversely with some reference interest rate or index. The coupon typically has a formula like this: Cap − Leverage × Index. The cap is the maximum coupon of the inverse. The leverage is the sensitivity to the reference index or rate. The leverage is generally greater than one since there are more floater buyers than inverse buyers. And the most common indices are LIBOR, Cost of Fund Index (COFI), prime rate, and Constant Maturity Treasury (CMT).

Most inverse floaters are created within a fixed-rate CMO by tranching out a complementary floater. The combined coupon of the floater and inverse floater must be equal to the underlying fixed-rate coupon at all times. The cap, leverage, index, and the underlying fixed rate are all critical pricing elements of the inverse and they are all interrelated to each other.

For illustration, one can construct a floater/inverse floater structure from a hypothetical $3.8 million of 7% fixed-rate cash flow/bond priced at $95. Assume that an investor wants $2.8 million of a COFI floater with a margin of 1.4% and a cap of 9.5% priced at $100. The size and price of the collateral (the 7% fixed-rate bond) as well as the size, price, margin, and cap requirements on the floater already dictate the leverage, size, and cap of the inverse. In this case, the inverse has a coupon formula of 22.68% − 2.8 × COFI with a floor of 0% and a cap of 22.68%. The coupon will hit the cap of 22.68% when the index COFI goes down to 0% and the coupon will go to zero when the index hits 8.1%. In this case, the inverse floater has two components: a long position on $3.8 million 7% fixed-rate bond and a short position on $2.8 million floater. The tranching of the floater and inverse are illustrated in Exhibit 3. Exhibits 4 and 5 illustrate the floater and inverse coupon relationships at various index levels.

Consequently, the price of the inverse is derived from its two components: primarily the underlying fixed-rate bond and secondarily the floater. The margin, size, and cap of the floater, which dictates the leverage of the inverse, helps fine tune the price of the inverse. The price and duration of this inverse can be written as:

Price(inverse) = 3.8 × Price(fixed) − 2.8 × Price(floater)
$Duration(inverse) = $Duration(fixed) − $Duration(floater)

The price and duration sensitivity of the inverse is illustrated in Exhibit 6.

Exhibit 3: Tranching of the Floater and Inverse

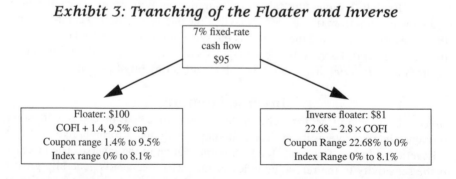

7% fixed-rate
cash flow
$95

Floater: $100
COFI + 1.4, 9.5% cap
Coupon range 1.4% to 9.5%
Index range 0% to 8.1%

Inverse floater: $81
22.68 − 2.8 × COFI
Coupon Range 22.68% to 0%
Index Range 0% to 8.1%

Exhibit 4: Floater and Inverse Coupon Relationships at Various Index Levels

Fixed Rate (%)	COFI (%)	Floater Coupon (%)	Inverse Coupon (%)	Combination (%)
7	0	1.40	22.68	7.00
7	1	2.40	19.88	7.00
7	2	3.40	17.08	7.00
7	3	4.40	14.28	7.00
7	4	5.40	11.48	7.00
7	5	6.40	8.68	7.00
7	6	7.40	5.88	7.00
7	7	8.40	3.08	7.00
7	8	9.40	0.28	7.00
7	9	9.50	0.00	7.00
7	10	9.50	0.00	7.00
7	11	9.50	0.00	7.00
7	12	9.50	0.00	7.00
7	13	9.50	0.00	7.00

Exhibit 5: Floater and Inverse Coupon Relationship

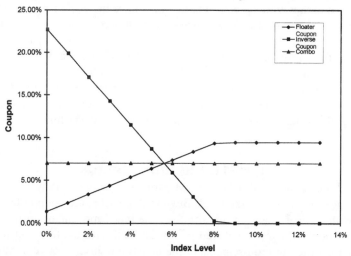

The observation of this component analysis is that the price of the inverse is most dependent on (sensitive to) the price of the fixed-rate bond component. A 1-point (1.05%) move in the underlying fixed-rate bond translates to a 3.8-point (4.5%) move in the inverse, holding the floater constant. A 1-point (1%) move in the floater translates to a 2.8-point (3.3%) move in the inverse. Clearly, inverse floaters are long duration securities; the higher the leverage, the longer the duration. The duration sensitivity in Exhibit 6 also illustrates the magnitude of the duration of the inverse being multiples of that of the underlying fixed-rate bond.

Exhibit 6: Price and Duration Sensitivity of the Inverse

Price (fixed)	Price (floater)	Price (inverse)
$95	$100	$81.00
$95	$99	$83.80
$96	$99	$87.60
Duration(fixed) Price = 95	Duration (floater) Price = 100	Duration (inverse) Price = 81
6	0	26.7
6	1	23.3
7	0	31.2

This component analysis also explains the price/yield behavior of inverse floaters and can be applied to relative value analysis. When the yield curve 'ˆ steep (low short-term rates and high long-term rates), long fixed-rate cash fl⌐ ⌐ (bonds) trade at a high yield (low price), assuming floaters still trade around par (except tight cap floater). Inverse floaters tend to trade at a very high static yield because of the low short-term reference rates. But the high yield does not mean the inverse is cheap. All it means is that a manager can borrow short and invest long and can earn a wide spread. Inverses may have better performance when the yield curve flattens (short rates go up and long rates come down) since the underlying fixed-rate bond will appreciate in price. Inverses tied to different indices also yield differently and the higher yielding one is not always the cheaper one. Higher leverage also contributes to higher yield. Therefore, a manger cannot perform any relative value comparison on inverses just by the static yield. Since the fixed-rate market and the floater market are fairly efficient, the component analysis illustrated earlier can be used to determine the relative richness and cheapness of an inverse.

Two-Tiered Index Bonds

Two-tiered index bonds (TTIBs) are CMO tranches whose coupons are fixed until the reference index hit a strike level. Beyond that strike, the coupon then deteriorates like an inverse floater at a multiple of the index movement until the coupon reaches zero. TTIBs are structured in conjunction with floaters and inverses to reconcile the different requirements of the floater and inverse buyers. Suppose the above floater buyer demands the same index, margin, and cap on the floater but the inverse buyer wants a different leverage (3.9) and a different index range (0 to 7). A TTIB can be structured to accomplish the difference. This is illustrated in Exhibit 7. The coupon relationship of the three tranches is in Exhibit 8.

Note that the combined coupon of all tranches is still 7% and the floater is identical to the previous structure. The introduction of a TTIB preserves the fixed-rate coupon and the structure of the floater while creating an inverse with a different leverage. The Inverse now has three components: a long position on $5.326 million 7% fixed-rate bond, a short position on $3.924 million floater, and a short position on \$0.40156 million TTIB. Assuming the price of the TTIB is known (which will be covered later in this chapter), the price and duration of this new inverse becomes:

$$\text{Price(inverse)} = 5.326 \times \text{Price(fixed)} - 3.924 \times \text{Price(floater)}$$
$$- 0.40156 \times \text{Price(TTIB)}$$

$$\text{\$Duration(inverse)} = \text{\$Duration(fixed)} - \text{\$Duration(floater)}$$
$$- \text{\$Duration(TTIB)}$$

The price and duration of the new inverse is illustrated in Exhibit 9.

Exhibit 7: Structuring of a TIBB

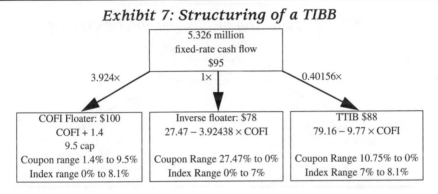

Exhibit 8: Floater, Inverse and TTIB Coupon Relationship

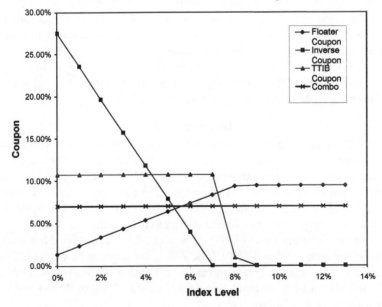

Exhibit 9: Price and Duration of the New Inverse

Price (fixed)	Price (floater)	Price (TTIB)	Price (inverse)
$95	$99	$88	$82.16
95	100	88	78.23
95	99	89	81.76
96	100	88	83.56
Duration(fixed) Price = 95	Duration (floater) Price = 100	Duration (TTIB) Price = 88	Duration (inverse) Price = 78.23
6	0	18	30.7
6	1	18	25.7
6	0	17	31.1
7	0	18	37.1

Exhibit 10: Tranching of Floater and Inverse IO

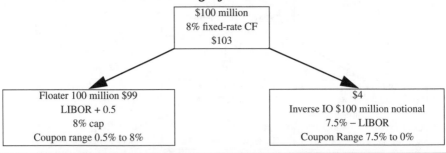

As discussed earlier, a higher leverage contributes to a higher yield (lower price) on the inverse. In this example, an increase of approximately one in the leverage lowers the price by about 3 points. Obviously, that also adds risk to the inverse. A 1-point (1.05%) move in the underlying fixed rate now translate to a 5.3-point (6.8%) move in the inverse, holding the floater constant. The extra leverage extends the base case duration from 26.7 to 30.7. This type of component analysis quantifies the effect of leverage and facilitates the relative value comparison of inverses with different coupon formula and leverage.

Inverse IO

An inverse IO is an interest only security (only notional principal) with an inverse floating coupon. It is created by carving out a floater with full principal from a fixed-rate bond. While first introduced in the CMO market many years ago, it became popular in the early 1990s when the yield curve was extremely steep. An inverse IO, like an inverse floater, offers an extremely high yield, sometimes in the 40% to 50% range, in a steep yield curve environment.

As an illustration using $100 million of a fixed rate 8% cash flow, a $100 million floater with a coupon of LIBOR + 0.5, 8% cap can be created. The left-over cash flows are used to create an inverse IO with a coupon formula of 7.5% − LIBOR on $100 million notional principal. The tranching of floater and inverse IO is illustrated in Exhibit 10.

Since both tranches have the same notional principal, the combined coupon is (LIBOR + 0.5) + (7.5 − LIBOR), which is always 8%. The two components of this inverse IO are a long 8% fixed-rate bond and short LIBOR floater. If the price of the fixed-rate bond is $103 and the price of the floater is $99, the fair price of the inverse IO should be around $4. A 1-point (1%) move in the fixed-rate bond translates to a 1-point (25%) move in the inverse IO. If the duration of the fixed-rate bond is 5 and the duration of the floater is 1, then the effective duration of the inverse IO should be around 104 (= (103 × 5−99 × 1)/4). The extremely long duration of the inverse IO — which caused a lot of problems for some hedge funds in 1994 — becomes apparent if a manager understands the component construction of an inverse IO.

Complex Floater

In most cases, the underlying collateral of a CMO is in the form of fixed-rate mortgage passthroughs. In general, any mortgage asset can be used as collateral for a CMO structure. As explained in Chapter 4, if the collateral is another CMO tranche, it is often called a re-REMIC.

FNR 94-97 FE is such a re-REMIC and can be used as a real life example. It is a floater/inverse floater hybrid-security. If LIBOR stays below 7.95%, it is a floater with a coupon of LIBOR + 1.95 subject to a 9.9% cap. If LIBOR goes beyond 7.95%, it becomes an inverse floater with a coupon formula of 38.52% − 3.6 × LIBOR subject to a coupon floor of 0. It is undoubtedly an interesting security, but is actually a fairly simple security to price if one can identify its constructing components. One would find that by reading the prospectus or Bloomberg, this is a re-REMIC of another floater FNR 94-42 FH. It is created by carving off a high cap floater (FNR 94-97 F) from a low cap floater (FNR94-42 FH). The tranching is illustrated in Exhibit 11. Exhibits 12 and 13 show the coupon relationship. Note that the combined coupon is equal to that of a LIBOR + 1.05 with a 9% cap floater.

Exhibit 11: Creation of FNR 94-97F

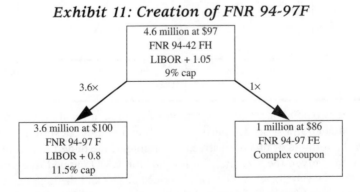

Exhibit 12: FNR 94-97F, FNR 94-97FE, and FNR 94-42FH Coupon Relationships at Various Index Levels

LIBOR (%)	FNR 94-97 F (%)	FNR 94-97 FE (%)	Combined FNR94-42 FH (%)
0	0.80	1.95	1.05
1	1.80	2.95	2.05
2	2.80	3.95	3.05
3	3.80	4.95	4.05
4	4.80	5.95	5.05
5	5.80	6.95	6.05
6	6.80	7.95	7.05
7	7.80	8.95	8.05
8	8.80	9.72	9.00
9	9.80	6.12	9.00
10	10.80	2.52	9.00
11	11.50	0.00	9.00
12	11.50	0.00	9.00
13	11.50	0.00	9.00

Exhibit 13: Coupon Relationship for FNR 94-97F, FNR 94-97FE, and FNR 94-42FH

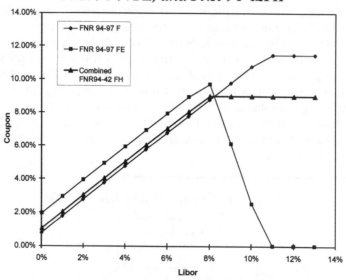

The two components of this complex hybrid security are long 4.6 parts of a low cap floater and short 3.6 parts of a high cap floater. Despite the complex nature of the formula of this derivative, the pricing of the underlying components are fairly easy given the size and liquidity of the CMO capped floater market. Suppose the low cap floater (collateral) is priced at $97 and the high cap floater is priced at $100, the fair price of the hybrid must be around $86(= 97 × 4.6 − 100 ×

3.6). Suppose the low cap floater has a duration of 2 and the high cap floater has a duration of 0, the effective duration of the hybrid is approximately 10.4 (= (4.6 × 97 × 2 – 3.6 × 100 × 0)/86).

DERIVATIVE COMPONENT APPROACH

All the previous illustrations applied the zero-sum principle on a structural component approach. By identifying and analyzing the components from which the CMO security is constructed and derives its value, a manager can perform pricing, relative value, duration and convexity assessment, and hedging analysis on the CMO. However, sometimes it may be hard to identify the components after the CMO deal has been carved into 50 to 100 tranches. Sometimes the components may not be straight forward by themselves, thus creating room for error. An alternative to structural component analysis is derivative component analysis. This approach does not require the identification of the complementary tranches. It values the CMO security by itself by decomposing the embedded derivative components such as cap, floor, and swap.

Inverse Floater with Embedded Swap and Cap

An inverse floater is equivalent to owning the underlying fixed-rate bond, entering into multiple notional principal of interest rate swaps equal to the leverage, and buying the same multiple notional principal of interest rate cap. Using the first inverse floater introduced in this chapter, the 22.68 – 2.8 × COFI, the same cash flow can be constructed by owning a 7% fixed-rate bond, entering into 2.8 times notional principal of interest rate swap to receive a fixed rate of 5.6% and pay floating at COFI, and buying 2.8 times notional principal of a COFI cap struck at 8.1%. The coupon formulae are:

Fixed Rate: 7%
Swap: 2.8 × (5.6 – COFI) or 15.68 – 2.8 × COFI
Cap: 2.8 × Max (COFI – 8.1, 0)
Net Coupon: Max (22.68 – 2.8 × COFI, 0)

The coupon relationship of the fixed-rate bond, the swap, and the cap is illustrated in Exhibit 14. Note that the combined coupon is exactly equal to that of an inverse floater with the formula of 22.68% – 2.8 × COFI subject to a cap of 22.68% and a floor of 0%.

In terms of pricing, the pricing formula of the inverse can be written as

Price(inverse) = Price(fixed) + 2.8 × Price(swap) + 2.8 × Price(cap)

If the price of the fixed-rate bond is $95, the price of the swap is –$7 and the price of each cap is $2.5, then the price of the inverse is roughly $82.4 [= $95 + 2.8 (–$7) + 2.8 ($2.5)].

Exhibit 14: Coupon Relationship of Fixed-Rate Bond, Swap, and Cap

COFI (%)	Fixed Rate (%)	Swap-Recv (%)	Swap Pay (%)	Cap (%)	Combined (%)
0	7	15.68	0.00	0.00	22.68
1	7	15.68	−2.80	0.00	19.88
2	7	15.68	−5.60	0.00	17.08
3	7	15.68	−8.40	0.00	14.28
4	7	15.68	−11.20	0.00	11.48
5	7	15.68	−14.00	0.00	8.68
6	7	15.68	−16.80	0.00	5.88
7	7	15.68	−19.60	0.00	3.08
8	7	15.68	−22.40	0.00	0.28
9	7	15.68	−25.20	2.52	0.00
10	7	15.68	−28.00	5.32	0.00
11	7	15.68	−30.80	8.12	0.00
12	7	15.68	−33.60	10.92	0.00
13	7	15.68	−36.40	13.72	0.00

Exhibit 15: Coupon Relationship of Fixed-Rate Bond, Short Cap, and Long Cap

COFI (%)	Fixed Rate (%)	Short Cap (%)	Long Cap (%)	Combined (%)
0.00	10.75	0.00	0.00	10.75
2.00	10.75	0.00	0.00	10.75
4.00	10.75	0.00	0.00	10.75
6.00	10.75	0.00	0.00	10.75
7.00	10.75	0.00	0.00	10.75
7.25	10.75	−2.44	0.00	8.31
7.50	10.75	−4.89	0.00	5.86
7.75	10.75	−7.33	0.00	3.42
8.00	10.75	−9.77	0.00	0.98
8.10	10.75	−10.75	0.00	0.00
9.00	10.75	−19.55	8.80	0.00
10.00	10.75	−29.32	18.57	0.00
11.00	10.75	−39.09	28.34	0.00
13.00	10.75	−58.64	47.89	0.00

TTIB with Embedded Corridor

A similar approach can be applied to value the price and duration of the TTIB example discussed earlier in this chapter. The TTIB has a fixed coupon of 10.75% until COFI hits 7%. Beyond 7%, the coupon will deteriorate at a leverage of 9.77 until the coupon reaches 0. The coupon has a cap of 10.75% and a floor of 0%. The coupon formula can be written as:

$$\text{Coupon} = \text{Min}[10.75, \text{Max}(0, 79.1591\% - 9.77273 \times \text{COFI})]$$

A close examination at the coupon formula reveals that it is a fixed coupon of 10.75% with two embedded options. One is a short position on the leverage notional principal of a COFI cap struck at 7%, and the other is a long position on the same leverage notional principal of a COFI cap struck at 8.1%. In option jargon, it is referred to as a 7 to 8.1 corridor. Exhibit 15 shows the coupon relationship. Note that the combined coupon is exactly equal to the above referenced coupon formula.

In terms of pricing, the pricing formula of the TTIB can be written as:

$$\text{Price(TTIB)} = \text{Price(fixed)} - 9.77 \times \text{Price(7-strike cap)} + 9.77 \times \text{Price(8.1-strike cap)}$$

If the price of the fixed-rate is $110, the price of the 7-strike cap is $4.75, and the price of the 8.1-strike cap is $2.5, then the price of the TTIB is roughly $88 [= $110 − 9.77 ($4.75) + 9.77 $(2.5)]. The dollar duration of the TTIB can be estimated by the same approach.

Inverse IO as Interest Rate Floor

As discussed earlier, an inverse IO has no principal. It receives a coupon such as 7.5% − LIBOR off some notional amount. Its coupon formula is equivalent to an interest rate floor struck at 7.5% (putting prepayment aside). The holder of a 7.5-strike floor receives the difference between LIBOR and 7.5% if LIBOR is below 7.5%. Otherwise the holder will receive no payments. The payout on the floor can be written as Max(7.5 − LIBOR, 0). The price of an equivalent average life floor generally serves as the upper boundary price of the inverse IO given that the inverse IO is prepayable.

Floater with Fixed Coupon Period

When the yield curve was extremely steep in 1992 and 1993, there was a high volume of issuance in LIBOR floater with a fixed coupon period. Due to the low LIBOR rates, a true LIBOR floater had a very low static yield. By fixing the coupon for one to two years, a higher initial coupon can be created.

To illustrate this, suppose current LIBOR is at a low 3% but the yield curve is so steep that the 2-year swap rate is at 5%. A par LIBOR flat floater will have a coupon of only 3%, thus a very low current yield. A LIBOR floater that offers an initial fixed coupon of 4.5% for two years seems to have a much higher current yield. However, the higher current yield does not mean that it is a cheaper bond. Whether one believes LIBOR would exceed 4.5% in the next two years is irrelevant. The fact is that the current 2-year swap rate is 5%. Any floater owner desires to lock in a fixed coupon for the next two years can enter into a 2-year swap to receive fixed (5%) and pay floating (LIBOR), thus creating the same floater with a 2-year fixed coupon period. By the same logic, if a manager can buy a floater with an above-swap-rate coupon, he can swap the initial fixed coupon back to floating to obtain LIBOR plus receipts.

HEDGING DERIVATIVE COMPONENT RISKS

As illustrated earlier in this chapter, many types of CMOs have embedded derivative components such as caps, floors, and swaps. It is logical to hedge out those risks with derivatives having the counter effects. Caps, floors, and swaps are fairly liquid and therefore can be used as hedging instruments.

Hedging an Inverse Floater with Interest Rate Swaps

As explained earlier in this chapter, an inverse floater is equivalent to the underlying fixed rate bond with a receiver swap and a cap. Let's use the previous inverse floater to see how this is done.

The coupon formula for the inverse floater is $(22.68 - 2.8 \times COFI)$. A portfolio manager can construct the same cash flows by owning a 7% fixed-rate bond, entering into 2.8 times notional principal of interest rate swap to receive a fixed rate of 5.6% and pay floating at COFI, and buying 2.8 times notional principal of a COFI cap struck at 8.1%. Assuming the price of the fixed-rate bond to be $95, the price of the swap to be −$7, and the price of the cap to be $2.5, the price of the inverse is roughly $82.4 [= $95 + 2.8 \times (−$7) + 2.8($2.5)]. If we also assume the duration of the fixed-rate bond to be 6, the duration of the swap to be 82, and the duration of the cap to be −40, the duration of the inverse is roughly 23 [= (95 \times 6 + 2.8 \times 7 \times 82 − 2.8 \times 2.5 \times 40)/82.4].

A specific hedge using swaps and caps can be constructed to convert this high leverage, long duration inverse back to a fixed-rate bond. The hedge will be to enter into 2.8 times notional payer swap (opposite to the embedded swap) and short 2.8 times notional COFI cap (embedded in the inverse). This will shorten the duration of the inverse from 23 back to that of a fixed-rate bond, which is around 6.

Hedging a TTIB with Corridors

As demonstrated earlier in this chapter, a TTIB is equivalent to a fixed-rate bond with a short position on a corridor. Therefore, a logical hedging strategy is to buy back the corridor. Using the hypothetical TTIB presented earlier with the 7 to 8.1 corridor, the portfolio manager can shorten the long duration of the TTIB from 18 back to the duration of the underlying fixed-rate bond, which is around 6.

Hedging an Inverse IO with Interest Rate Floor

An inverse IO coupon is equivalent to an interest rate floor. Therefore, an effective hedge to an inverse IO is to short an interest rate floor with the same strike. Since an inverse IO is prepayable, this may have to be a dynamic hedging process. The portfolio manager has to dynamically adjust the notional principal of the interest rate floor to the outstanding notional balance of the inverse IO. The portfolio manager also has to construct a projected amortization schedule for the amortizing floor in order to match the projected paydown of the inverse IO.

Exhibit 16: Illustration of an Amortizing Floor Schedule to Hedge an IO Inverse

Year	Remaining Not. Amt. IO	Floor Notional Principal Amounts by Expirations					Cumulative Floor Not. Face Amount
		1 year	2year	3year	4year	5year	
Initial	100	10	15	25	30	20	100
1	90		15	25	30	20	90
2	75			25	30	20	75
3	50				30	20	50
4	20					20	20
5	0					0	0

For example, an inverse IO may have an initial notional balance of $100 million, an average life of three years, and a final maturity of five years. Instead of hedging it with a 3-year floor, an amortizing floor schedule can be created as shown in Exhibit 16.

By hedging with a ladder of floors with different expirations, the portfolio manager can match the projected notional balance of the IO. Note in Exhibit 16 that initially there is a total of $100 million notional principal of floors for the hedge. At the end of one year, the 1-year floor will expire leaving only $90 million notional principal of floor outstanding, which is also the remaining balance of the IO. By the end of year 4, only $20 million of the 5-year floor will still be outstanding which matches the projected balance of the inverse IO. Of course, this is not a perfect match of the IO balance as prepayments are less predictable and occur on a monthly basis. However, the portfolio manager would not want to match the monthly balances of the IO, as the hedge will have small pieces of floors that the portfolio manager must unwind if the hedge needs to be adjusted.

Hedging a Complex Floater with Interest Rate Caps

Another example for hedging complex securities with interest rate derivatives can be illustrated using the complex floater discussed earlier in this chapter, the FNR 94-97 FE. This security is a floater/inverse floater hybrid security. If LIBOR remains below 7.95%, it is a floater with a coupon of LIBOR+1.95 subject to a 9.9% cap. If LIBOR rises above 7.95%, it becomes an inverse floater with a coupon formula of 38.52% − 3.6 × LIBOR. Also recall that it has a long duration of about 10.4, even though it behaves like a floater in the current rate environment. A hedge can be constructed using caps to convert this complex floater back to a plain uncapped LIBOR plus floater, therefore reducing the duration to near zero.

When LIBOR hits 7.95% and higher, the complex floater starts to lose coupon at a 3.6 times leverage. To offset that, the manager can buy 4.6 times the notional principal of LIBOR cap struck at 7.95%. The 3.6 parts cap neutralizes the 3.6 leverage inverse component, while the one part cap effectively uncaps the floater. Since the complex floater has a coupon floor of 0 when LIBOR hits 10.7%, the manager can sell 3.6 times the notional principal of LIBOR cap struck at 10.7% to finance the purchase of the 7.95% caps. The net result will be an uncapped agency floater with near 0 duration. The cash flows of the various components of the hedge are illustrated in Exhibit 17.

SUMMARY

The CMO market is a huge market by outstanding volume as well as issuance. It is also a very complex market due to its structure and derivative nature, and it is this complexity that creates opportunities. The value of one tranche often depends not just on its own characteristics, but also on other tranches in the same deal. It is impossible to assess the value of a complex CMO derivative by the traditional yield and average life comparison. The structural and derivative component analysis discussed in this chapter offers a more reliable valuation methodology since the underlying components such as fixed-rate bonds, floaters, caps, floors, and swaps tend to be more efficiently priced. Component analysis is not complete or conclusive by any means and should be used in conjunction with other analyses discussed in earlier chapters such as OAS and vector analysis. Finally, we illustrated the use of interest rate derivatives to hedge out the undesirable components embedded in specific CMO derivative structures.

Exhibit 17: Illustration of Hedging a Complex Floater with Caps

LIBOR (%)	FNR 94-97FE (%)	Long 7.95% cap 4.6 times (%)	Short 10.7% cap 3.6 times (%)	Net Coupon LIBOR+1.95% (%)
0.00	1.95	0.00	0.00	1.95
1.00	2.95	0.00	0.00	2.95
2.00	3.95	0.00	0.00	3.95
3.00	4.95	0.00	0.00	4.95
4.00	5.95	0.00	0.00	5.95
5.00	6.95	0.00	0.00	6.95
6.00	7.95	0.00	0.00	7.95
7.00	8.95	0.00	0.00	8.95
7.95	9.90	0.00	0.00	9.90
8.00	9.72	0.23	0.00	9.95
9.00	6.12	4.83	0.00	10.95
10.00	2.52	9.43	0.00	11.95
11.00	0.00	14.03	−1.08	12.95
12.00	0.00	18.63	−4.68	13.95
13.00	0.00	23.23	−8.28	14.95
14.00	0.00	27.83	−11.88	15.95
15.00	0.00	32.43	−15.48	16.95

Chapter 13

Total Return Analysis and Portfolio Construction/Optimization

The first main step in the investment management process is setting investment objectives. Investment objectives will vary by type of financial institution and are essentially dictated by the nature of an institution's liabilities. For institutions such as banks and thrifts, the objective is to earn a return on invested funds that is higher than the cost of acquiring those funds. For institutions such as pension funds, the investment objective will be to generate sufficient cash flow from the investment portfolio to satisfy its pension obligations. Life insurance companies sell a variety of products guaranteeing a dollar payment or a stream of dollar payments at some time in the future. Premiums charged policyholders depend on the interest rate the company can earn on its investments. To realize a profit, the company must earn a higher return on the premium it invests than the implicit (or explicit) interest rate it has guaranteed policyholders.

Neither the static cash flow yield methodology nor the option adjusted spread methodology will tell a money manager whether investment objectives can be satisfied. We explain why in our discussion of the limitations of each methodology. The potential return of an individual MBS or an MBS portfolio requires specification of an investment horizon, whose length for most financial institutions is dictated by the nature of its liabilities. For example, a life insurance company issuing a 4-year guaranteed investment contract (GIC) would use a 4-year investment horizon. For money managers who face no liabilities but are instead evaluated in terms of some benchmark index, the relevant investment horizon is typically one year.

The measure that should be used to assess the potential return of a security or a portfolio over some investment horizon is the total return.[1] The purpose of this chapter is to discuss the total return framework and to show how total return is measured for mortgage-backed securities. We also show how to incorporate the option-adjusted spread methodology into the total return framework.

TOTAL RETURN MEASURE

An investment in a fixed income security has three potential sources of return: the coupon income, reinvestment of coupon and any interim cash flows, and the price return (gain or loss) at the end of the holding period. These three sources of return together make up the total return of a fixed income security.

---

[1] The total return is also called the horizon return.

The total return can be illustrated by an example using the on-the-run 10-year Treasury. Let's assume that an investor purchases $5,000,000 par amount of a 6.125% 10-year Treasury and that the last coupon payment for this security was 144 days ago. Assuming the price of the Treasury is 103½, the total investment would be $5,295,822, which is the clean price ($5,000,000 × 103.5%) plus accrued interest ($5,000,000 × 6.125% × 144 days/365 days). Let's calculate the potential 1-year total return.

The investor will earn coupon interest over the one year of $306,250 (= $5,000,000 × 6.125%). The coupon interest will then be reinvested at short-term rates, say 3-month LIBOR. Assume that this generates reinvestment income of $10,950. Assuming no changes in rates over the year, this Treasury security would have a price of 103.24 (premium amortization) at the end of the 1-year holding period. The price return (loss) would be –$13,170, which is $5,000,000 × (103.24 – 103.5). The total dollar return on the investment would be $304,030 (= $306,250 + $10,950 – $13,170). This is an annualized return of 5.74% (= $304,030/$5,295,822) or a semiannual bond equivalent return of 5.66% (= $2 \times ((1.057)^{\frac{1}{2}} - 1)$).

The above example is fairly straight forward because the 10-year Treasury has a bullet final maturity and no amortization of the principal. When it comes to the calculation of total return for mortgage-backed securities such as passthroughs and CMOs, there is one extra component. The amortization of the principal due to regular repayments and accelerated prepayments has to be taken into account and paydown gains or losses are often generated. Since all principal is repaid at par, if the passthrough or CMO is purchased at a premium, any paydown in principal, whether scheduled regular payment or prepayment, would generate a paydown loss. If the passthrough or CMO is purchased at a discount to par, any paydown would generate a paydown gain. The end-of-holding period price gain or loss would only affect the remaining outstanding balance at the end of the holding period.

For example, suppose a CMO is purchased at a premium, say 103, and 20% of the initial principal is paid back or amortized during the holding period. At the end of the holding period, assume the price of the CMO appreciates to 104. There will be a paydown loss of 3 points on 20% of the balance and a gain of 1 point on 80% of the balance. The total return of a passthrough and CMO typically has a bigger component on reinvestment since the repaid principal (together with the coupon) has to be reinvested. The amount of principal to be reinvested obviously depends on the prepayment assumption and, in the case of a CMO tranche, the structure.

SCENARIO TOTAL RETURN ANALYSIS

The total return calculation requires that several assumptions be made. These include assumptions regarding the holding period, reinvestment rate, reinvestment horizon, prepayment rate, and horizon price. In the case of a floating-rate security and inverse floating-rate security, the reference rate over the holding period that determines the coupon rate must be assumed.

To test the sensitivity of total return to alternative assumptions, a technique known as *scenario analysis* is helpful. It is basically a "what-if" analysis. What if interest rates go up 100 bps in a parallel fashion? What if interest rates go down 50 bps in a parallel fashion? What if the yield curve inverted 75 bps? What would be the likely total return of an MBS holding or the entire portfolio under these scenarios? A common practice by portfolio managers is to generate the total returns given parallel shifts in the yield curve in 50 bps to 100 bps increments.

Projection of Price at the Horizon Date

The most difficult part of estimating total return is projecting the price of an MBS at the horizon date, particularly for a CMO tranche. The price depends on the characteristics of the tranche and the spread to Treasuries at the end of the holding period. The key determinants are the "quality" of the tranche, its average life (or duration), and its convexity.

In the case of a CMO tranche, quality refers to the type of CMO bond. Consider, for example, that an investor can purchase a CMO tranche that is a PAC bond but as a result of projected prepayments, could become a sequential-pay tranche. As another example, suppose a PAC bond is the longest average life tranche in a reverse PAC structure. Projected prepayments in this case might occur in an amount to change the class from a long-term average life PAC tranche to effectively a support tranche. The converse is that the quality of a tranche may improve as well as deteriorate. For example, the effective collar for a PAC tranche could widen at the horizon date when prepayment circumstances increase the par amount of support tranches outstanding as a proportion of the deal.

OAS-Total Return

The total return and OAS frameworks can be combined to determine the projected price at the horizon date. This requires an OAS model and a prepayment model. At the end of the investment horizon, it is necessary to specify how the OAS is expected to change. The horizon price can be "backed out" of the OAS model. We discussed this in the previous chapter in explaining how to obtain the two prices needed to calculate effective duration and effective convexity. This technique can be extended to the total return framework by making assumptions about the required variables at the horizon date.

Assumptions about the OAS value at the investment horizon reflect the expectations of the money manager. It is common to assume that the OAS at the horizon date will be the same as the OAS at the time of purchase. A total return calculated using this assumption is referred to as a *constant-OAS total return*. Alternatively, active total return managers will make bets on how the OAS will change — either widening or tightening. The total return framework can be used to assess how sensitive the performance of an MBS is to changes in the OAS.

Exhibit 1 shows the 1-year total return profile of $5 million of a 10-year Treasury assuming a parallel shift in rates by (1) plus or minus 150 bps, (2) plus or minus 100 bps, and (3) plus or minus 50 bps shifts. The exhibit also shows the 1-year total return profile of $10 million original face of FNMA 7. The total return is computed assuming constant OAS horizon pricing. Note that the total returns of FNMA 7 include a paydown gain/loss component. Also, the lower the interest rates, the faster the prepayment, and reinvestment becomes a bigger component of the total return.

PORTFOLIO CONSTRUCTION AND OPTIMIZATION

The single security total return scenario analysis illustrated above can be performed on a portfolio basis. The total return profile of each security in the portfolio can be generated individually and the results can then be aggregated to form a portfolio. This is helpful in the portfolio construction process. Individual securities that may be too volatile on a stand alone basis may fit into a portfolio. Options and swaps may be volatile leveraged products but serve as good risk-control instruments within a portfolio. Portfolio managers should be more concerned with the performance and the total return profile of the entire portfolio than of any individual security.

Exhibit 1: Scenario Analysis Assuming Constant OAS for a FNMA 7 and 10-Year Treasury: 1-Year Total Return

Rate Change (bps)	−150	−100	−50	Base	+50	+100	+150
10-year Treasury 8/07							
Initial Price				$103.50			
Initial Balance/Face Amount				5,000,000			
Coupon Income	306,250	306,250	306,250	306,250	306,250	306,250	306,250
Reinvestment	7,967	8,963	9,961	10,950	11,959	12,960	13,963
Horizon Price	$114.21	$110.40	$106.75	$103.24	$99.87	$96.63	$93.53
Price Change	535,430	345,012	162,262	(13,170)	(181,594)	343,328)	(498,653)
Total Dollar Return	849,647	660,225	478,473	304,030	136,615	(24,118)	(178,440)
Total % Return	15.448	12.101	8.840	5.661	2.563	(0.456)	(3.398)
FNMA 7							
Initial Price				$100.9688			
Initial Balance/Original Face Amount				10,000,000			
Initial Balance/Current Face Amount				8,236,329			
Coupon Income	523,035	539,609	552,530	563,041	565,843	566,905	567,510
Reinvestment	33,726	29,571	25,641	21,759	21,845	22,882	24,163
Projected Balance as % of Current	72.1%	81.1%	88.3%	94.1%	95.6%	96.1%	96.4%
Projected Remaining Balance	5,938,393	6,679,663	7,272,679	7,750,386	7,873,931	7,915,112	7,939,821
Horizon Price	$104.56	$103.67	$102.47	$100.82	$98.72	$96.35	$93.82
Price Change	213,314	180,625	109,229	(11,827)	(177,126)	(365,887)	(567,963)
Paydown Gain/Loss	(22,286)	(15,073)	(9,379)	(4,736)	(3,543)	(3,107)	(2,856)
Total Dollar Return	747,789	734,732	678,021	568,237	407,019	220,793	20,854
Total % Return	8.789	8.638	7.984	6.712	4.830	2.635	0.250

Values obtained using *Derivative Solutions Fixed Income System.*

A constrained optimization is basically a process to optimize (maximize or minimize) the value of an objective function by varying the dependent variables of the objective function subject to various constraints. The technique used for solving constrained optimization problems is called *mathematical programming*. If the objective function and constraints are linear, the problem is solved by using a technique called *linear programming*, a special case of mathematical programming. For example, the return of a portfolio is a linear combination of the returns of the underlying bonds. The duration of the portfolio is a linear combination (weighted average) of the durations of the underlying bonds. The constraints are usually linear too. For example, the sum of the bond holdings values must be less than $100 million or each holding cannot be more than 10% of the portfolio.

The mostly wide accepted algorithm to solve a linear programming problem is the simplex method. Most common linear programming softwares used by academics in decision and management science are Lindo, QSB, and SAS. However, in the business world these days, optimization problems including situations involving non-linear constraints and/or objective function (i.e., non-linear programming) can be handled by Excel or Lotus123. The simplex method is still used (Lotus calls it Logical method). But any more complicated problems and non-linear programming can be solved by numeric iteration given the fast speed computer these days.

The portfolio construction process is similar to an optimization exercise. Given the investment objective, guidelines, and restrictions, what portfolio composition would the portfolio manager construct to have the best shot of beating the liability, benchmark, index, or bogey. In optimization terms, the portfolio manager may want to maximize the expected total return of the portfolio subject to the constraints implied by the investment guidelines and restrictions; the portfolio manager may want to minimize the variability of the total return under various scenarios; or the portfolio manager may want to minimize tracking error against an index. The solutions to these optimization exercises often depend on the flexibility of the guidelines.

For example, suppose a portfolio manager uses the 10-year Treasury as the benchmark or bogey. Suppose further that the following restrictions are imposed:

1. at least 70% of the portfolio must be invested in the 10-year Treasury
2. the portfolio's duration must match the 10-year Treasury's duration of 7.08 within ±0.1 (i.e., 6.98 to 7.18)
3. the portfolio credit quality must be government/agency
4. no interest only products may be included in the portfolio due to the lack of guarantee of the proceeds invested
5. no derivatives or leverage (no shorts) are permitted

Moreover, suppose the portfolio manager wants the portfolio to outperform the 10-year Treasury within a ±100 bp movement in rates. The portfolio manager is willing to take the risk of slight underperformance beyond the 100 bp movement given the low volatility in the market.

All these requirements can be set up as constraints to perform the optimization process to maximize the expected return of the portfolio. For purposes of this illustration only a few securities are considered for inclusion in the portfolio. These securities are shown in Exhibit 2. The exhibit also shows the result of the optimization over a 1-year horizon and assuming constant OAS pricing. The resulting portfolio still consists primarily of the 10-year Treasury (71.6%) with the rest of the portfolio in various mortgage passthrough securities. It also has 9.5% mortgage POs. The expected 1-year total return of the portfolio exceeds the expected total return of the 10-year Treasury benchmark by 12 bps given the probability distribution shown in Exhibit 2. The portfolio outperforms the benchmark within ±100 bps movements in rates. The portfolio also has a duration of 7.06, which is only 0.02 different from that of the benchmark 10-year Treasury.

If the investment guidelines and restrictions are more flexible, there will be a different set of constraints and a different optimal expected total return. For instance, if the manager is allowed to invest up to 50% of the portfolio in non-Treasury securities, and a small amount in IO products, he can construct the portfolio to have an excess expected return of 15 bps (see Exhibit 3). The portfolio manager would still outperform the benchmark within ±100 bps movements in rates.

As a further example suppose that the guidelines and restrictions are relaxed as follows:

1. the portfolio may include up to 10% in IO products
2. only 20% must be invested in the 10-year Treasury
3. a bigger interest rate bet may be made by permitting a 0.2 band on the duration (i.e., 6.88 to 7.28)

Moreover, the manager is allowed to make a volatility bet by accepting 100 bps underperformance in total return under the ±150 bps scenarios.

With all the extra flexibility, the optimized portfolio has 71 bps of excess expected total return against the benchmark 10-year Treasury (see Exhibit 4). However, the portfolio underperforms significantly in the −150 bps scenario. The portfolio also has added liquidity risk on the IO products which is not quantified in this optimization process. Also, when volatility changes in the market, the probability distribution changes and will alter the expected total return. Volatility changes will also impact the horizon pricing of the securities. Holding OAS constant, a higher volatility would lower the price of MBS products with embedded short positions on options. In addition, the OASs on IOs and POs would tend to widen and tighten in bullish and bearish markets. Many refinements can be made to this optimization process.

Exhibit 2: 1-Year Total Return Results for Optimal Portfolio

Pricing Date 1/2/98

Security	Tranche Type	Coupon	WAC	Collateral Type	Original Face	Current Factor	Current Face	Effective Duration	Market Price	Market Value	% Orig. Portfolio
10-Year Treasury 8/07	Govt	6.125	6.125	Govt	50,000,000	1.00000	50,000,000	7.08	—	51,750,000	71.6%
FNMA 30-Year 7%	Pass Thru	7.000	7.000	Pass Thru	5,000,000	0.82363	4,118,165	3.95	—	4,158,059	5.8%
FNMA 30-Year 8%	Pass Thru	8.000	8.000	Pass Thru	5,000,000	0.51352	2,567,576	2.86	—	2,662,255	3.7%
GNMA 30-Year 7%	Pass Thru	7.000	7.000	Pass Thru	5,000,000	0.81051	4,052,564	4.35	—	4,096,889	5.7%
GNMA 30-Year 8%	Pass Thru	8.000	8.000	Pass Thru	5,000,000	0.53449	2,672,428	2.90	—	2,775,149	3.8%
FNR 94-108 S	PAC Inv IO	8.250	7.000	30-year	—	1.00000	—	37.35	36.000	—	0.0%
FNR 93-8 HA	PAC IO	1,200	7.500	15-year	—	1.00000	—	-15.50	5,300.0	—	0.0%
FNR 97-78 PR	Interm PAC	6.500	7.000	30-year	—	1.00000	—	3.25	—	—	0.0%
FNS 240 PO	Trust PO	—	7.000	30-year	13,000,000	0.72875	9,473,776	13.77	72.438	6,862,566	9.5%
Portfolio					83,000,000		—	7.06			100.00%

Constant OAS Horizon Prices

Security	-150	-100	-50	Base	+50	+100	+150
10-Year Treasury 8/07	114.21	110.40	106.75	103.24	99.87	96.63	—
FNMA 30-Year 7%	104.56	103.67	102.47	100.82	98.72	96.35	—
FNMA 30-Year 8%	107.17	106.10	104.96	103.67	102.10	—	—
GNMA 30-Year 7%	105.20	104.35	102.97	101.04	98.70	96.14	—
GNMA 30-Year 8%	106.98	105.94	104.84	103.56	101.92	99.91	—
FNR 94-108 S	41.66	42.31	38.85	32.97	26.53	20.49	—
FNR 93-8 HA	3,484	3,784	4,203	4,634	4,919	5,056	—
FNR 97-78 PR	101.96	102.15	101.44	100.65	99.19	97.45	—
FNS 240 PO	86.71	82.63	77.61	72.43	67.70	63.54	—

Constant OAS 1-Year Total Return (%)

Security	-150	-100	-50	Base	+50	+100	+150
10-Year Treasury 8/07	15.448	12.101	8.840	5.661	2.563	(0.456)	(3.398)
FNMA 30-Year 7%	8.789	8.638	7.984	6.712	4.830	2.635	0.250
FNMA 30-Year 8%	7.249	7.099	6.947	6.606	5.791	4.394	2.606
GNMA 30-Year 7%	9.618	9.428	8.477	6.821	4.705	2.329	(0.218)
GNMA 30-Year 8%	7.823	7.632	7.341	6.852	5.719	4.040	2.032
FNR 94-108 S	48.362	45.752	33.538	14.449	(8.155)	(32.574)	(58.447)
FNR 93-8 HA	(11.543)	(5.601)	2.389	10.283	15.363	17.785	18.989
FNR 97-78 PR	7.609	7.804	7.143	6.399	4.997	3.329	1.505
FNS 240 PO	25.729	20.304	12.861	5.128	(1.504)	(7.325)	(12.415)
Portfolio	15.12	12.17	9.02	5.82	2.67	0.42	(3.43)
vs. 10-Year Treasury Benchmark	(0.33)	0.07	0.18	0.16	0.11	0.03	(0.04)
Probability of Scenarios	2%	5%	20%	43%	18%	8%	4%
Expected Return of Portfolio				5.53			
Expected Return of 10-Year Treasury				5.41			

Values obtained using *Derivative Solutions Fixed Income System*.

Exhibit 3: 1-Year Total Return Results for Optimized Portfolio Allowing up to 50% Non-Treasuries and Other Constraints Relaxed

Pricing Date   1/2/98

Security	Tranche Type	Coupon	WAC	Collateral Type	Original Face	Current Factor	Current Face	Effective Duration	Market Price	Market Value	% Opt. Portfolio
10-Year Treasury 8/07	Govt	6.125	6.125	Govt	34,929,913	1.00000	34,929,913	7.08	—	36,152,460	50.0%
FNMA 30-Year 7%	Pass Thru	7.000	7.000	Pass Thru		0.82363		3.95	—		0.0%
FNMA 30-Year 8%	Pass Thru	8.000	8.000	Pass Thru	39,329,762	0.51352	20,196,431	2.86	—	20,941,174	29.0%
GNMA 30-Year 7%	Pass Thru	7.000	7.000	Pass Thru		0.81051		4.35	—		0.0%
GNMA 30-Year 8%	Pass Thru	8.000	8.000	Pass Thru		0.53449		2.90	—		0.0%
FNR 94-108 S	PAC Inv IO	8.250	7.000	30-year		1.00000		37.35	36.000		0.0%
FNR 93-8 HA	PAC IO	1.200	7.500	15-year	4,695	1.00000	4,695	-15.50	5,300.0	248,825	0.3%
FNR 97-78 PR	Interm PAC	6.500	7.000	30-year		1.00000		3.25	—		0.0%
FNS 240 PO	Trust PO	—	7.000	30-year	28,343,913	0.72875	20,655,683	13.77	72.438	14,962,460	20.7%
Portfolio					28,343,913		20,655,683	7.16			

Security	Constant OAS 1-Year Total Return (%)							Constant OAS Horizon Prices						
	-150	-100	-50	Base	+50	+100	+150	-150	-100	-50	Base	+50	+100	+150
10-Year Treasury 8/07	15.448	12.101	8.840	5.661	2.563	(0.456)	(3.398)	114.21	110.40	106.75	103.24	99.87	96.63	—
FNMA 30-Year 7%	8.789	8.638	7.984	6.712	4.830	2.635	0.250	104.56	103.67	102.47	100.82	98.72	96.35	—
FNMA 30-Year 8%	7.249	7.099	6.947	6.606	5.791	4.394	2.606	107.17	106.10	104.96	103.67	102.10	—	—
GNMA 30-Year 7%	9.618	9.428	8.477	6.821	4.705	2.329	(0.218)	105.20	104.35	102.97	101.04	98.70	96.14	—
GNMA 30-Year 8%	7.823	7.632	7.341	6.852	5.719	4.040	2.032	106.98	105.94	104.84	103.56	101.92	99.91	—
FNR 94-108 S	48.362	45.752	33.538	14.449	(8.155)	(32.574)	(58.447)	41.66	42.31	38.85	32.97	26.53	20.49	—
FNR 93-8 HA	(11.543)	(5.601)	2.389	10.283	15.363	17.785	18.989	3.484	3.784	4.203	4.634	4.919	5.056	—
FNR 97-78 PR	7.609	7.804	7.143	6.399	4.997	3.329	1.505	101.96	102.15	101.44	100.65	99.19	97.45	—
FNS 240 PO	25.729	20.304	12.861	5.128	(1.504)	(7.325)	(12.415)	86.71	82.63	77.61	72.43	67.70	63.54	—
Portfolio	15.11	12.29	9.10	5.84	2.70	(0.41)	(3.45)							
vs. 10-Year Treasury Benchmark	(0.34)	0.19	0.26	0.18	0.14	0.05	(0.05)							
Probability of Scenarios	2%	5%	20%	43%	18%	8%	4%							
Expected Return of Portfolio				5.56										
Expected Return of 10-Year Treasury				5.41										

Values obtained using *Derivative Solutions Fixed Income System.*

Exhibit 4: 1-Year Total Return Results for Optimized Portfolio Allowing 80% to be Invested in Non-Treasury Securities and Other Relaxed Constraints

Pricing Date   1/2/98

Security	Tranche Type	Tranche Coupon	Tranche WAC	Collateral Type	Current Factor	Original Face	Current Face	Effective Duration	Market Price	Market Value	% Opt. Portfolio
10-Year Treasury 8/07	Govt	6.125	6.125	Govt	1.00000	14,042,132	14,042,132	7.08	—	14,533,606	20.1%
FNMA 30-Year 7%	Pass Thru	7.000	7.000	Pass Thru	0.82363			3.95	—	—	0.0%
FNMA 30-Year 8%	Pass Thru	8.000	8.000	Pass Thru	0.51352			2.86	—	—	0.0%
GNMA 30-Year 7%	Pass Thru	7.000	7.000	Pass Thru	0.81051			4.35	—	—	0.0%
GNMA 30-Year 8%	Pass Thru	8.000	8.000	Pass Thru	0.53449	59,528,130	31,816,928	2.90	—	33,039,892	45.7%
FNR 94-108 S	PAC Inv IO	8.250	7.000	30-year	1.00000	8,041,103	8,041,103	37.35	36.000	2,894,797	4.0%
FNR 93-8 HA	PAC IO	1,200	7.500	15-year	1.00000	70,951	70,951	-15.50	5,300.0	3,760,395	5.2%
FNR 97-78 PR	Interm PAC	6.500	7.000	30-year	1.00000	—	70,951	3.25	—	—	0.0%
FNS 240 PO	Trust PO	—	7.000	30-year	0.72875	34,242,435	24,954,243	13.77	72.438	18,076,230	25.0%
Portfolio							—	6.88			

Security	Constant OAS 1-Year Total Return (%)							Constant OAS Horizon Prices						
	-150	-100	-50	Base	+50	+100	+150	-150	-100	-50	Base	+50	+100	+150
10-Year Treasury 8/07	15.448	12.101	8.840	5.661	2.563	(0.456)	(3.398)	114.21	110.40	106.75	103.24	99.87	96.63	—
FNMA 30-Year 7%	8.789	8.638	7.984	6.712	4.830	2.635	0.250	104.56	103.67	102.47	100.82	98.72	96.35	—
FNMA 30-Year 8%	7.249	7.099	6.947	6.606	5.791	4.394	2.606	107.17	106.10	104.96	103.67	102.10	—	—
GNMA 30-Year 7%	9.618	9.428	8.477	6.821	4.705	2.329	(0.218)	105.20	104.35	102.97	101.04	98.70	96.14	—
GNMA 30-Year 8%	7.823	7.632	7.341	6.852	5.719	4.040	2.032	106.98	105.94	104.84	103.56	101.92	99.91	—
FNR 94-108 S	48.362	45.752	33.538	14.449	(8.155)	(32.574)	(58.447)	41.66	42.31	38.85	32.97	26.53	20.49	—
FNR 93-8 HA	(11.543)	(5.601)	2.389	10.283	15.363	17.785	18.989	3,484	3,784	4,203	4,634	4,919	5,056	—
FNR 97-78 PR	7.609	7.804	7.143	6.399	4.997	3.329	1.505	101.96	102.15	101.44	100.65	99.19	97.45	—
FNS 240 PO	25.729	20.304	12.861	5.128	(1.504)	(7.325)	(12.415)	86.71	82.63	77.61	72.43	67.70	63.54	—
Portfolio	14.45	—	9.81	6.66	3.22	(0.46)	(4.21)							

	-150	-100	-50	Base	+50	+100	+150
vs. 10-Year Treasury Benchmark	(1.00)	0.44	0.97	1.00	0.66	(0.00)	(0.81)
Probability of Scenarios	2%	5%	20%	43%	18%	8%	4%
Expected Return of Portfolio				6.12			
Expected Return of 10-Year Treasury				5.41			

Values obtained using *Derivative Solutions Fixed Income System.*

MONTE CARLO SIMULATION

The performance of an MBS or MBS portfolio depends on the outcome of a number of random variables.[2] A portfolio's total return will depend on the magnitude of the change in Treasury rates, the spread between MBS and Treasury securities, changes in the shape of the yield curve, and actual and expected prepayment speeds. Moreover, each random variable may have a substantial number of possible outcomes. Consequently, evaluation of all possible combinations of outcomes in order to assess the risks associated with an MBS portfolio may be impractical.

Suppose that a portfolio manager wants to assess the performance of an MBS portfolio over a 1-year investment horizon. Suppose further that the portfolio's performance will be determined by the actual outcome for each of nine random variables, and that each of the nine random variables has seven possible outcomes. There would then be 4,782,969 (= 9^7) possible outcomes representing all possible combinations of the nine random variables. Furthermore, each of the 4,782,969 outcomes has a different probability of occurrence.

One approach for a portfolio manager is to take the "best guess" for each random variable, and determine the impact on the performance measure. The best-guess value for each random variable is usually the expected value of the random variable.[3] There are serious problems with this shortcut approach. To understand its shortcomings, suppose the probability associated with the best guess for each random variable is 75%. If the probability distribution for each random variable is independently distributed, the probability of occurrence for the best-guess result would be only 7.5% (= 0.75^9). At this level of probability, no portfolio manager would have a great deal of confidence in this best-guess result.

Between the extremes of enumerating and evaluating all possible combinations and the best-guess approach is the simulation approach. Simulation is less a model than a procedure or algorithm. The solutions obtained do not represent an optimal solution to a problem. Rather, simulation provides information about a problem so that a portfolio manager can assess the risks associated with an MBS or an MBS portfolio.

There are many types of simulation techniques. When probability distributions are assigned to the random variables, the simulation technique is known as a Monte Carlo simulation, named after the famous gambling spot on the French Riviera. Monte Carlo simulation enables portfolio managers to determine the statistical properties of various investment characteristics such as total return and average life of an MBS portfolio. Armed with this information, a portfolio manager can assess the likelihood of meeting an investment objective.

---

[2] A random variable is one that can take on more than one possible outcome.

[3] The expected value of a random variable is the weighted average of the possible outcomes, where the weight is the probability of the outcome.

Steps for Monte Carlo Simulation

There are 12 steps in a Monte Carlo simulation:[4]

Step 1. A performance measure must be specified. The performance measure could be total return over some investment horizon or net interest (spread) income.[5]

Step 2. The problem under investigation, including all important variables and their interactions, must be expressed mathematically. The variables in the mathematical model will be either deterministic or random. A deterministic variable can take on only one value; a random variable can take on more than one value. The variables that are typically assumed to be deterministic in a Monte Carlo simulation to assess the total return performance of an MBS include:

- the volatility of short-term Treasury rates
- the volatility of long-term Treasury rates
- the correlation between the movement in short-term and long-term Treasury rates
- a prepayment model

The random variables are typically:

- short-term rates
- long-term rates
- the shape of the yield curve
- the relationship between long-term Treasury rates and mortgage rates

The horizon price of a security can be calculated using the static cash flow yield methodology or the OAS methodology. The interest rate paths generated in the simulation can be used to determine the horizon price, but an OAS value at the horizon date must be assumed.[6]

Step 3. A probability distribution for the random variables must be specified.

Step 4. Probability distributions for random variables must be converted into cumulative probability distributions.

Step 5. For each random variable, representative numbers must be assigned on the basis of the cumulative probability distribution to each possible outcome specified.

Step 6. A random number must be obtained for each random variable.

---

[4] A more detailed explanation and illustration is provided in Frank J. Fabozzi, *Introduction to Quantitative Methods for Investment Managers* (forthcoming, Frank J. Fabozzi Associates, 1998).

[5] Liabilities can also be simulated, particularly when liabilities exhibit interest rate sensitivity.

[6] For an illustration of how this can be done to assess the performance (as measured by total return) of an interest-only (IO) trust under various yield curve scenarios, see: Lakhbir Hayre, Charles Huang, and Vincent Pica, *Realistic Holding-Period Analysis: Technology and Its Impact on Valuation Metrics*, Study #14, Financial Strategies Group, Prudential Securities, August 13, 1992.

Step 7. For each random number, the corresponding value of the random variable must be determined.

Step 8. The corresponding value of each random variable found in the previous step must be used to determine the value of the performance measure mathematically expressed in step 2.

Step 9. The value of the performance measure found in step 8 must be recorded.

Step 10. Steps 6 through 9 must be repeated many times, say, 100 to 1,000 times. The repetition of steps 6 through 9 is known as a trial.

Step 11. The values for the performance measure for each trial recorded in step 9 become the basis for construction of a probability distribution and cumulative probability distribution.

Step 12. The cumulative probability distribution constructed in step 11 is analyzed in terms of summary statistics such as the mean, standard deviation, and the range.

Usually more than one simulation analysis is undertaken in order to test for the sensitivity to changes in the deterministic variables. A portfolio manager may rerun the simulation using a different volatility assumption for short-term and long-term rates. To test sensitivity to prepayment rates, the simulation could be rerun assuming prepayment rates that are a specified percentage higher or lower than that projected from the model (e.g., 80% lower or 120% higher).

In order to implement step 6, it is necessary to have a procedure to obtain random numbers. Monte Carlo simulation software takes care of this. If a Monte Carlo simulation is performed on an electronic spreadsheet, there is a random number generator feature.

Illustrations

To illustrate the application of simulation, we use several total return simulations provided by David Canuel and Charles Melchreit.[7] In all illustrations, the investment horizon is two years. Interim cash flows are assumed to be reinvested in Treasury strips that mature at the horizon date. The total return for each trial is calculated assuming a constant OAS. There are 200 trials for each simulation.

In the first example, FHLMC 151 C tranche (a PAC tranche) is compared to a U.S. Treasury benchmark consisting of a combination of 3-year and 5-year on-the-run Treasuries. The coupon rate for the tranche and the passthrough coupon rate are both 9%. Exhibit 5 graphs the results of the simulation, a total return distribution for the tranche versus the U.S. Treasury benchmark. The PAC tranche has a total return distribution similar to that of the Treasury benchmark because of the high degree of prepayment protection at the time of issuance (an initial collar of 90 to 270 PSA).

---

[7] David E. Canuel and Charles F. Melchreit, "Total Return Analysis in CMO Portfolio Management," Chapter 12 in Frank J. Fabozzi (ed.), *CMO Portfolio Management* (Summit, NJ: Frank J. Fabozzi Associates, 1994).

Exhibit 5: Total Return Distributions: FHLMC 151 C versus U.S. Treasury Benchmark

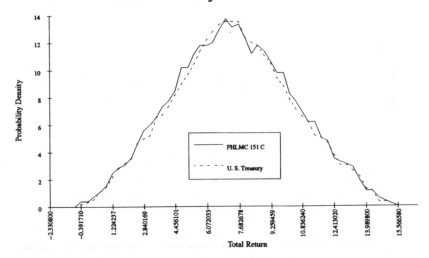

Exhibit 6: Total Return Differences: FHLMC 151 C versus U.S. Treasury Benchmark

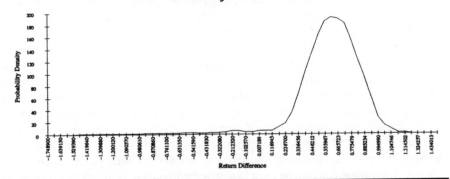

Exhibit 6 shows the distribution for the spread between the tranche and the Treasury benchmark for each trial. This exhibit provides further insight into the relative performance of the tranche and the Treasury benchmark that is not evident from Exhibit 5. The distribution has a tail to the left, due to the negative convexity of the PAC tranche, which reduces the mean of the distribution significantly. The mean of the PAC distribution is 59 basis points above that of the Treasury distribution, while the cash flow yield spread of the PAC was 75 basis points. The difference between the cash flow spread and the spread between the two distributions is attributable not only to the option cost (i.e., negative convexity of the distribution), but also to the fact that the Treasury benchmark rolls down the yield curve more rapidly than the PAC over a 2-year horizon.

Exhibit 7: Total Return Distributions: FHLMC 151 D versus FNMA 8.5

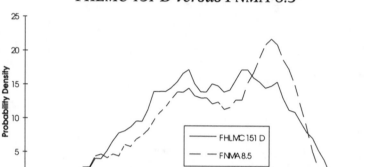

Besides comparing a CMO tranche to a Treasury benchmark, simulation can be used also to look at the relative performance of competing mortgage-backed securities. Exhibit 7 graphs the total return distributions for FHLMC 151 D tranche (a PAC tranche) and a newly originated FNMA 8.5% passthrough. Both mortgage-backed securities exhibit a slight negative convexity, but the passthrough exhibits more. This difference reflects differences in (1) option exercise during the horizon, (2) option cost embedded in the end-of-horizon price, and (3) rolling down the yield curve. Assumptions regarding reinvestment of cash flows also affect the difference between the distribution means. For example, if the reinvestment rate was 0% over the horizon, the difference would be large, and the security with more rapid prepayments would experience low realized returns. If reinvestment occurred at the Treasury rate plus a fixed spread, the difference between distribution means is a rough measure of the differences in option cost. It is sensitive to other factors as well.

Simulation can also be used to assess the impact of differences in collateral on total returns. Exhibit 8 shows results of two simulations of an actual sequential-pay tranche returns, assuming collateral of 9% and 9.5%.[8] The exhibit indicates that in rising interest rate environments, the nature of the collateral makes little difference in performance. In declining interest rate environments, however, the tranche with the lower-coupon collateral will outperform the tranche with the higher-coupon collateral. The mean difference in total return is 20 basis points. The tranche at the time of issuance had 50% of 9% collateral and 50% of 9.5% collateral. With seasoning of mortgages and interest rate changes, the character of the collateral will change over time, so in the future simulation results may be quite different.

---

[8] The deal used in this illustration was Kidder Peabody Mortgage Assets Trust Three issued in 1987. The tranche that was simulated is Class D.

Exhibit 8: Sequential-Pay Total Returns:
Impact of Collateral Differences

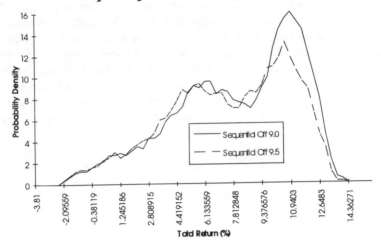

Exhibit 9: PAC-IO Total Returns:
Impact of Collateral Differences

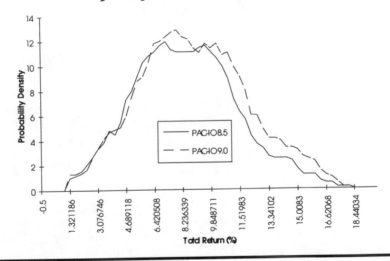

The same type of analysis for PAC IOs appears in Exhibit 9. The exhibit shows the total return distributions for FHLMC 194 F tranche. At issuance, the average life for this tranche was 16 years. The passthrough rate for the collateral is 8.5%. Shown in the exhibit are total return distributions assuming passthrough coupon rates of 8.5% and 9% (with the WAC 50 basis points higher). The mean difference in the total return distribution over the two years is 24 basis points.

SUMMARY

Total return is the correct measure for assessing the performance of an MBS or MBS portfolio over a specified investment horizon. The option-adjusted spread methodology can be incorporated into a total return framework to calculate the price of an MBS at the horizon date. Scenario analysis is one way to evaluate the risk associated with investing in an MBS or MBS portfolio, but the dynamics of interest rates cannot be captured by scenario analysis. Monte Carlo simulation provides a better assessment of potential return performance through generation of a total return distribution. An optimal portfolio can be constructed given the investment objective, guidelines, and restrictions.

Index

Coverage You Can Count On.
Accuracy You Can Trust.

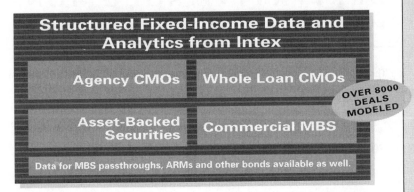

Structured Fixed-Income Data and Analytics from Intex

Agency CMOs   Whole Loan CMOs

OVER 8000 DEALS MODELED

Asset-Backed Securities   Commercial MBS

Data for MBS passthroughs, ARMs and other bonds available as well.

Before you build or buy your next fixed-income system, call Intex first. Intex provides the industry's most accurate and complete database of deal models for residential CMOs, asset-backed securities and commercial mortgage-backed securities of any complexity. All models are updated in a timely manner with information gathered from a variety of independent sources.

Intex clients have a choice of data interfaces and analytics including flexible **C++/C-Callable Subroutines**, ready-to-use applications like **Intex Trader™** and **CMO Analyst™**, built-in access from a variety of well-known **third-party products**, and the **Intex Structuring Tool™** for deal creation. So whether you wish to build your own system or buy an existing one, Intex has a solution that's right for you.

Intex has long been recognized as the premier provider of structured data and analytics to the fixed-income market. In fact, most leading broker/dealers, issuers, banks, insurance companies and money managers rely on Intex for their essential fixed-income applications.

For bond administration, trading support, portfolio management, risk management, structuring and a host of other front- and back-office applications, make Intex a part of your solution.

Intex is an independent company located near Boston, MA. For over a decade, Intex has provided high quality products and support to the fixed-income industry.

For more information, call or write:

Intex Solutions, Inc.

35 Highland Circle
Needham, MA 02194
Tel: 781 449-6222
Fax: 781 444-2318
E-mail: desk@intex.com
Web: http://www.intex.com

Successfully Manage Your MBS Portfolio with the

DERIVATIVE SOLUTIONS
FIXED INCOME SYSTEM

The Derivative Solutions Fixed Income System provides an arsenal of portfolio level value & risk analytics in an easy to use Windows environment. A highly adaptable set of term structure, prepayment, & option pricing models allows the unique characteristics of different security types to be correctly & rigorously handled. While the specific nuances of each security type are individually considered in generating cashflows, the resulting value & risk calculations are consistently generated to be directly comparable across all securities in all sectors. The general assumptions, scenarios, calculators, & even the user interface are the same for all security types. Only the cashflow algorithms differ according to a security's specific features. This level of rigor & consistency is essential to the integrity of relative value comparison, portfolio hedges, & risk management.

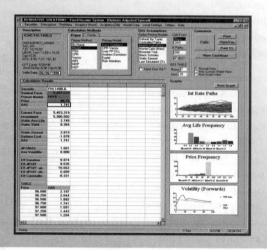

DERIVATIVE SOLUTIONS

140 S. Dearborn Street, Suite 310, Chicago, IL 60603 · (312) 739-9393 · Fax: (312) 739-1330 · E-mail: sales@dersol.com

Key Features for MBS

- **All MBS types handled** including Agency & Whole Loan CMOs, ABS, Passthroughs, Strips, Callable Passthroughs, ARMs, & Mortgage Loans.

- Multiple **Prepayment Model** choices include the Derivative Solutions Models, user customized models, & third party vendor models.

- Multi-Factor **Monte Carlo Options Pricing Model** incorporating the Term Structure of Volatilities from the Cap & Swaptions markets.

- **Loss Analysis** for Credit Sensitive MBS including user customizable default and loss severity models.

- **Portfolio calculations** consistently applied to all security types including short positions & repos.

- All **Hedging Vehicles** supported including Interest Rate Swaps, Caps, Floors, Swaptions, Futures, & Options.

- **Customized Portfolio Reports** via Windows point & click technology.

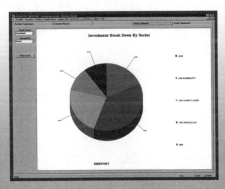 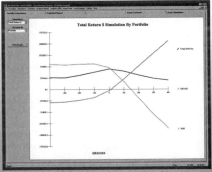

- Comprehensive leading edge **Analytics** including:

⇢ Pricing	⇢ Twist Duration (Sensitivity to Curve Twists)
⇢ Static Yield, Duration, Average Life, Spreads, etc.	⇢ Prepayment Duration (Sensitivity to Prepayment Modeling)
⇢ Options Adjusted Spread (OAS)	⇢ Vega (Sensitivity to Volatility)
⇢ Static Spread (Zero Volatility Spread)	⇢ Spread Duration (Sensitivity to OAS)
⇢ Options Cost	⇢ Partial Durations (Sensitivity to parts of the curve)
⇢ Total Rates of Return (Horizon pricing at OAS or Spread)	
⇢ Effective Duration (Sensitivity to Parallel Shifts)	

FOR MORE INFORMATION

Call Derivative Solutions at *(312) 739-9393* or visit our website at *www.dersol.com*

Interactive Data is unsurpassed in its coverage of taxable fixed income securities. In both global and domestic markets, we have a passion for accuracy that is second to none.

We cover North American corporate, government, and agency fixed income instruments, pass-through securities (FNMA, GNMA, FHLMC, and SBA) and structured finance securities (CMOs), as well as international corporates, convertible debentures, Eurobonds, and government bonds in over twenty currencies.

With a team of professionals working in all major international markets, Interactive Data

Taxable Fixed Income: no one covers the world like we do.

offers unbiased evaluations you won't find anywhere else.

Don't just take our word for it. The 1997 vendor survey published by Securities Operations Letter awarded Interactive Data 55 awards for coverage, accuracy, reliability, and service.

To find out more, call Interactive Data today.

THE MEASURE OF THE MARKET. WORLDWIDE.

Call 781-687-8670 or visit www.intdata.com

Interactive Data
FINANCIAL TIMES Information

As an experienced industry leader in fixed income evaluations for 30 years, Interactive Data continues to be the best source of International Fixed Income information.

Today, we lead the pack by providing pricing and descriptive data in over twenty currencies. We use models developed with many years of experience to provide daily evaluations that truly reflect the market. Not only is accuracy a hallmark, but our international fixed income evaluations are typically available by 2:00 pm ET, two hours ahead of the competition.

Every business day, teams in London and New York bring international fixed income market expertise to our clients. At the end of their day, our London evaluators electronically transfer their workbook to our professionals in New York to provide clients with fast, accurate customer support.

Experience, speed, accuracy, and service. Interactive Data has redefined the world of international fixed income data.

To find out more, call Interactive Data today.

Global data that's ahead of the curve.

THE MEASURE OF THE MARKET. WORLDWIDE.